Equipping Christians *for*
KINGDOM PURPOSE
in Their Work

A GUIDE
FOR ALL WHO
MAKE DISCIPLES

Tom Lutz & Heidi Unruh

HENDRICKSON
PUBLISHERS

an imprint of Hendrickson Publishing Group

THEOLOGY OF WORK   PROJECT

Equipping Christians for Kingdom Purpose in Their Work: A Guide for All Who Make Disciples

© 2022 Tom Lutz and Heidi Unruh

Published by Hendrickson Publishers
an imprint of Hendrickson Publishing Group
Hendrickson Publishers, LLC
P. O. Box 3473
Peabody, Massachusetts 01961-3473
www.hendricksonpublishinggroup.com

ISBN 978-1-68307-399-4

Printed in the United States of America

First Printing — January 2022

Library of Congress Control Number: 2021948463

*To Sherry, my beautiful wife of many years, our seven children,
and (at current count) our twelve grandchildren—
the purpose behind my kingdom purpose.*

—Tom

To my daughter, Elise, whose life gives delight.

—Heidi

CONTENTS

Part Three. DISCIPLESHIP CORE QUESTION #2: WHAT IS YOUR PURPOSE?

(Helping People Understand How Their Job Gets God's Kingdom Work Done)

Part Four. DISCIPLESHIP CORE QUESTION #3: HOW WILL YOU FULFILL YOUR PURPOSE?

(Helping People to Faithfully and Fruitfully Live out Their Calling)

Part Five. VOCATIONAL DISCIPLESHIP THAT LEADS TO TRANSFORMATION

APPENDICES: TOOLS FOR VOCATIONAL DISCIPLESHIP

PREFACE: TELLING OUR STORY

Tom's Story

As a young man in high school, I had the honor of being viewed as a leader in most of my group activities, whether Young Life or Sunday school. As a result, I was frequently told by mature Christians whom I admired and trusted, "If you really want to serve God, you'll become a pastor." I was flattered, but I didn't really know what to do with this. Of course, I wanted to "serve God," but I didn't sense that pastoral leadership was where God was leading me. I frequently asked myself: Is there anywhere besides church to fully serve God? Where could I find my purpose?

Feeling pushed in this direction of "serving God," I eventually attended seminary and gained my master of divinity degree. After graduation, I ultimately was ordained as a teaching elder in the Presbyterian Church. The church was in the inner city of Baltimore and was not able to pay me very much. At that time, several Christian friends of mine were starting a business. They offered to allow me to work for them with flexible hours, to enable me to continue to work at church. When I entered the workplace, I recognized almost immediately that this was what God had put me on earth to do. I had truly found my kingdom purpose. I told my pastor friends, "After several years in the pastorate, God called me to the ministry."

As I developed my workplace ministry, I began reading the Bible quite differently from many of my pastor friends. They tended to read and teach the Bible as if it were written only to church members, while I learned to read it and to teach it as if it were written to every individual created in God's image, charged with doing God's work in the world he created.

So, my passion has become discipling image-bearers who are also church members. I want others to experience hearing God say "Well done, good and faithful servant" as they leave their place of work.

Heidi's Story

As a ministry consultant and trainer specializing in helping Christians care well for their neighbors, my career has primarily centered on the world of churches, parachurch organizations, and nonprofits. My abiding passion is to see struggling communities and families restored in the abundance that God intended when he pronounced creation "very good."[1] This passion led me to a master of arts in theological studies at Palmer Seminary to become biblically anchored and spiritually prepared for this work. My college and seminary work focused on how Christians participated in the kingdom of God through mission work, volunteerism, and civil service.

Outside of church-based job training ministries, I had little experience with the faith and work arena—until I was asked to write a faith and work curriculum for a church! In the crash course that followed, I found many assumptions in my worldview being challenged and reconstructed.

I had accepted the hierarchy that puts "worldly," profit-seeking work at the bottom of the God-serving pyramid, and reveres church ministry positions at the "spiritual" peak (bonus points if unpaid!). Since I rarely heard church sermons and teachings meaningfully reference the world of work, I assumed it was peripheral to spiritual growth. I presumed that the main value of work (outside of meeting basic needs) was to supply funds and develop skills useful for the ministry of the church.

I needed my eyes opened to a new way to read the Scriptures about our anointing for God's kingdom purpose! I needed a spark to light up my imagination for work that is "well done," at the nexus of productivity, innovation, justice, and faithfulness. Becoming a student of the faith and work movement vastly expanded my vision for the "good works" to which each image-bearer is called (Eph. 2:10). Tom's insights bring exceptional clarity and drive to that vision.

Now, *you*—as a vocational discipler—can help others find that spark!

I am excited and honored to be a part of the development of this book, because it breathes fresh life into our calling to join Jesus in his work of reclaiming and restoring a very good world. "As the Father has sent me, so I send you" (John 20:21). My dream is that vocational discipleship can ignite a movement where showing up for work means showing up for love of God, creation, and neighbor.

Why This Book?

Throughout twenty years of building and then selling a business, and then another twenty years of coaching other business leaders, I (Tom) have had a ringside seat to the kingdom battle. God has enabled me to disciple people who work outside the church into an understanding that their work is an integral part of God's kingdom purpose for their lives. Over the years, this discipling has occurred in many arenas—Christian CEO Roundtable groups, discipleship groups, one-on-one conversations, and conferences.

The call to write this book came to me at one such event. While attending a faith at work conference here in Atlanta, I was struck by several things.

Over the past thirty years, I had been involved with many such conferences, and while hundreds had come to hear and understand the faith at work message, our movement essentially remained static. In fact, I noticed that most of the attendees at this conference were the same people I had seen at all the other conferences. We were, proverbially, preaching to the choir. We needed to figure out a way to send more laborers into the fields of kingdom purpose.

At that point, I heard a voice say to my spirit, "Until every Sunday, from every pulpit, every sermon is illustrated from and applied to the workplace, the work will not be done." I heard it as a call to turn my attention to discipling the disciplers.

My first step on that road was to return to graduate school to earn a doctorate. In 2017, I completed my doctoral dissertation "Discipling Christian C-Level Business Executives," from Covenant Theological Seminary. The vocational discipleship curriculum I developed and tested for my dissertation became the foundation for this book.

My desire to share this resource more broadly led to a collaboration with Heidi. Though our backgrounds are quite different, we discovered a convergence on the main ideas and goals of vocational discipleship.

We agree with Amy Sherman's blunt assessment: "Discipleship that doesn't equip people for the activity they spend forty percent of their waking hours doing is not discipleship." Together, we dream of a critical mass of Christians who are influencing church culture from within while impacting their workplaces and communities through the vocation in which God has called and equipped them to be productive. We dream that as more church leaders develop a focus on vocation, the prevailing paradigm of discipleship will shift to include following Jesus on the job as a matter of course. We envision a future in which every book written about discipleship includes a chapter (or several) about work, every church conference has a track dedicated to vocational ministry, every seminary program equips pastors to preach and teach about vocation, and the term "vocational discipleship" becomes redundant.[2]

ACKNOWLEDGMENTS

As I sit here at Corners End, as we call our little oasis north of Atlanta, I am humbly aware of the many tools God has used to craft in me a kingdom purpose.

It started with Vernon and Rose Lutz, who welcomed me into a special, totally functional family of origin. The educators who invested in me at Calvert Hall High School, University of Maryland Baltimore County, and Covenant Theological Seminary. Professor John Sanderson of Covenant Seminary, who instilled in me what has become the lifelong thrill of reading the Scriptures as God intended them to be read. Uncle Ron Hastie, who taught me that businesses are an essential element in the flourishing of a community. Arol Wolford, my senior partner at CMD Group and friend of many years, and our other partners, who collectively taught me that you can lead a business with godly integrity. The members of Faith Christian Fellowship in Baltimore, Maryland, where I was at one time active in leadership, who allowed me the privilege of testing out the formational ideas that became *Equipping Christians for Kingdom Purpose*.

Randy Pope, long-time lead pastor of Perimeter Church, who taught me what it means to disciple another Christian. Randy Schlichting, my pastor and the president of Atlanta Metro Seminary, as well as many seminary students, who gave me the opportunity to test out many of these kingdom purpose ideas in the laboratory of my classroom. Each of the godly business leaders who have allowed me to walk alongside them through the Convene organization, and the staff and co-chairs at Convene who make it easy for me to do so. The men who were the "guinea pigs" for my doctoral research.

Heidi Unruh, my collaborator on this project, who made the book better than it would have been otherwise through her many contributions, and who truly thought my thoughts after me, making me sound so much wiser than I really am.

And of course, my wife of nearly forty-six years, who not only bore a total of sixty-three pounds of Lutz children, but who was also active in developing them into the seven wholesome individuals of whom we could not be prouder.

Tom Lutz
Peachtree Corners, Georgia
September 2021

To my wise, gracious and patient colleague, Dr. Tom Lutz: Our collaboration has been a blessing. May your vision continue to lead many—including me—to approach work with renewed devotion.

Tracing the roots of this project, I am grateful to Travis Vaughn for introducing me to the faith and work arena, as well as to Tom. Collaboration with Travis and Chip Sweney at Perimeter Church laid the groundwork for my part in this book and opened doors to conversations with great thinkers and practitioners. Gratitude also to my colleague Andy Rittenhouse, who first sparked my interest in discipleship for mission in the workplace.

Given the richness of the faith and work community, nearly every sentence in this book deserves a footnote. Special thanks to the brilliant Amy Sherman for taking time to comment on early drafts; to pioneer Tom Nelson and the innovative team at Made to Flourish; and to the incomparably thorough Theology of Work Project, whose print and online resources I frequently consulted.

To all who provided feedback on our outline and drafts, and who allowed us to share your quotes: Your insights made this a better book.

We are grateful to Hendrickson Publishers for your patient partnership, and for paving the way with your investment in faith and work resources.

On a different note, I offer tribute to the many image-bearers I know who struggle daily with difficult, unfulfilling jobs. As you work so hard to make ends meet for your families, you motivate me with a reminder of what is at stake.

As always, deep gratitude to my husband, Jim, for sharing your wisdom, keeping me grounded, and supplying me with coffee. Your encouragement helped keep my writing candle burning through a difficult season. And loving thanks to Yu'Nique, Elise, Jacob, and Maurice, for hanging in there through another writing project. You are all in this world for a very good purpose.

Finally, honor is due to all in my life story who have taught and modeled what it means to do good work in a good way.

HEIDI UNRUH
HUTCHINSON, KANSAS
SEPTEMBER 2021

PART ONE

VISION AND INVITATION

1

WHAT COULD BE POSSIBLE?

This book aims to help you equip other followers of Christ to live out their kingdom calling through their vocation. What does this look like? Rather than sketching out a vision for vocational discipleship in abstract terms, let's tell a story.[1]

Imagine Christians with Clarity around Their Kingdom Purpose

The adult Sunday school class at Northside Presbyterian, a mix of white-and blue-collar workers, had always featured lively discussions. One week, their long-time class instructor, Herb, announced they would be starting a new series on God's calling into ministry.

Robert squirmed uncomfortably. When he accepted Christ in college, he had felt a tug to dedicate his life to serving God, bu exploring what that meant kept getting postponed while he pursued a career in business—first to pay off student loans, then to raise a family, and now because he was a leader of the company.

Miranda also felt a twinge. She and her husband had talked about signing up together for a summer mission project overseas, but she had just accepted a promotion with significant responsibilities and didn't know if she could leave.

Meanwhile, Craig was wondering if he might skip class the next few months, since he knew this topic didn't apply to him. He figured he would write a support check to whoever accepted the call to ministry.

Herb started the series by reading Ephesians 2:10: "We are God's handiwork, created in Christ Jesus to do good works, which God prepared in advance for us to do." Then he said something that got Craig's attention. "What is the good work that God has prepared for us? This doesn't just mean work in or for the church. This includes work in the office and the factory and the garden. Your calling to good work begins when you wake up on Monday morning." That's when Craig realized he was not off the hook.

Six weeks into the study, Robert's vague sense of guilt was replaced by a growing excitement. He had never imagined that "God's calling into ministry" might mean God's plan for his work. No one had ever shown him in Scripture how he served God through his business. Before, he had assumed that "good works" meant volunteering or making a generous donation. Now he could see how his business—manufacturing retail shelving—was a part of God's good design for feeding and clothing people.

When Robert saw a newspaper article about a neighborhood near the church being a food desert, he felt a nudge from the Spirit. He began envisioning ways his company might partner with local retail entrepreneurs to spark economic development. He found himself looking forward each week to learning more about how to dedicate himself to his ministry at work.

Imagine Church Members Whose Work Is Their Ministry

Miranda found the concept of her work as ministry difficult to absorb. She took notes as Herb taught: "Like God, we are also workers. He made us with creative minds. He created us with the ability to solve problems. We honor and glorify God when we use the skills and passions that he has given us to be productive and efficient. We bring him glory when we commit to giving our all no matter what the task or job."[2]

For the first time, she began to look at her promotion as an opportunity to glorify God with her skills. But she couldn't stop thinking about that opportunity for summer service with their sister church in Honduras. She finally approached Herb about this after class.

"What's the purpose of mission?" he asked.

Miranda answered with confidence—she had thought about this for a long time. "To share the good news of the gospel with others. To love our neighbors around the world."

"What kinds of things would you do on a mission trip to pursue this purpose?"

Again, Miranda's reply was eager. "I want to help out any way I can, of course. But I'm especially drawn to studying the Bible with other women."

"Is anything stopping you from doing that at your workplace?" Miranda didn't have an answer. At that moment, a young woman in her workplace, a new believer, came to mind. Miranda decided she would delay her plans for a mission trip—but she wouldn't wait to pursue her mission.

Imagine Discipling People Where They Minister—at Their Work

"Hello, Robert." Members of Northside had gotten used to seeing their pastor show up at their workplace. Today, Rev. Park had arranged to meet Robert for coffee in the company break room.

Robert looked frustrated. His pastor listened as he described a competitor whose underhanded practices had cost his company a major customer. Some *in the company wanted to retaliate against the competition; others were pressuring Robert to imitate their tactics. This led to an energetic conversation with Rev. Park about productivity versus prosperity, revenge, praying for those who mistreat you, and the cost of integrity. Rev. Park opened the Bible app on his phone to Luke 16 and read a story Jesus told that related to dealing with dishonesty in business.*

"As you consider how to respond," the pastor advised Robert as he got up to leave, "remember that you bear God's image and your actions will reflect that."

Robert returned to work with greater peace and clarity.

Meanwhile, Miranda invited Caroline, the young woman God had put on her heart, to meet for lunch. Caroline was thrilled to get to know a mature Christian in the office. They hit it off and decided to meet for bagels and Bible study every Thursday morning.

A church member who worked nearby asked to join them. That week, sitting in a corner booth at the deli next to Miranda's investment firm, the three women read through Psalm 8. When they reached verse 5—"You have given them dominion over the works of your hands"—the conversation steered toward best leadership practices. As Miranda shared points from a recent management seminar, the newest member of their trio grew increasingly impatient. Finally she burst out: "I thought this was going to be a spiritual group!" Gently, Miranda invited her into a new understanding of how every domain of life—including management—is intended for God's glory.

Imagine God's Image-Bearers Enabling the World to Flourish

When Craig opened his eyes on Monday morning, he felt something was different. After a moment, he realized he didn't hate the prospect of going to work today.

As he put on his uniform, he reflected on the change in his attitude. He usually dreaded the question, "What do you do for a living?" Having the title of "sanitation engineer" helped, until people figured out what it meant. But Herb's teaching had given him a new lens to view his work. The turning point had been the question: What would happen if no one did your job? In his case, the answer was obvious! The image of a world overrun with trash spurred him on as he headed to work.

Herb had encouraged Craig to memorize Genesis 1:28: "God said to them, 'Be fruitful and multiply; fill the earth and subdue it.'" Knowing that his work was part of how God had designed humankind to bring order to creation led Craig to perform his tasks with more care. He became less touchy and disagreeable. That Monday morning, his partner on the sanitation truck even joked how it was nice not having to work with Oscar the Grouch.

Craig considered this for a moment and then said to his partner, "Every day, we make this city cleaner. People rely on us to keep out rats and bugs and disease. It's God's work, and we're good at it. Why shouldn't I be in a good mood?"

As the truck made its next stop, Craig said a prayer for the household as he disposed of their trash. It was a habit he had started recently. He thought about talking to his partner about that too.

Imagine Every Worker Making This World More Like Heaven

Rev. Park launched into his annual sermon on heaven. In previous years, he had preached about what it took to enter heaven, how God would bring an end to mourning and pain, or the joy of living eternally in God's presence.

This year, in consultation with Herb and after paying many visits to various members in their workplaces, a different sermon emerged. He talked about how the work done by people in his congregation reflected the kingdom of God that would be realized fully in heaven.

Rev. Park started by pointing out those who continue the work originally commissioned to Adam and Eve at creation: from landscapers to store shelving manufacturers to sanitation engineers. Wouldn't God's New Jerusalem still need its residents to work to keep the city beautiful, orderly and well provisioned? What could be more meaningful than working to create, cultivate, organize, build, manage, and discover in the "new heavens and new earth"?

He closed by encouraging those members whose work foreshadowed God's kingdom of perfect love, healing, and justice: counselors, healthcare providers, law enforcement, social workers. Rev. Park added that he himself might be unemployed on entering heaven, since everyone would already know the Lord!

Individuals in the pews nodded as they heard a reference to their line of work. Miranda thought about her job at the investment firm. Surely there was no money in heaven, so what was the eternal relevance of her career?

Then she tuned into the pastor saying, "Heaven will be like Jesus' story of selling our entire livelihood to gain the pearl of great price. Everything we work for our whole lives is not lost when we die—it is transformed, and its kingdom value is revealed." That sounded like investment work to Miranda. She made a mental note to talk to Herb further about how to bring this heavenly perspective into her daily efforts on behalf of clients.

Inviting God's People to the Vision

This story, while fictional, draws from real experiences with vocational discipleship. It illustrates what is possible when church leaders focus on the goal to "help God's people work well for Him" (Eph. 4:11–12 NLV), and when members take ownership of doing God's kingdom ministry through their daily occupations (whether paid or unpaid).

The vision for how church and community could thrive as followers of Christ live out their kingdom calling is compelling. The role of intentional discipleship in shepherding this vision is vital. That's why we wrote this book.

We envision churches and disciple-makers teaching people how their so-called secular jobs honor God, helping their fragmented lives come together around their kingdom purpose. We envision Christians animated by how their job matters to God and to the flourishing of the world. More workers will be invited to discover and reflect the image of a God who also is a laborer. Workplaces will be endowed with greater dignity, joy, fairness, and productivity. And out of all this, we envision communities reaping the benefits of God's design for effective, eternally meaningful work.

As someone committed to vocational discipleship, sharing this vision and bringing it to fruition is your work.

RESOURCE

Start with Listening: Faith at Work Interviews

In their book *Discipleship with Monday in Mind: How Churches across the Country Are Helping Their People Connect Faith and Work* (Made to Flourish, 2017), Skye Jethani and Luke Bobo share stories about churches that feature faith and work interviews with members. These interviews serve "to communicate the sacredness of work," to affirm workers in various occupations, and to influence the culture of the church around the purpose of work.

We have adapted their questions below for usage in a vocational discipleship context. Engaging in this kind of conversation—and really listening to what workers have to say—could be encouraging and eye-opening. Some of the questions may be challenging, however, for those who have seldom been asked to consider their day-to-day workplace experience from a theological framework. Regardless of whether or how they answer, merely asking the questions can be transformative.

1. Describe what your work day is like on a day-to-day basis.
2. How did you come to be in this work? Do you feel called to do what you're doing?
3. What does it mean to you to do your work as a Christian?
4. How does sin affect your work? Where do you experience brokenness?
5. Where do you experience restoration and redemption in the work you do?

6. What opportunities or obstacles are you facing in your work?
7. How do you try to serve others through your work?
8. In what ways can you express the gospel in relation to your work?
9. How do you experience the presence of God, or reflect God's image, as you work?
10. How would you like prayer in relation to your work?

2

A CALLING FOR THOSE WHO DISCIPLE WORKERS

CASE STUDY

After Herb retired from his career in sales, he poured himself into his gifts of teaching and discipling. Every week, he encouraged his Sunday school class to trust in their salvation through Christ and their hope of heaven. He emphasized the practical applications of faith, unpacking what the Scriptures said about their worship, family life, ethical choices, even their finances. His class members listened and engaged, and he was grateful for the opportunity to strengthen their faith.

Then one day he went shopping at a store managed by one of the regular attenders in his class, whose name was Julie. Herb was just wondering if he might get a chance to say hello to her when he heard her voice. It was hard to miss. Julie was royally chewing out one of the clerks, who looked on the verge of tears. Herb caught the two other clerks exchanging a mortified glance, as if anxious they might be next. "Now get back to your station, and you'd better get things right this time!" Julie snapped.

Herb's class had been going through the book of Ephesians, and last week they had studied chapter 4, including verse 2: "Be completely humble and gentle; be patient, bearing with one another in love." Herb had shared an example from how he learned to be humble in arguments with his wife. This then led to an intense discussion of how to resolve a congregational dispute involving the church budget.

Never had he considered how this passage might apply to a workplace. And apparently, neither had Julie. "Humble," "gentle," and "patient" were definitely not words Herb would use to describe how she treated her employees.

That's when Herb resolved to look more intentionally at what the Scriptures said about work, so he could influence the members of his class to behave more like Christ on the job.

What Is Vocational Discipleship?

The goal of discipleship is to equip people to follow Christ day by day, building their life on the good news of the gospel by the power of the

Spirit.[1] Discipleship is not just about what people believe, but how their faith leads them "to will and to act in order to fulfill [God's] good purpose" (Phil. 2:13). Discipleship is for the whole of life, because "through [Christ] God was pleased to reconcile to himself *all things*" (Col. 1:20; italics added).

This book focuses on the particular arena of *vocational discipleship*. Vocational discipleship equips people to do good work in a good way that serves the purposes of God's kingdom, based on how God has specifically called, gifted, and positioned them for impact in their job. Discipleship leads people to view their vocation as an arena where "the gospel is bearing fruit and growing" (Col. 1:6), and to be transformed by the Spirit for ongoing fruitfulness in the ministry of their work.

The Scope of Vocational Discipleship

A vocational discipler is anyone who influences the faith of another related to their life in the workplace. If you help Christians to work out their faith in the context of their work, then we have you in mind!

"Discipleship" is too often narrowly associated with activities that take place at church, led by church staff. Being a vocational discipler is not necessarily linked with a position, title, or program, but with a goal: "to equip the saints" for the work they are called to do (Eph. 4:12). The category of vocational disciplers is broad. In addition to church personnel (pastors, discipleship staff, Sunday school teachers, Bible study leaders), it includes Christian life coaches, Christian employers and workplace mentors, chaplains, Christian business groups and vocational networks, campus ministers, parents of working-age offspring, teachers and students at seminaries and Christian colleges, and faith and work consultants.

In the context of this book, vocational discipleship addresses not only paid jobs but also unpaid work that is a person's primary labor: the work of stay-at-home parents, family caretakers, interns, and retirees with volunteer placements. The point of work, from the perspective of vocational discipleship, is not that it earns an income but that it accomplishes tasks that need to be done in God's kingdom.

Because vocational discipleship focuses on how God is moving in the workaday world, it often takes place outside the church building. It might look like arriving at work early to meet with a new Christian in your warehouse for Bible study, or having lunch regularly with a fellow business owner you met at church to share and pray together, or leading a small group in your living room for other stay-at-home parents to discuss biblical perspectives on parenting.

The last decade has seen dynamic growth in the faith and work movement, through the efforts of dedicated visionaries to spread the message through a variety of innovative programs and media. We seek to build on, rather than replicate, this strong foundation. Thus this text assumes a basic understanding of core faith and work principles. We touch on key concepts but refer you to other excellent resources for a deeper dive (see Appendix C). The intent of this book is *to equip readers to equip others* to absorb and apply these important ideas. One way to look at it: Our aim is not to reinvent the faith and work wheel, but to help more people get their driver's license!

Why Is Vocational Discipleship Essential?

The church's track record on discipleship in the area of vocation has not been stellar. Church-goers might participate actively in "discipleship activities" from childhood on without any significant application to the vast part of their life that is spent at work. Beyond generalities such as "don't cheat customers," "don't lie on your timesheet," and "avoid extra-marital affairs with coworkers," Christians typically don't get much help applying biblical principles to the specific issues they face at work. For too many church-goers, work is out of sight on Sunday, and faith is out of mind on Monday.

The Judeo-Christian heritage provides an overarching sense that working hard develops good character and pleases God. Scratch a little deeper, however, and few people can trace the biblical roots of this belief. Thus many Christians have a vague ethic of work, but no real theology of work, and little guidance for how faith is practiced at work.

In the absence of overt discipleship, Christians absorb many unbiblical ideas about work. Chief among these is the belief that work in the for-profit arena is not by definition *ministry*. Church teachings tend to imply that people with "secular" jobs are second-class citizens in the spiritual world: people either work in the world or they work for God.

When Christians have their eyes opened to who God created them to be and how God called them to work in his kingdom, it is a transformative experience. As one executive who participated in Tom's Kingdom Purpose Workshop expressed:

> In terms of the strategic impact that this could have, not only on our church but in our community and in the world, this is a conversation that the world has been desperate for. . . . What does our faith say about where we spend half of our waking hours?

The world needs a church that sends out image-bearers who are productive in God-honoring, kingdom-purpose-focused work. Vocational disciplers are the hands and feet of this mission.

Job Description for Disciplers: Equip
God's People for *Ergon*

A key verse for vocational discipleship is Ephesians 4:11–13. In the NIV (italics added), this reads:

> Christ himself gave the apostles, the prophets, the evangelists, the pastors and teachers, *to equip his people for works of service,* so that the body of Christ may be built up until we all reach unity in the faith and in the knowledge of the Son of God and become mature, attaining to the whole measure of the fullness of Christ.

The King James Version renders this italicized phrase: "for the perfecting of the saints, for the work of the ministry." This version has influenced the typical interpretation for this verse, that to "equip people for works of service" means *church-centric work*: that is, activities connected with a congregation, mission agency, or nonprofit. Skye Jethani notes the implications of this interpretation for discipleship:

> Most of our church ministries are designed to make people into little pastors. We take our calling as pastors to teach the Bible, to evangelize, to teach the faith, and we replicate ourselves in our people. We teach them how to study the Bible, how to teach the Bible, how to lead small groups, how to share their faith. . . . When you and I hear the word *ministry* we think of church work. That's not what Paul meant. There were no institutional churches when he wrote that.[2]

Rather, the Greek term for work, *ergon,* has the broader sense of "business, employment, that with which anyone is occupied," according to *Thayer's Greek-English Lexicon of the New Testament. Ergon* includes that which is accomplished or produced as a job. The second part of the phrase, *diakonias,* indicates tasks done for the benefit of others or at another's command. Together, they have the sense of intentional effort that serves a good purpose.

The mission statement for vocational disciplers is summarized in Ephesians 4:12: "To help [God's] people work well for Him" (NLV). Vocational disciplers must avoid "kingdom purpose projection," or the assumption that our goal is to help others to do what *we* are called to do. Rather, we prepare God's people to do the *ergon* work that God has gifted and called *them* to perform. Our role is to "come alongside them, validate their communion with Christ, validate their calling in the world, and equip them to meet with God and to carry his glory into the midst of a world that desperately needs him."[3]

Qualifications for Vocational Discipleship

One who disciples others must commit to follow Jesus, grow in faith, have healthy relationships, and remain accountable to responsible church leaders.[4] Vocational disciplers must be able to share from the Scriptures and the fullness of the gospel story. A level of familiarity with the theology and principles of faith-work integration (or willingness to learn) is assumed. Being able to guide people in a process of biblical discovery and application is far more important than having all the answers yourself.

Excellent vocational disciplers are servant leaders, as described in Philippians 2:3: "In humility regard others as better than yourselves." The discipling relationship is not about you. It's about the image-bearer sitting across from you—and the valued kingdom purpose that God has uniquely fashioned them to pursue.

Servant leaders need patience, because growth toward kingdom purpose rarely comes easily or quickly. As Randy Pope observes, "The process of discipleship is more like a marathon than a sprint."[5] Corollary qualities are wisdom and discernment to know when to listen, when to teach, when to encourage, when to prod, and when to step back and let the Holy Spirit work—and always how to speak the truth in love (Eph. 4:15).

The Calling to Vocational Discipleship

Are you called to be a vocational discipler? Can you see yourself meeting with believers to support their ministry of work, examine how Scripture enlightens their daily challenges, explore key questions about vocation, challenge them to do good work in a good way, and equip them to be productive in their kingdom purpose?

In *The Disciplemakers Handbook*, coauthor Josh Patrick describes a difficult period in his life:

> I felt the weight of the world crushing me down. All I could do was drop to my knees and cry out to God. . . . My church attendance record was nearly perfect, but my faith was weak and undeveloped. I had more than a decade of Christian education under my belt, but I had no clue how to apply what I already knew. I needed someone to meet me where I was and make an intentional effort to invest in my spiritual maturity. God answered my cry of need and despair, and he sent several people into my life to disciple and mentor me. Today, he's sending me back out, into the lives of others. That's how it works.[6]

A vocational discipler is one who is "sent" (John 20:21) to working Christians, many of whom are crying out to God in pain, frustration and confusion. Followers of Jesus need more than good sources of instruction; they need someone to walk alongside them as they translate biblical wisdom to the messiness of their workplace. They need someone who will believe in their potential as an image-bearer, affirm their unique calling, and hold them personally accountable to their kingdom purpose.

This is not discipleship for the status quo. Inviting people to follow Jesus in their work may lead to radical shifts in how believers see themselves (and others), their vocational ministry, and how their work connects with the gospel story. Disciple-makers may be called on to challenge unbiblical assumptions, attitudes, and actions and invite repentance. This calling requires people who have the courage of their convictions as well as openness to ongoing renewal in their own lives.

RESOURCE

"Life on Life" Discipleship: The TEAMS Model

Personal discipling relationships are a high-impact strategy for helping people apply their faith to their work at a deeper level.

Randy Pope, founding pastor of Perimeter Church and president of Life on Life Ministries, has developed a helpful model that lends itself to vocational discipleship. This framework for "life-on-life discipleship" includes five components forming the acronym TEAMS: Truth, Equipping, Accountability, Mission, and Supplication.[7] The purpose of this framework is "to see them become mature and equipped followers of Christ, committed to doing the same in the lives of others."[8]

While there are many possible variations on this framework, it offers a helpful foundation for understanding the role of the discipler in the working life of a follower of Jesus.

Truth: Discipler as Teacher

While discipleship is more than Bible study, we turn to the word of God for guidance in the truth. Read Scripture together to learn to see the world through God's perspective. While the Bible is the foundation, truthful wisdom can also be found in research, reflection, and experience.

Equipping: Discipler as Coach

As Jesus' parable of the soils indicates (Matt. 13:1–23), there is a difference between merely hearing the truth and being equipped to put truth into action. People need help unpacking the meaning of Scripture so they can apply it to their lives. Explain, demonstrate, challenge, prod, inspire, and encourage—whatever someone needs to move toward active practice.

Accountability: Discipler as Sponsor

Pope compares the discipler to a sponsor in the Alcoholics Anonymous Twelve Steps model: asking incisive questions to invite an individual to examine their thinking and behavior. Without accountability, people can get mired in unbiblical, unproductive patterns. This role does not mean passing judgment, but offering feedback that exposes sin and empowers change to "provoke one another to love and good deeds" (Heb. 10:24).

Mission: Discipler as Sender

Pope says of the mission component: "In my opinion this is the most challenging of the five emphases. In a certain respect, it is the lead domino of spiritual formation."[9] Mission is where individual spirituality is turned outward toward sharing the fullness of the gospel in word and deed with the world. The disciple becomes one who disciples others. "As the Father has sent me, so I send you" (John 20:21).

Supplication: Discipler as Intercessor

Pray with each other, for each other, and for others. Prayer reminds us that we are coworkers with God and that apart from Jesus we can do nothing (John 15:5). Prayer teaches trust and patience. Be intentional about praying over the needs, dilemmas, hardships, and triumphs of those you disciple, as well as interceding for the world.

3

THREE CORE QUESTIONS OF VOCATIONAL DISCIPLESHIP

CASE STUDY

Melissa took a deep breath and prayed for wisdom as she opened her twelve-year-old son's door. "Let's talk about the garden," she said calmly as Derek looked up from his iPad.

"Yeah, I kind of forgot about weeding," he said, his attention going back to the screen. "Sorry. I'll finish it later."

Melissa sorted through her thoughts. It was his third time "forgetting" tasks that week. Should she yell at him? Impound his iPad?

"Derek, you are God's unique creation and our beloved child, and you are a vital part of our family." Melissa could see Derek's expression was wary. He wasn't sure where his mother was going with this. She continued speaking calmly. "Everyone in our family has their work to do. What makes your job of weeding the garden important?"

"It . . . helps the plants grow better, I guess."

"Fewer weeds, more produce! Every time we eat a tomato, your work helped put it on the table. So we depend on you doing it well. Here, read this."

She handed her son her Bible, open to Genesis 2:15. He read aloud, "The Lord God took the man and put him in the garden of Eden to till it and keep it."

"See," she said, smiling, "assigning you to weed the garden is not just my idea. You inherited the job from Adam, who got it from God. You are just the right person to do it." There was a pause. "NOW."

As Derek scrambled out the door, Melissa thought: "And my assignment from God is tending this kid as he grows."

Core Discipleship Questions

Vocational discipleship invites people to reclaim their identity as redeemed image-bearers and to discover their kingdom calling so they can fruitfully enact God's purpose through their work. In this book, we lay out a model of spiritual growth anchored in three core questions:

1. *Who Are You?* Disciplers help people regard themselves as God's redeemed image-bearers.

2. *What Is Your Purpose?* Disciplers help people understand the kingdom purpose of their work.

3. *How Will You Fulfill Your Purpose?* Disciplers walk with people to carry out the kingdom purpose of their work more faithfully and fruitfully.

Parts two, three, and four of this book are organized according to this discipleship model, equipping disciplers to engage with people around these three core questions. Part five examines how disciplers can enable this model to sink in and produce change, including confronting false narratives about work. The appendices and the resource pages throughout the book provide practical tools to help carry out this approach to vocational discipleship.

Being, Knowing, Doing

One cannot be an authentic follower of Jesus and not experience change (Mark 8:34). Disciples experience transformation in three arenas: our being, our knowing, and our doing.

Christians often have a vague sense of *how* they're supposed to behave at work, but not *who* they should be at work. The first role of discipleship is to open their eyes to claim *who they are as God's redeemed image-bearers*. Disciplers help people discover this powerful, foundational truth in a biblical context and how it relates to faithfulness in vocation. Disciplers support reflection on what it means to be an image-bearer on the job.

At the end of my (Tom's) class, one student wrote:

> I am always convicted, humbled, and encouraged by remembering that I bear God's image. It is both a simple concept and a deeply moving concept, because remembering that you bear the image of God himself changes the implication of your entire life. It allows me to read the Scriptures in a new light, it allows me to work in a new light, and it allows me to be a believer in a new light.[1]

As this student discovered, seeing ourselves as God's redeemed image-bearers can be a starting point for further growth.

We're immersed in a secular culture that drives people to seek success defined by profit, prestige, and comfort. Christians are also typically steeped in a religious culture that defines the aims of spiritual maturity in terms of being church-centered and other-worldly. In this context, discipleship searches the Scriptures and invites the Holy Spirit to help people to *know God's kingdom purpose for image-bearers.*

This transformative process involves more than sharing a few key verses or principles about faith-based work. Discipleship is rooted in a story that gives image-bearers purpose. Disciplers help people locate their specific vocational calling within the biblical "Big Story" (the gospel told in four chapters—creation, fall, redemption, restoration). From start to finish, from creation into new creation, the Bible points to four kingdom purposes for work:

1. Glorify God

2. Bless people

3. Draw people to Christ

4. Enable the world to flourish (build abundant community, establish order, develop potential from creation, and restore brokenness)

Vocational discipleship takes these big ideas and zooms into the specific things people do every day to restore the goodness and cultivate the potential of God's creation.

In God's kingdom, it's never enough just to have spiritual insight or a pure heart—faithfulness is always revealed in action. Jesus declared, "Everyone who hears these words of mine and puts them into practice is like a wise man who built his house on the rock" (Matt. 7:24). As people grasp that they are made in God's likeness, equipped and empowered by loving grace to serve God's kingdom purpose, they can dedicate themselves to pursuing it effectively. Disciplers guide people to *faithfully and productively live out their calling,* doing good work in a good way.

How people work matters to God. Since work carries out God's agenda, God wants to see it done well, and in a manner that reflects his image. Vocational discipleship cultivates Christ-likeness in people's attitudes and actions in the workplace. A discipler must be prepared—like the prophets and like Jesus—to address tough issues of productivity, wealth, ethics, excellence, generosity, and fairness. Encourage people in practicing disciplines that will "keep [them] from being ineffective and unfruitful in [the] knowledge of our Lord Jesus Christ" (2 Pet. 1:8).

Characteristics of Discipleship Built around Being, Knowing, and Doing

Vocational discipleship in this model possesses four characteristics: (1) Relational; (2) Contextualized; (3) Integrative; and (4) Transformational.

Relational

Vocational discipleship cannot be just a program or a curriculum. It requires a personal investment of time, transparency, and mutual accountability. "Disciples are made in relationships through personal, eyeball-to-eyeball invitation."[2]

Relational investment allows the discipler to customize to the person's personality, needs, questions, and unique work situation. A relational approach also means that people will learn from your life as much as from your words. "The key to equipping is modeling. Most of what we learn is observed—caught, not taught. Jesus said, a disciple is not above his teacher but when he is fully trained he will be like his teacher (Luke 6:40)."[3]

Above all, discipleship requires you to authentically, self-sacrificially care for those God has entrusted to you. Work in this world is hard, and people are hurting. Sometimes a listening ear and affirming word is worth a hundred principles.

Because the essence of discipleship is relational, this means you don't have to wait for your church to start a faith and work program. Launching yourself as a vocational discipler is as simple as setting a time to connect.

Contextualized

Vocational disciplers should seek to go to their workers' turf and focus on their issues. Timothy Keller observes, "Many churches do not know how to disciple members without essentially pulling them out of their vocations and inviting them to become heavily involved in church activities. In other words, Christian discipleship is interpreted as consisting largely of activities done in the evening or on the weekend."[4]

Learn as much as you can from the people you disciple about the jobs they do. Discipleship doesn't consist simply of imparting wisdom; spend a good amount of time asking questions and listening. Whenever possible, vocational disciplers should enter the world of their workers because that is where God is moving. One way to contextualize discipleship is through a "Gospel@Work Day" (see Appendix B).

Integrated

Vocational discipleship integrates big ideas into the level of daily choices. Although it is rooted in broad theological principles, it always leads toward practical application in the work world. The focus on *who people are* as image-bearers also helps connect their work more seamlessly with other roles of their life (see Appendix B for an integrative Life Plan).

Executive coach Daniel Steere noted after participating in Tom's kingdom purpose discipleship group, "I'm more consistent now, because I have a better narrative to tie it back to. . . . I've done the homework, to go from a 30,000-foot view of my calling down to what do I do today." The discipleship process gave him a "holistic framework for why I do what I'm doing."[5]

Transformational

I (Tom) had a professor who said the job of a teacher is to create cognitive dissonance: if you walked out of his class and your head wasn't spinning, then he hadn't done his job. As disciplers, we follow in the footsteps of Jesus, who sure made a lot of heads spin!

We aren't trying to be controversial or flashy for its own sake. But if we're doing our job, then we're going to challenge people's assumptions and the false paradigms surrounding work. We're going to unmask and confront idolatry and sin in the workplace. Disciplers have to be prepared to generate friction in order to shed light.

As people grasp their kingdom purpose as redeemed image-bearers, they may be open to reconsider aspects of their working life: what work they do, how they do it, how they treat others on the job, what motivates them to work, and what they believe God expects from them as a worker. A vocational discipler walks with people through these shifts.

Clear Purpose, Flexible Path

There is no set program or model for vocational discipleship. To pursue their goal of "helping God's people work well for him," disciplers have a range of options for effective formats.

- *Structure:* one-on-one, small group, class

- *Style:* teacher, coach, chaplain, spiritual advisor, mentor, peer support

- *Substance:* Bible study, book study, prepared curriculum, informal conversation

There is no single correct order for tackling topics, or even a clear starting point, as people will best learn their kingdom purpose out of whatever their working life is throwing at them in the moment.

Whatever path you walk with a follower of Jesus, you can find your way by returning to these three core markers of spiritual maturity in the ministry of their vocation:

1. Who are you as a redeemed bearer of God's image as you engage in your work?

2. What is God's kingdom purpose that you are called to fulfill through your work?

3. How can you work productively, so that God is glorified and his beloved world flourishes?

RESOURCE

Principles for Effectively Connecting with Adult Learners

Disciples are learners, but adults learn differently than children. Effective disciplers don't simply model their teaching methods after the ways they learned Bible stories as a child. According to Malcolm Knowles,[6] a pioneer in the field of adult education, and other researchers, adults learn best when:

- *They are motivated to learn.* Adults don't just want information; they want to understand why this information is important. Discipleship reaches to their goals and passions.

- *They are respected partners in learning.* Adults resist being talked down to. Engage disciples in drawing on their own stock of life experiences and perspectives to make discoveries.

- *Learning is practical and relevant.* Adult learners have limited time and many responsibilities, so they need to "keep it real." Effective discipleship bridges biblical wisdom with here-and-now applications to the workplace.

- *Instruction is adapted to their personal learning style.* Some disciples are readers who thrive on book studies, some learn best through listening and dialogue, some are visual learners who click with graphics and diagrams, and some are kinesthetic learners who focus best when their bodies are in motion. Find out what method works best for each individual discipling relationship.

- *Learning is relational.* Discipling adults must mean more than just getting through the material and checking off the boxes. They want to know that you are sincerely invested in them as a person. Discipleship is strengthened by authentic connection.

PART TWO

DISCIPLESHIP CORE QUESTION #1: "WHO ARE YOU?"

(Helping People See Themselves as Image-Bearers Who Work)

4

DISCIPLESHIP LEADS PEOPLE TO DECLARE "I AM AN IMAGE-BEARER!"

CASE STUDY

Colin joined Marcus at the table in the student center, lunch in hand. Colin knew Marcus from the campus ministry team, but this was his first time meeting with him as Colin's spiritual advisor. As they ate, Colin filled Marcus in on how his junior year was going. As a good student, he had the opportunity to apply for a paid internship but was wrestling with the choice of various options. Each represented a different career path within his field. Though he had prayed about the decision, he couldn't discern a direction. He laid out his dilemma to Marcus.

Colin expected Marcus to say something like, "What career would please God more?" or, "What's the best fit with the gifts God has given you?" or even, "Which kind of job would give you the most joy?"

Instead, Marcus started with the question Colin least expected. Leaning in, he asked, "Who are you when you are working?"

What It Means to Be an Image-Bearer

Human beings appear as the apex of all of God's acts of creation: "Let us make humankind in our image, according to our likeness" (Gen. 1:26). Before we know anything else about these new creatures—before we are told what they are called to *do*—we are introduced to the essence of who they *are*: the bearers of God's likeness. This is the starting block for everything we know about humanity, our relationship with God, and our place in the world. Similarly, in vocational discipleship, the foundation is to help people see themselves as God's image-bearers. This may not be the first topic you explore together, but once it's on the table, it holds everything else together.

What does it mean to be an image-bearer? The *imago Dei* has innumerable implications—from the sanctity of life to racial justice to self-care to religious liberty.[1] Here are three corollary affirmations to emphasize in the context of vocational discipleship.

1. "As an Image-Bearer, I Am Designed to Work."

If we reflect God's image, then this means our identity is uniquely based on who God is and what God does. Of course, we realize this doesn't mean that we *are* God, but that we are *like* God.

At the beginning of the biblical story, how are we introduced to God? As a worker. God envisions, designs, creates, assesses, establishes, blesses, distributes, directs—all in the first chapter of Genesis. When we work, we reflect God's likeness. We can't fulfill our purpose as image-bearers without working.

Jesus, as the "exact imprint of God's very being" (Heb. 1:3), models this. In John 5:17 he declares, "My Father is still working, and I also am working." There are many ways to unpack this passage in context, but one clear application is that Jesus affirms that God is a worker and thus we also are workers. This gives work inherent dignity and worth.

2. "As An Image-Bearer, I Work to Make God's Creation Very Good."

At the conclusion of each of the first five days of creation, God's work is pronounced "good." On the sixth day, God breathes life into a human created in his image. And then what is the assessment? "Indeed, it was very good" (Gen. 1:31). The thing that takes God's garden from *good* to *very good* is the presence of the image-bearer. That is a testimony to our inherent value, our vast potential, and our sacred responsibility.

Working is part of our created nature that makes us very good. The more image-bearers align their work with God's purpose, the more the world is restored to its "very good" status. (The ways that disciplers help people discover their purpose and specific calling as workers will be fleshed out in part three.)

3. "As I Work, I Am an Image-Bearer—and So Is Everyone Else."

Being created in God's image means that people cannot *not* be image-bearers! We may certainly act otherwise, but no matter what we do, we can't change or erase what we are at the core.

So, there is no hierarchy between "Christian image-bearers" and "secular image-bearers." There are no arenas in our lives, like church services, where we bear God's image more than others. Each human being, whether working in a coffee shop or a coal mine or a corner office, has been equally made in God's likeness. We are image-bearers before we are sinners, before we are saved, before we are aware of whose image we bear.

As disciplers, we encourage people to walk with Jesus in the process of "being transformed into his image" (2 Cor. 3:18), so that we may be restored and empowered to carry out our created purpose. We are not just redeemed souls—we are redeemed image-bearers! The ultimate destiny of this spiritual journey is to live and work in unity with God with no more separation between the Creator and the people who bear his image (Rev. 21:3).

The resource that follows below provides a list of Bible passages and reflection questions for you to study with someone to introduce the idea of being an image-bearer. It may be necessary to bring up these concepts repeatedly, until they really begin to sink in. We are changing the way people see themselves (and others) at the core, and that is no simple matter. But once grasped, it leads to indelible change. The next chapter looks at the transformational impact of being an image-bearer.

RESOURCE

Selected Scripture Passages on Being an Image-Bearer

These passages (and others) can be helpful to walk through with a disciple, to show how the unique status of human beings created in the image of God rings throughout Scripture.

- Being made in God's image gives us a special, intimate bond with our Creator. We recognize this when Adam's first son is described as being "in his likeness, according to his image" (Gen. 5:3).

- Being image-bearers is the foundation for law and social order: "Whoever sheds the blood of a human, by a human shall that person's blood be shed; for in his own image God made humankind" (Gen. 9:6).

- Being created in the image of God gives humans unique status in creation: "You have made them a little lower than God, and crowned them with glory and honor" (Ps. 8:5).

- We look to Jesus as the perfect reflection of God's likeness, to show us who God is: "If you know me, you will know my Father also. . . . Whoever has seen me has seen the Father" (John 14:7–9).

- The Spirit of Christ gives us freedom to live more fully as image-bearers, as we are "transformed into the same image" (2 Cor. 3:18).

- Jesus, "though he was in the form of God," modeled for us that image-bearers don't live for themselves but for God. "Being born in human likeness, and being found in human form, he humbled himself" (Phil. 2:6–8).

- Being an image-bearer guides our personal relationships and social ethics—integrity is demanded of those whose identity is being renewed "according to the image of its creator" (Col. 3:9–10).

- Being an image-bearer is inextricably linked with the work of creation. Jesus is "the reflection of God's glory and the exact imprint of God's very being" and also the one "through whom he also created the worlds" (Heb. 1:2–3).

- Our status as image-bearers continues into eternity: "When he is revealed, we will be like him, for we will see him as he is" (1 John 3:2).

5

HELPING PEOPLE SHIFT TO AN IMAGE-BEARER PERSPECTIVE

Mark Salcedo took Tom's Kingdom Purpose Workshop. One of the course assignments is to write about Bible passages that hold fresh meaning for them after developing an image-bearer perspective. Here is Mark's testimony.

MARK'S STORY

This class helped me understand in a much more meaningful way what is meant by "image-bearer," that we were made in the image of God. One of aspect of God is that he is creator. His "work" was creation. What really hit home for me was the simple statement that we were designed and made in the image of God to work, to create. Our individual work is our calling, the thing that God has designed us each to do, the thing we feel passion for. And it doesn't necessarily have to be something related to the church to have value.

Now when I read Genesis 1:26–31, where God tells us to "be fruitful and multiply and fill the earth and subdue it," I think of my calling—the passion God has given me in particular for music and also for technology. For a long time, I felt these passions would only be truly useful in the context of church service. If I was building technology for use at church, or if I was serving in worship services with the piano or voice, that's when I thought I was doing what God had called me to do.

But now I understand how narrow that thinking is. I can utilize these talents anywhere, anytime, for the glory of God. In the concert hall—wonderful! In the public schools—awesome! Of course, in our church buildings is still great as well, but I'm not limited there. My "music ministry" doesn't have to be in the church; it can be out in the world, and that is very freeing.

This concept brings new depth of meaning to a Scripture like Romans 8:18–25—"The creation waits with eager longing for the revealing of the sons of God." Our "work" is to beautify this world, and the creation has been waiting for us to do our work. It will be done in even more fullness at the return of Jesus. Meanwhile, I can continue to apply my talents, gifts, and passion to the work God has given me . . . to do my absolute very best in both information technology and music.[1]

Shifting to an Image-Bearer Perspective

One of the key tasks of a vocational discipler is to help people shift from a "church-centric perspective" to an "image-bearer perspective." Many Christians come to the discipling relationship with a church-centered perspective. They assume:

- God's work takes place mainly in and by the church; our kingdom purpose flows through the church.

- The focus of "Christian work" is activity that draws people into the church or builds up the church.

- "Good works" that please God are those commissioned by the church or by nonprofit ministries.

- The value of work outside the church arena is measured by how it supports the church (e.g., by enabling people to make financial contributions, or giving people skills and influential connections that help the church's ministry thrive).

- The Bible is primarily written to the church, about the church.

Steven Garber summarizes the critique of this church-centric perspective:

> Vocation is integral, not incidental, to the *missio Dei*. Most of the time, all over the world, the church teaches otherwise, that vocation is incidental, not integral, to the missio Dei. It is always a compartmentalizing of faith from life, of worship from work, and it has tragic consequences for the church and the world.[2]

We advocate discipleship that reflects an image-bearer perspective:

- God's work is done by image-bearers, only some of whom are in the church.

- The focus of Christian work is activity that fulfills God's kingdom purpose for all of creation.

- God delights in good work in every arena that helps his world flourish.

- The vital role of the church is to invite, prepare, and send out image-bearers to do the work that fulfills our kingdom purpose.

- The Bible is a book written to image-bearers, some of whom are in the church.

It must be emphasized that challenging a church-centric perspective does not by any means make us anti-church. The church is the body of Christ, the bride of Christ, a household built on Christ the cornerstone. Without the church, there is no growth into maturity. Without the church, there is no equipping and sending into mission. In the church, we can experience authentic community, freedom of prayer and worship, and the joyful celebration of our Creator and Redeemer that anticipates heaven like nothing else on earth.

So, the church and its ministries are vitally, irreplaceably important. *But it is not at the center of our kingdom purpose.* Church-related activities are not the only focal point of our relationship to God and faithfulness to his commands.

People once called it heresy to say that the earth revolved around the sun, fearing this perspective would diminish the value of the earth and its inhabitants. But, of course, our uniqueness as image-bearers circling around the sun remains intact. Here, we highlight that the fullness of God's kingdom work is not limited within the boundaries of church-related activities. But this could never diminish all that makes the church uniquely beloved to Christ (Eph. 5:25) or essential to his followers (Heb. 10:25).

A Transformative Perspective

Shifting to an image-bearer perspective may not be easy, especially for those who have been taught within a church-centered framework all their lives. The journey, however, is transformative. People's beliefs and behavior change as they discover the fullness of what it means to declare, "I am an image-bearer!"

It Revolutionizes How People See Themselves and Their Value

From a church-centric perspective, God interacts with people primarily when they're engaged in "spiritual" activities, meaning individual devotional acts or involvement with church ministries. Many imagine that God only pays attention to them at work to make sure they're not breaking ethical rules or being a bad witness to Christ.

In Tom's long experience with discipleship, when people grasp an image-bearing perspective, you can actually see their countenance change. A look of peace and a smile of contentment break out on their face as they discover, and really absorb, that they matter to God as image-bearers during the majority of their lives: when they are on the job. God actually cares deeply about their investment in the work to which he has gifted and uniquely called them.

For example, after studying with Tom, one professional who had been discouraged by his work gained a radically new and energizing perspective:

> *God is definitely involved in my work. God is very much concerned with what I do. It is my ministry. God has helped me to be good at it. He designed me that way. . . . Now I have a certain joy or appreciation that God is in my work and my work is my ministry for God.*[3]

It Illuminates Their Reading of Scripture

Most Christians read Scripture through a church-centric lens. They assume that the Scriptures were written to and for the people of God—Israel in the Old Testament, the body of Christ in the New Testament. Thus Christians read the Bible for guidance and inspiration on spiritual, church-related topics. But what if the Bible is a book written *to image-bearers*—some of whom are in the church?

> *Paul Minear once said that the Bible is "an album of casual photographs of laborers. . . . A book by workers, about workers, for workers—that is the Bible." This being the case, it is rather stunning that we are able to leaf through most of the major Bible dictionaries and find absolutely no articles on work at all! It is as if the Bible had nothing to say on the subject.* [4]

When people learn to read the Bible through an image-bearing lens, they immediately become more interested in what the Bible has to say to the whole of their lives.

It Strengthens Their Connection with God

The more people live with the awareness of bearing God's image, the more they go through their day with a sense of closeness to God—even in seemingly trivial activities. They discover that there is no part of life outside their image-bearing relationship with their Creator.

> *The more I am reminded of being an image-bearer and recognizing that I bear the characteristics, desires, and wants of God, I realize that the things I should be praying for should align more with God's heart for the world and God's heart for his people. I begin to see that my prayers are less self-focused and more God-focused.*[5]

As image-bearers, people's hearts can be more tuned to the living presence of the Spirit during their hours on the job.

Their Spiritual Growth Is Revitalized

If their faith is irrelevant to their work, then how can people grow in their faith during their hours spent at work? Since God is a worker, there are spiritual insights that people can discover only as they reflect God's image and pursue God's purpose on the job. When they stop regarding spiritual disciplines as an end in themselves, but as a vital part of how their work matters to God, their motivation to pursue spiritual maturity is recharged.

Gaining "a better understanding of who I am and what I'm supposed to be doing" made a significant difference in how Daniel Steere regarded spiritual growth:

> *It gives context and . . . meaning to personal time of worship. Before, I just did it because I'm good at keeping rules. . . . I'm not saying that my spiritual disciplines are better; I would say that I'm looking at a different set of metrics to define what my spiritual state looks like.*[6]

Their Spiritual Life Becomes More Integrated and Balanced

Once people realize that they are image-bearers all the time—not just when doing "church-y" things—they're relieved from the burden of feeling that spiritual formation is in competition with work. They can follow Jesus into their workplace and every area of life. Seeing themselves as image-bearers leads to a more seamless faith. One of Tom's students described it this way:

> *It is a new thought process to think of myself as an image-bearer. It causes me to no longer keep church ministry and daily life work as two separate things. As an image-bearer all that I do is to be for God.*[7]

Image-bearers are free to discover the spiritual dimensions of their work, as well as their family and leisure time. A busy executive described a practical effect of this integrated approach:

> *Now, for the first time in my life, I'm actually thinking about things like getting up and going to the gym. . . . I've always felt guilty; I thought maybe that was my vanity. No—this is caretaking. It's helping me to see the spiritual dimension to all of the practical things that I've been doing.*[8]

They Are More Motivated to Work

After a study of Ephesians 2:10, a student wrote:

Understanding my calling as God's image-bearer, this verse just jumps off the pages. It's no longer just about being good or doing good from a moral standpoint. Instead, I see that purposefulness with which God has rescued me. . . . It's good work! Work that I can be proud of. Work that is a significant part of his master plan.[9]

When a disciple says, "I am God's image-bearer," this means acknowledging that their life belongs to the God who is a worker, who has gifted and called them for tasks that serve a meaningful purpose. This creates more accountability and a desire to work well.

It Transforms Their Relationships with Others

Learning to see each human as an image-bearer has profound implications for how we treat the people around us. All image-bearers deserve to be regarded as having unique and inestimable value. A hospital chaplain in Tom's class remarked,

This class has really opened my eyes to what I am as an image-bearer and how it relates to patients at the hospital. Every time I now visit a patient I think of them as made in the image of God, no matter what their skin color, deformity, or beauty.[10]

This perspective puts everyone on equal spiritual footing, whether Christian or not, whether working in the church or out in the world. A pastor in Tom's class shared this new conviction:

Now I can help a disciple see that my job as a minister is not of greater value than the job they hold as a parts handler for Boeing aircrafts. I can now see that God has not only gifted Christians with talents and gifts; He has also gifted non-Christians . . . because they are created in the image of God and also contribute to creating culture.[11]

Instead of seeing unchurched people in the workplace only as targets of mission, Christians can also appreciate how as image-bearers, their coworkers are also designed to be co-participants in God's purpose. This means that Christians are always on mission as they engage with "outsiders" in the context of their work.

They Discover New Doors for Sharing the Gospel

The question we ask in discipleship—*"Who are you when you are working?"*—is one with profound evangelistic implications as well. It is a question that gnaws at many people we encounter in the workplace who feel the emptiness of their lives, even if they can't quite put it into words.

From an image-bearer perspective, everyone who does good work contributes to God's kingdom purpose. This opens doors to affirm to others the value of their work—and their value as a person—in God's eyes. When we approach people as fellow image-bearers, we encounter unexpected opportunities to share about how knowing God imbues work with a sense of purpose. What an affirming way to introduce people to God—by showing them how their work reflects their Maker!

A Living Offering

In Romans 12:1–2, Paul appeals to disciples "to present your bodies as a living sacrifice, holy and acceptable to God, which is your spiritual worship." Being an image-bearer is a life of offering, of spiritual worship expressed through the physical work of our bodies. As our minds are renewed in this understanding, God's Spirit transforms us to share in God's good, acceptable, and perfect will.

None of these transforming effects happen automatically or overnight. The role of the discipler is to walk with image-bearers at work, as they grow in an ongoing process of offering, renewal, and discernment.

RESOURCE

Image-Bearer Discipleship Questions

Questions to discuss what it means to be an image-bearer:

- Say out loud, "I am God's image-bearer." What does this mean to you? What reaction does this spark in you?

- Where in Scripture do you see God doing work similar to yours? What does this say about how you reflect God's image?

- How does the awareness of being God's image-bearer in your workplace affect how you view your work?

- How does the awareness that each person is God's image-bearer affect how you view others in your workplace?

- Who in your workplace could you reach out to affirm as being a valued image-bearer?

- What conclusions about God could others draw from observing you at work?

- As you review your work life, are there ways in which you have not acted consistently with bearing God's likeness? How is God inviting you to repent and be transformed?

- Who are you at work? Is this seamless with who you are at church? At home? With your friends?

- How can claiming your identity as an image-bearer lead to more consistency and balance?

6

HELPING IMAGE-BEARERS APPRECIATE GOD'S DESIGN FOR WORK

CASE STUDY

Shannon showed off her vacation pictures at the Wednesday evening Bible study. "If only I could have just stayed on that beach," she sighed. "I hated going back to work."

"Just wait until we get to heaven," said her friend helpfully. "Then you'll get to just hang out on beautiful beaches forever."

"But for now, we have to take our punishment and stay on the job," someone else commented. This led to a litany of general complaints about work from around the room.

"If I didn't have to pay rent, I'd quit tomorrow and never look back."

"I live for the weekends."

"I can't wait to retire and never have to work another day."

Mandy, the facilitator for the Bible lesson that week, decided to put the curriculum aside for the moment. Instead, she asked, "According to the Bible, is work a blessing or a curse?"

Vocational disciplers help people realize they are image-bearers whose work matters to God. Yet probably 95 percent of work-related discipleship conversations revolve around frustrations and failures on the job. The issues on the front burner of people's attention at work tend to expose the worst of the human condition, not the qualities that reflect God's image.

It is thus important to help disciples grasp *what God designed work to be*. We need this in order to be proactive in pursuing God's purpose, rather than merely reacting to the problem of the day.

Taking on the Creation Mandate

The starting point for exploring God's design for work with disciples comes right after God makes the first image-bearers (Gen. 1:26–28), in a passage often known as the "creation mandate":

Then God said, "Let us make humankind in our image, according to our likeness; and let them have dominion over the fish of the sea and over the birds of the air, and over the cattle, and over all the wild animals of the earth, and over every creeping thing that creeps upon the earth."

So God created humankind in his image, in the image of God he created them; male and female he created them.

God blessed them, and God said to them, "Be fruitful and multiply, and fill the earth and subdue it; and have dominion over the fish of the sea and over the birds of the air and over every living thing that moves upon the earth."

Right after giving image-bearers life, God gives them an assignment. Because God is a worker, he put them to work. This is foundational to shaping image-bearers' attitude toward work.

The task that God gives to the first humans may seem specific to their unique place in history. Their workforce of two is the entire global population. Their work setting is an abundant wilderness, unspoiled by pollution or decay. This scene takes place before their disobedience led to the scarcities, hardships, and corruption of the world that shape our work today.

Yet from a theological perspective, our commonality with God's first workforce is greater than our differences. Our essential identity as image-bearers is unchanged. We still live in the world that God designed and loves. The entrance of sin and its consequences made carrying out God's directive more difficult and painful, but did not negate it. This creation mandate—sometimes also called the cultural mandate—still applies to all image-bearers today. (See the questions on the resource page below to help people grasp the significance of this for themselves.)

Chapter 7 describes in more detail how to help disciples apply the creation mandate to their own employment. employment. Here, we consider how God's design for work can shape disciples' attitudes, including receiving work as God's blessing, honoring work as God's provision, and appreciating how work connects people with one another and the created environment.

Receive Work as God's Blessing

When supervisors hand out work assignments, they hardly expect the response, "Thanks! What a blessing!" But in Genesis 1:28, right before Adam and Eve get their assignment, we read, "God blessed them, and God said to them . . ." Do the people you disciple think about work as a blessing? Not just because it pays the bills, but because it is an expression of the goodness of God's design?

Timothy Keller and Katherine Leary Alsdorf point out that the Bible was unique among ancient philosophies in asserting that people work in paradise:

It is part of the blessedness of the garden of God. Work is as much a basic human need as food, beauty, rest, friendship, prayer, and sexuality. . . . Many people make the mistake of thinking that work is a curse and that something else (leisure, family, or even "spiritual" pursuits) is the only way to find meaning in life.[1]

So having to work is *not* a punishment. Work, in itself, is good.

But the story goes on. After sin entered the world, work fell under the curse, along with every other aspect of paradise. To assert that God designed work to be a blessing is not a glib dismissal of the bitter hardships and heartaches that come with work. Disciplers must acknowledge the reality that "work in a fallen world can be degrading, boring, unjust, stressful, and ugly"; thus we must "never instruct a suffering worker to 'whistle while you work.'"[2]

Rather, this calls for resolute effort to close the gap between God's intentions for work and the common experience of "painful toil" (Gen. 3:17). *Every Good Endeavor* by Keller and Alsdorf provides a thorough review of how sin subverts the joy, dignity, meaning, and fruitfulness of labor, and how the gospel restores the goodness of working for God. Christ will "redeem all things that had been broken," and that includes our work.[3]

Despite the prevalent misconception of heaven as an eternal day off, the Bible suggests that the blessing of meaningful work will continue into our resurrected existence. Image-bearers will work in a way that engages all their gifts, finally free from the curse and the limitations of mortality. A Christian's resentment at *having to work* now is inconsistent with the everlasting gift of *getting to work* in their future.

Honor Work as God's Provision

In Genesis 1:29, right after God issues his commands to humans—to be fruitful, multiply, fill, subdue, and have dominion—he says, "I have given you every plant yielding seed that is upon the face of all the earth and every tree with seed in its fruit; you shall have them for food." Food follows work.

God could simply supply our every need and solve our every problem. But our God invites us into a creative partnership with him. He supplies the earth, the air, the water, the sun and our strength and then asks us to work with Him.[4]

God set up a sustainable system—sunlight and plants that produce food and seeds—and then put people in charge of turning it into a regular source of food. God takes delight in seeing how people multiply value from the raw materials he has created, and learning about this system can enhance people's satisfaction as participants in it (more on this in chapter 7).

In a complex economy, people rarely step back and see their tasks as a link in this larger system of provision. Pay scales are rarely a simple measure of how a person's effort contributes to productivity. Thus it is easy for people to become discouraged about their ability to provide for their family, or cynical about the value of their labor. (This is especially true for those who do unpaid work such as raising children.) Disciplers can help people untangle the goodness of God's system of provision from the imperfections in our current economic system.

Many aspire to make the most money with the least effort. In fact, our culture tends to equate success with the ideal life of enjoying wealth without needing a job, as if there is something distasteful about working for a paycheck to put food on the table. As disciplers, we can affirm that the "working class" has its roots in God's very first speech to his people. Only God can make something out of nothing; everyone else has to work for it.

Scripture makes this quite clear: "Anyone unwilling to work should not eat" (2 Thess. 3:10). If the person you are discipling is resistant to the idea of work—to put it bluntly, if they have a tendency toward idleness—this is a point you may want to emphasize.

Value How Work Connects Us with Other People

Another aspect of work that precedes the curse and reflects God's very good design is how work connects people together. While each individual is a unique creation, God's image binds them together: "God created humankind in his image, in the image of God he created them" (Gen. 1:27). Genesis 2 expands on the story to describe how God put the first human, Adam, in the garden with the charge to "till it and keep it" (v. 15). But in that context, God then declared, "It is not good that the man should be alone; I will make him a helper as his partner" (Gen. 2:18). Human community is built around work.

Have you ever heard someone say, "I hate my job, but I just keep it because I like the people"? Or "I like my job but can't stand the people I work with"? Workplace relationships are part and parcel of God's design for work. Even those who work for themselves are "not alone," because God's system of provision inevitably creates connections.

Learning to relate with one another in a Christlike way on the job is integral to what it means to work as an image-bearer. This explains why a major source of unhappiness on the job involves workplace relationships—the more important something is in God's design, the more grief it causes when it is warped by sin. Help disciples view their coworkers as more than "people I happen to work with" but partners in kingdom purpose. Every coworker (no matter how difficult they are to work with) bears God's image.

Beyond interpersonal relationships, workplace connections build social capital.[5] Social capital is the bonds of trust and belonging that make enterprise possible, and thus is essential to flourishing communities and economies. "It's not what you know, it's who you know" is a saying often uttered cynically to explain why some people seem to advance in their careers due to connections rather than merit. However, helping people understand God's design for connectedness may encourage them to be more intentional about strengthening their own (and others') vocational networks.

Enjoy How Work Connects Us with Nature

A final observation that disciplers can make about work before the curse is that human work is intertwined with the nonhuman creation. The creation mandate involves interactions with animals, plants, land, and elements. The garden God made was "pleasant to the sight and good for food" (Gen. 2:9), and its abundance was freely available to the humans God appointed to develop its potential. God intends every image-bearer to enjoy and enhance the beauty and usefulness of nonhuman creation.

Yet people typically think of nature as an escape from their job, something to be appreciated outside of working hours. Or, they view nature as the source of problems to be solved by human enterprise. The realm of nature and the world of work are disconnected. It is hard to even talk about how Christians relate to nature in their work without getting embroiled in conflicts.

We say more about the relationship between work and nonhuman creation in the next chapter. The main point here is to help image-bearers begin to view the natural world from the perspective of God's design, as integrally and positively connected with work. This leads to thinking more intentionally about how they experience natural elements *on the job.*

Encourage people to do what they can to enjoy God's nonhuman creation in the context of their work. Ideas include bringing potted plants into their work area, planting flowers and greenery around the building, taking walks outdoors during breaks, displaying nature-themed artwork, having pets at work, partnering with a local farmer's market, adding more natural light, or designing outdoor work spaces. It is well-documented that being around nature improves mental and physical health, as well as worker productivity.[6] Attitudes toward work may improve when more of God's creation is in the picture.

Humanizing Work

God created image-bearers to cultivate and enjoy a world of abundance and beauty by working in partnership. Leading disciples to awareness of this good design does not mean glossing over the realities of work under the curse of sin.

As prisoners entered the concentration camp at Auschwitz during World War II, they passed under these words, worked in iron letters over the gate: *Arbeit Macht Frei*, meaning "Work Sets You Free." Of the 1.3 million people who saw those mocking words as they entered the camp, 1.1 million died there. Those who were not killed in the gas chambers succumbed to the long hours of forced labor under conditions of starvation, exposure, and rampant disease. They toiled solely for the benefit of those who viewed them as less than human.

This grotesque example is a stark contrast to the connection our Creator intended between work and the *imago Dei*. Our identity as image-bearers motivates us to work as a source of blessing, meaning, and provision. The creation mandate directs humankind to offer our labor in reverence to a Maker who lovingly designed and gifted us for work. But whenever people are dehumanized in any way (whether employers, employees, or customers), our relationship to work becomes twisted and destructive.

A grievous example is the estimated 25 million people worldwide who are trapped in forced labor or sex trafficking.[7] This is a gross violation of God's design for image-bearers. This desecration is amplified by those who depend on this labor, knowingly or unknowingly, for their own profits.

In the United States, we see the cost of a culture that anchors identity to having a good job, rather than being an image-bearer. People who lose their livelihood often start to question their value to God and others. Tragically, one in three people who take their own life are unemployed at the time.[8] Even people who appear to have a successful career often struggle with feeling hollow, lonely, and fearful of losing it all.

As you walk with people through difficult work situations, take note that *why* we work is always tightly connected with *who* we are as valued, redeemed image-bearers, sent into the world to work with kingdom purpose. Matt Rusten writes about holding fast to our "gospel-shaped identity," which keeps us grounded in both sober humility and unshakeable confidence in Christ's sacrificial love. "Though all of us experience discouragement and despair . . . the gospel provides a strong ballast against despair by reminding us of our true identity."[9] Only this truth will truly set anyone free.

RESOURCE

Creation Mandate Discipleship Exercises

It's one thing to understand the creation mandate as a theological concept, but another to grasp it as a practical reality. Try these questions and exercises to help those you disciple to personalize what Genesis 1 teaches about work:

- Do you consider work as a blessing or a curse? Try to go through a week without grumbling about your job.

- Write down all the ways that God has blessed you in your work.

- If you supervise others, what do you do to make work a blessing for your employees?

- How is your work linked with others in the chain of provision? List every industry connected with your job.

- Imagine doing your job in heaven. What might that look like?

- In what way do your interactions with your coworkers reflect the character of Christ? What is the Spirit inviting you to improve? How might that change impact your workplace relationships?

- Name ten people you work with. For each name, think, "_____ is God's image-bearer and my partner in the work God has called us to do. May God bless _____ in their work."

- Think about all the ways you encounter God's nonhuman creation while you are at work. What ideas do you have for expanding your interactions with nature on the job?

- What is the gap between God's intentions for work, and what you have experienced or observed? What could you do to bring your workplace closer to God's design?

- How would you answer the question: "Why do you work?"

- "*Why* we work is always tightly connected with *who* we are as valued, redeemed image-bearers, sent into the world to work with kingdom purpose." What does this statement mean to you in your current work context?

7

A CREATION MANDATE FRAMEWORK FOR IMAGE-BEARERS

The previous chapter showed how disciplers can explore general ideas about work based on the creation story. This chapter offers a framework (not *the* framework, but one possibility) for unpacking the creation mandate, so people can begin to see more clearly how their work fits into God's design.

Fill It! Subdue It! Cultivate It!

In the garden, God gave image-bearers three basic instructions: fill the earth, subdue it, and exercise dominion over it. Each mandate is a response to the context in which God placed human beings. Each also reveals something vital about them as image-bearers.

Biblical mandate	Context for work	Image-bearer action	Quality of image-bearers
"Fill the earth . . ."	This place is empty	Create abundance!	Great worth
" . . . and subdue it"	This place is wild	Bring order!	Empowered
" . . . and have dominion"	This place is incomplete	Cultivate potential!	Creative

The following overview provides talking points for each part of the mandate that disciplers can use as they walk through this concept with others. At the end of the chapter, the resource page provides a list of questions to spur comprehension and conversation about this creation mandate.[1]

"Fill the Earth . . ."

Image-bearers have great worth and multiply the abundance of creation.

God makes it abundantly clear with a succession of commands (be fruitful, multiply, fill the earth) that he wants lots of image-bearers around. Why? Because image-bearers are of great value to God. And because there is lots of work to be done!

Point #1: Raising Families Is Part of Our Core Work

The creation mandate depends on having people around who are ready and able to serve God's purposes! Anyone who has been in charge of raising children knows that this is flat-out hard work. Yet it is not often considered a "job," or even a vocation. But God doesn't divide life into discrete realms the way that we do. God's calling is consistent across the whole of our lives.

This point needs emphasizing, especially when someone feels the tension between their job and their home life (which is pretty much all the time for nearly everyone). The way we talk about work—e.g., "I'm leaving work to go home now"—underscores the assumption that caring for family is not really work. Similarly, the phrase "work-life balance" implies that work is segregated from real life.

Disciplers affirm that full-time caregiving or sharing in household duties is not simply a "support role" or a distraction from a "real job." Exploring how this image-bearing work equally fulfills God's creation mandate may bring greater peace. We suggest a shift in perspective, from balancing competing realms to integrating various facets of the same purpose.

Point #2: People Are the First Product

Those you disciple need to understand that nothing they make, sell, or service will be of greater value than God's image-bearers. Valuing people is always foundational to any type of work.

"Fill the earth" does not indicate that God merely wants a large population. "Fill" implies an optimal capacity, a sense of fulfillment and completion. God wants a world of image-bearers actively invested in bringing his intentions to fruition. God entrusted the first humans not only with multiplying new image-bearers but also with passing on his mandate. We fill the earth as we enlarge the scope of kingdom purpose work.

Thus this part of the creation mandate is not just about parenting. It is also about promoting the potential, safety, health, and welfare of others in our workplaces and through our work. Discipleship leads image-bearers to act on the question, "How can I invest in the well-being and capacity of people connected with my work?"

Moreover, "multiplying" connotes generational succession. Disciplers should also ask people to consider how their work impacts the well-being of image-bearers in future generations.

Point #3: Being "Fruitful" Means Building Abundant Community

No one can be a fruitful image-bearer alone. Everyone's work connects them with others. Even the most solitary of occupations touches many others behind the scenes. "Then the LORD God said, 'It is not good that the man should be alone; I will make him a helper as his partner' " (Gen. 2:18). While the immediate application of this passage is to marriage and family, the implications are far-reaching. Individuals and families are all embedded in a rich fabric of culture, social networks, and systems.

For example, when a couple "multiplies" in the literal sense of bearing a child, consider how the impact ripples beyond the parents to intersect with multiple industries: healthcare, textiles, waste disposal, transportation, communications, utilities, government, retail, legal, insurance, furnishings, home décor—and that's just in the first week!

As we will discuss in the chapters on productivity, disciplers help people grasp that our mandate goes beyond "making more" to "being fruitful." Like raising a family, cultivating social connections and culture is not in tension with work, but rather is a key reason why we all work. Image-bearers are generators of culture, builders of community, and designers of systems and infrastructure that enable abundant life for everyone.

Point #4: Being "Fruitful" Means Growing the Family of God

Another aspect of the work associated with the command "fill the earth" is how it anticipates the outcome God desires for his kingdom. "Go out into the roads and lanes and compel people to come in, so that my house may be filled" (Luke 14:23). "There . . . was a great multitude that no one could count, from every nation, from all tribes and people and languages, standing before the throne and before the Lamb" (Rev. 7:9).

The Creator doesn't simply want to multiply the population of people who live and die on earth. He values the presence of image-bearers "on earth *as it is in heaven*" (Matt. 6:10). Disciplers help people become aware of the opportunities afforded by their work to point other image-bearers toward God's kingdom, to fill up the household of God.

". . . and Subdue It"

Image-bearers are empowered to bring order to creation.

Point #1: Image-Bearers Tame Creation

Children's books often depict the Garden of Eden as a genteel place, with grassy meadows, orderly fruit-laden trees, and gentle brooks. But when Scripture describes nature, it highlights its wildness—not as a result of the fall, but because this is how it sprang from God's creative will. "Fire and hail, snow and frost, stormy wind fulfilling his command!" (Ps. 148:8).

God creates forces of immense power—water, electricity, wind, fire, atomic energy, crabgrass—and then tells his image-bearers, "You are the most powerful thing I have created. Your work is to tame and harness these forces to make the world habitable and fruitful."

> It may be easy enough today, in a civilization of air-conditioners, to imagine that "the environment" is naturally hospitable to humans, and that humans add nothing to nature but to pollute it. . . . Wind, flood, desert and erosion needed to be tamed; resources hidden in nature needed to be brought to human usefulness.[2]

Disciplers help people to see how their work makes the world safer, more enjoyable, and more sustainably useful. I (Heidi) knew a young man who developed a passion for lawn care. He would post pictures on social media of the neatly latticed rows left by his mower and before-and-after pictures of the hedges he trimmed. One day I commented, "Did you ever stop to think that you are doing the very first job that God invented?" My friend is a Christian but had never before connected the pride and satisfaction he felt in his work with faithfulness to God.

Point #2: Image-Bearers Study Creation

Jesus is Lord of creation. When he commanded the stormy waves to "be still!," they obeyed (Mark 4:39). We, of course, don't have that kind of power to subdue creation. Instead, God equipped humans with the capacity to adapt and make use of just about any natural environment—from the Atlantic to the Arctic to the Sahara.

How do image-bearers do that? God equips us with the aptitude to be continual learners about all that God has made. We explore the world with our minds and senses before we can subdue it with our hands and tools. We see this exhibited in Genesis 2:19–20, when God assigns Adam the work of cataloguing and naming the animals.

Disciplers affirm those whose work involves understanding the world to improve how we interact with it. We also lift up the goodness of exploring God's creation for sheer delight, as modeled by wisdom personified in Proverbs 8:31—"rejoicing in his inhabited world and delighting in the human race."

Point #3: Image-Bearers Respect Creation

Why do image-bearers subdue creation? So that it becomes a place where they can multiply and build fruitful community. Thus "to subdue" in the context of Genesis 1 is the opposite of exploiting or abusing creation. We are to tame the forces of nature so they contribute to human flourishing, not bend them to selfish or destructive ends. Such exploitation is not compatible with being sustainably fruitful.

Disciplers encourage image-bearers to sustain the perspective that God has toward the world—that it is very good.

Point #4: Image-Bearers Restrain Harm from and to Creation

God's mandate did not put humanity on a quest to domesticate every bit of wildness out of the planet—nor to preserve it in its pristine state. Rather, image-bearers bring that wildness into alignment with the needs of a flourishing community.

After the fall, however, new enmity arose between humans and other aspects of the created order. The entrance of sin meant additional dangers and adversities standing between people and a flourishing community. It meant that subduing would always come at a cost. Just ask a nuclear safety inspector or a firefighter!

Humanity's rebellion against God also made the world vulnerable to human excesses. Humanity and the rest of creation were supposed to be very good *together*. It was not God's intention for the different parts of his creation to compete with one another for survival.

Discipleship leads people to submit themselves to God to subdue the destructiveness of sin within ourselves. Then we can be empowered by his Spirit to carry out the work of restraining the impact of sin around us.

". . . Have Dominion"

Image-bearers generate value by cultivating the potential in creation.

God created a world of astounding beauty and abundance—but it was, by design, incomplete. It is up to the image-bearers to cultivate its potential and put it to (very) good use.

Point #1: God Appoints Image-Bearers as Co-Creators

Creation is good, but it is not very good until the image-bearer does work to develop it. Image-bearers are generative—they imitate God by creating new arenas for fruitfulness that didn't exist before.

Genesis 2:4–9 highlights this potent role of the image-bearer. Up until day six of the creation, there were no plants for food, "for the LORD God had not sent rain on the earth and there was no one to work the ground." After bringing his image-bearer to life, God planted a garden to be his home, with "every tree that is pleasant to the sight and good for food."

You'd think that a garden hand-planted by God could not be improved on. But God made people in his image to be his co-creators. "The LORD God took the man and put him in the garden of Eden to till it and keep it" (Gen. 2:15). Without the image-bearer to do the work, the goodness of the garden could not be cultivated and sustained.

Where people might see their work as messy and unfinished, a discipler helps them look at things closer to the way Adam might have viewed his assignment in the garden: as a never-ending process of development.

Point #2: God Creates Potential, Not Finished Products

God could have simply rained down manna or sandwiches. Instead, God says: "I have given you every plant yielding seed" (Gen. 1:29). In the divine division of labor, God creates an abundance of raw materials, and it's our job to get from the seed to bread for the table. Somewhere along the way, this involved adding fertilizer researchers, tractor manufacturers, truckers, food safety regulators, agricultural policymakers, investors, nutritionists, marketers, grocery stockers, and checkout clerks.

God designed image-bearers with the unique capacity to modify the world in ways that can and ought to lead to flourishing. Cultivating the treasures implanted in creation draws on every human faculty—observation, imagination, technology, extraction, organization, allocation, collaboration. As we develop the world, we develop social systems and culture.

Disciplers help people see how their jobs add value to the original materials that God created. For example, computer programmers enhance the productivity of technology built with silicone, which comes from sand. Their job cultivates the potential that existed in the dirt that God created on day one of the universe.

Point #3: "Dominion" Implies Responsibility

The word for "dominion" is often translated "rule." As image-bearers, humankind reflects the likeness of God's sovereignty over the earth and its creatures. In what way does God intend us to exercise this rule or dominion? We find the same word applied to the good king in Psalm 72:8: "May he have dominion from sea to sea." This psalm gives a model for how rulers should use their dominion: to bring protection and prosperity to all of creation. Godly dominion brings justice, righteousness, prosperity, peace, tribute, abundance, and blessing, and it vanquishes threats to these good outcomes.

Dominion is not simply "power over" but "power to use well." Dominion is always exercised in the context of the other two clauses of the creation mandate: to fill the earth and to subdue it. If the exercise of power makes places uninhabitable, or creates messes for others to clean up, or unleashes destructive forces, or inhibits productivity, then it is not faithful to the creation mandate.

"From everyone to whom much has been given, much will be required" (Luke 12:48). The greater the scope of authority in one's job, the higher the expectation for responsible dominion. You can encourage people to be aware of the impact of their work (whether planned or unintentional) on the natural world and its inhabitants.

Point #4: Dominion Is Eternal

The Bible suggests that image-bearers will continue to exercise dominion in heaven. Citizens of the New Jerusalem "will reign forever and ever," caring for the beautiful city with the garden at its heart (Rev. 22:5).

We have every reason to expect that the creation mandate will continue in the new creation, freed from the curse of sin and death. The work of extracting potential from God's creation is never-ending because God is endlessly creative. Our imagination and capacity to improve on our work has no limits. Heaven will still need the image-bearer "to till and to keep" the unfolding wonders of God's dwelling place. What a thrill! Disciplers help people to cultivate an eternal perspective on their vocation.

Life in Abundance

As image-bearers, we have inestimable value as we are empowered to productively develop and responsibly enjoy God's very good creation. We are called to work that multiplies fruitfulness, harnesses energies, and cultivates potential. Such work blesses people and honors God.

Selfish defiance of God's creation mandate does the opposite. Sin leads to people's image-bearing capacity being suppressed, neglected, or diminished. Wherever people are not fully valued, productive, empowered, or responsible—this points to the need for redemption.

"The thief comes only to steal and kill and destroy," Jesus declared. "I came that they may have life, and have it abundantly" (John 10:10). The picture that emerges from the creation mandate is life in abundance. Jesus, in the perfect likeness of his Father, redeems and reclaims image-bearers so they can continue their God-appointed work.

Disciplers, urge people to rise to God's summons: "I redeemed you to do what I created you to be. You have work to do! Get going! Go raise families, produce goods, construct buildings, invent devices, overcome diseases, create beauty, bring order. Make my world a marvelous place!"

RESOURCE

Discipleship Questions:
The Creation Mandate and Vocations

Help the people you disciple connect their daily work to the creation mandate of Genesis 1:26–28. These questions can spark meaningful discussion:

- How does the organization you work for fulfill one or more aspects of the creation mandate? (Create abundance! Bring order! Cultivate potential!).

- In what practical ways does this work contribute to abundant life or the flourishing of God's creation?

- How does your role in the organization where you work contribute to this function?

- When do you see these qualities reflected in your work as an image-bearer?
  - ✓ I have great worth and multiply the abundance of creation.
  - ✓ I am empowered to bring order to creation.
  - ✓ I create value by cultivating the potential in creation.

- What can you (or the organization you work for) do to be more intentional and effective in how you fulfill the creation mandate?

- What difference does it make that you approach your work as an image-bearer?

8

KEY PRINCIPLES FOR IMAGE-BEARERS IN THE WORKPLACE

CASE STUDY

Kurt, an only child, grew up helping out with the family business of custom paint sales and house painting services. His father, Joseph, had started the business and built it into a success, and it was his passion. Kurt didn't mind the work, but he always felt he was destined for something more, something greater.

Stirred by an appeal for "more workers in God's harvest field" at church camp his senior year, he told his parents that he felt called to full-time ministry. After college, he went to seminary and then accepted a pastorate in a town a few hours from home.

But then a terrible car accident took his mother's life and hospitalized his father. Kurt took a leave of absence from his church to help run the business while his father recovered. However, he soon grasped the reality of the situation: his father wasn't ever going to fully recover. Without a full-time partner, he would lose his business. And the only one Joseph trusted with his life's work was Kurt.

Kurt loved his father. He felt he had no choice but to give up his pastorate to run the company. As he settled into the job, he struggled with the feeling that he had left his ministry—that he had betrayed God.

The Value of Key Principles

Vocational discipleship asks people to absorb new teachings, to reassess long-held assumptions, to read the Bible with fresh eyes, to hold a biblical light to areas of their life previously unexamined. This is energizing—but it can also be overwhelming.

People have only so much mental bandwidth. We have limited tolerance for material that feels too abstract. We therefore tend to tune out input that doesn't fit our pre-existing ideas. We look for ways to break down complex concepts into bite-sized pieces we can mentally organize.

As a tool for discipleship, this chapter presents a set of core principles that streamline the teachings about being an image-bearer in the workplace.[1]

Core principles are like a filing cabinet for big ideas. Even if people don't fully grasp the principles at once, they can return to these foundational concepts as they continue learning and growing.

Five Key Principles for Faith and Work

For a more detailed discussion of these principles, we refer you to the excellent faith and work resources listed in Appendix C. Our goal here is not to unpack each principle, but to lay out a useful framework for organizing the content as you share it with others.

1. God Is a Worker, and God's Image-Bearers Work

- You are made in the image of a God who works; when you do good work, you resemble your Maker.
- The mandate to work given to the first image-bearers at the time of creation still applies: all image-bearers are called to work, though not all have paid jobs.
- Each of your coworkers is also an image-bearer, worthy of dignity and respect.
- God intended image-bearers to find satisfaction and joy in their work, just as he does.

2. Work Is a Part of God's Good Design

- Work, in rhythm with Sabbath rest, is part of God's original plan for paradise—not a punishment or a curse.
- God's design for abundance was to empower image-bearers to bring forth the vast potential he implanted in the world.
- Image-bearing work is an essential part of what makes creation "very good."
- Image-bearers will do good work in the new creation; your work has eternal significance.

3. The Gospel Is Good News for Your Work!

- Every aspect of work has fallen under the curse of sin; work brings you distress, and you bring your brokenness to your work.

- Jesus brings healing and transformation to your identity as a worker, your perspective on work, your behavior at work, and your purpose for work.

- You are redeemed by Jesus to partner with his Spirit for the restoration of God's intentions for the flourishing of all creation (*shalom*).

- Redeemed image-bearers will find great reward and joy in being able to work in heaven unhindered by sin and free from the effects of the curse.

4. Your Work Matters to God

- All work that serves God's kingdom purpose has equal dignity and value.

- There is no hierarchy between "spiritual" and "secular" vocations; faith and work are not in competition for God's approval.

- God is present with you, and you are important to God, just as much at work as at church.

- God holds you accountable for what work you do, how you do it, how *well* you do it, and how it intersects with the rest of your life.

5. Your Work Is Your Ministry

- You offer service, honor, and glory to God by doing faithful, fruitful work, so you must not compromise.

- God blesses you by providing for your needs and enriching your life through your work.

- God calls you to work that blesses others in your workplace and contributes to the flourishing of your community, making "on earth" more like "in heaven."

- God uses you in the workplace to help people discover who they are as image-bearers and who Jesus is as their Redeemer, so they can join in working for his kingdom purpose.

These principles flesh out the question, "Who am I as an image-bearer created to be a worker?" Knowing these principles lays the foundation for the next question, "What kind of work am I called do?" How disciples pursue God's kingdom purpose through their specific vocational calling will be developed more fully in part three.

How to Use Key Principles as a Discipleship Tool

You can use these key principles in developing curriculum and in lesson plans. You can use them to assess understanding of the theology of faith and work. You can also draw on them when helping someone through a challenge at work.

While general principles are a useful tool, overuse may lead to oversimplification. Don't reduce these to mantras that are never really applied in the messiness of the real world. We offer some suggestions for how to use these principles meaningfully as an aid in discipleship:

- Connect each principle to Scripture (see the list of faith and work passages at the end of chapter 22).

- Ask questions to help the individual apply key principles to their personal work context (see the lists of discipleship questions in chapters 11, 12, and 13).

- Contrast these principles with other perspectives (church-centric, prosperity mindsets).

- Refer to relevant principles in addressing everyday situations that arise at work.

- Invite people to examine themselves and be transformed by the Spirit—move from "head" to "heart."

- Encourage the person you disciple to share these ideas with others (disciple people to be disciplers).

Best practices of adult learning remind us that each person absorbs these principles in their own way. Some (like Heidi) prefer logical, orderly outlines; others are more intuitive, artistic processors who visualize ideas as graphic representations; while others are "doers" who focus on what these principles look like in action. Your role as discipler includes helping people connect with the learning style God designed in them.

CASE STUDY REVISITED

Let's return to the case study at the beginning of the chapter. How could a discipler work with Kurt to apply these principles to his situation?

First, Kurt needs the reminder that *his work matters to God*. He needs the assurance that he's just as important to God when filling requisitions for materials as when writing a sermon. His work matters to God now no less than it did when he was pastoring. He didn't abandon God when he went into business—nor did God abandon him.

A discipler could challenge Kurt to apply the principle that *work is a part of God's good design.* Kurt can explore how working with paint reflects God's creativity and abundance in the rich spectrum of colors. He could even imagine how the services offered by his business might contribute to the beauty and grandeur of the eternal New Jerusalem. This would bring him closer to his father, whose passion for his vocation Kurt had never taken seriously before.

A discipler could also encourage Kurt to examine what it means that *his work is his ministry.* He could stop assuming that he had "left the ministry" and start focusing on doing his business to the glory of God, with the kingdom purpose of helping the world God created to flourish. He could begin to appreciate the value that paint brought to customers and their neighborhoods. And he could look for ways to bless his community by donating paint. He could even start a program enabling college students to support themselves by working as house painters.

Instead of feeling he had betrayed God, Kurt could be helped to see how he honored God and served others by running an excellent business.

RESOURCE

Workplace Values from Paul's Letter to Titus

Paul's letter to Titus provides detailed guidance for how Christian conduct in response to God's grace enables people to "be ready for every good work" (3:1). Almost any workplace looking for a statement of organizational values and good practices could begin drawing from Titus, as demonstrated in this excerpt from the *Theology of Work Bible Commentary.*[2] These values show what the core principles of faith and work look like in practice.

Respect

- Show respect to everyone (3:1)
- Be hospitable (1:8)
- Be kind (2:5)
- Don't engage in conflict about inconsequential matters (3:9)
- Don't be arrogant, quick tempered, or obstinate (1:78)
- Don't use violence as a means of supervision (1:7); use gentleness instead (3:1)

Self-Control

- Be self-controlled (1:8; 2:6)
- Don't be greedy for gain (1:7)
- Don't become addicted to alcohol (1:7; 2:3)
- Avoid envy and ill will (3:3)

Integrity

- Act with integrity (1:8)
- Love goodness (1:8)
- Submit to those in authority over you in the workplace (2:9)
- Obey the civil authorities (3:1)
- Respect others' property (2:10) and manage it faithfully on their behalf if you have a fiduciary duty (2:5)

Authority and Duty

- Exercise the authority you have been given (2:15)
- Be prudent (1:8)
- Silence rebellious people, idle talkers, deceivers, slanderers, and those who intentionally cause personal divisions (1:10; 2:3; 3:10)
- Hold people accountable (1:13)
- Train others under your leadership in these same virtues (2:2–10)

PART THREE

DISCIPLESHIP CORE QUESTION #2: WHAT IS YOUR PURPOSE?

(Helping People Understand How Their Job Gets God's Kingdom Work Done)

9

DISCIPLESHIP LEADS PEOPLE TO AFFIRM "I UNDERSTAND MY KINGDOM PURPOSE!"

CASE STUDY

Anthony already had a name picked out for his boat: the Daisy May. *He and his wife were counting down the years. His management position at a regional auto parts supplier hadn't made him rich, but it provided enough to look forward to retiring in comfort.*

A friend invited him to the annual Christian business association conference. He had become a member of the association for the networking, but this was his first time going to any of the events. The way they talked about faith at the conference was completely new to Anthony. He couldn't decide if he was inspired, challenged, or just confused, so he signed up for a small group for Christian businessmen to sort it out.

A few sessions into the group, the facilitator asked, "What gives your work meaning? What is the purpose of your job?" The first thing that came to Anthony's mind was the automatic deposit from his paycheck to the savings account for his boat. Beyond that, he struggled to come up with anything that didn't sound trite.

It wasn't like he was a doctor saving lives or a teacher guiding kids. He filled out forms, negotiated contracts, and maintained inventory. Big deal. Who said work had to have a grand purpose? He was honest with clients, wrote solid contracts, and tried to be nice to his coworkers—wasn't that enough?

Discovering That the Work Itself Is the Ministry

The idea that their daily work can serve a purpose in God's kingdom may come as a surprise to many of the people you disciple. Christians tend to assume that God's kingdom is synonymous with the church. In a church-centric context, the main purpose of employment is to fund the personnel and activities of the church, and to prepare people for church ministry roles. Church-goers are also urged to see their workplace as a mission field and to invite people into a relationship with Christ. People may feel called to be "in ministry" at their job, but seldom do they recognize how *their job itself is their ministry*.

In the absence of a clear sense of how their work matters to God, people often attach meaning to their work from a worldly success narrative. Work is significant if it pays well, or opens doors to social advancement, or maximizes their sense of personal satisfaction. Sometimes people find meaning in working for a cause or a person they admire. On the flip side, many have abandoned hope of finding any meaning in their job. Their main purpose is to get through another day of work so they can get back to their "real" life.

Vocational disciplers help people connect the joy of salvation with the meaning of work. As the next chapter will address, salvation encompasses all of our being. A redeemed life is not defined by weekly church involvement and private devotions on the side, while spending the majority of time on one's own objectives. Disciples are redeemed to live 24/7 with kingdom purpose. They honor God with the whole of their lives. Disciples start each workday knowing they are called, literally, to be "laborers together with God" (1 Cor. 3:9 KJV), as ministers of his kingdom.

What Do We Mean by "Kingdom Purpose"?

Once disciples recognize that God has a stake in their working life, the next step is to help them grasp *how* their job fits into God's design. We call this working with kingdom purpose.

The word *kingdom* refers to the reality that God is sovereign. God is boss. God's kingdom is the realm where people who have been created in God's image carry out the work that God commands. Vocational disciplers encourage and equip people to fulfill God's kingdom purpose through their work in alignment with their gifts. The simplest definition of fulfilling our kingdom purpose is "working well to bring about what God wants to see done."

Disciples collaborate with God through their work. But you can't collaborate well with someone unless you know what they want to accomplish. To fulfill their kingdom purpose, disciples have to know what God intends for his creation and then discern their specific role in these plans. Discipleship leads people to be able to affirm, with confidence and specificity, "I am fulfilling my kingdom purpose as an image-bearer at work when I . . ."

Here we outline *four foundational categories of kingdom purpose*. There are a number of ways of framing God's purpose for work, so this is not the *only* way to present it, but we believe it can be helpful in a discipleship context. These categories take big ideas about aligning our work with God's design and make them concretely applicable to people's everyday labor. What does God want image-bearers to accomplish through their work?

- To glorify God

- To bless people

- To draw others to Jesus

- To enable God's world to flourish (build community, bring order, cultivate potential, and restore brokenness)

The first two categories of kingdom purpose—*glorifying God* and *blessing people*—correspond broadly with the Great Commandment to love God and love others as you love yourself (Mark 12:30–31), which we will explore in chapter 11. Chapter 12 will look in depth at the purpose of *drawing others to Jesus*, which fulfills the Great Commission to take the good news of the kingdom into the world (Mark 16:15). And chapter 13 will unpack the ways that image-bearers enable God's world to flourish consistent with the creation mandate (Gen. 1:26–28).

Helping People Work with Kingdom Purpose

As a discipler, how do you help image-bearers find and fulfill their calling to work with kingdom purpose? Let's return to the model of discipleship outlined in chapter 3: disciplers help people become rooted in their *being* as God's redeemed image-bearers, leading to growing alignment in *knowing* God's purpose for their vocation and then effectively *doing* God's work in the world.

The following chapters support disciplers in the process of helping people know God's purpose for their work. As the next chapter explains, this starts by walking with people through the big picture of creation, fall, redemption, and restoration—the biblical story of God establishing his kingdom among his image-bearers, from the Garden of Eden to the New Jerusalem. Vocational discipleship highlights the vital role of work in this story of God's kingdom, and how this translates to the categories of vocational purpose. Disciplers can then help people see how they fit into this biblical story and help them discover their personal vocational calling, based on how God has gifted and positioned them for kingdom work.

This process of exploring vocation with kingdom purpose can be envisioned as a funnel (see next page). Sometimes discipleship follows this funnel, from teaching big ideas to finding application in daily life. Probably more often, a person will bring a specific challenge or decision faced in their workplace, which the discipler can lead them to explore in the light of foundational theological principles of kingdom purpose. In these chapters, we are able to present the content in a neat progression—but we know that real life is messy and so is discipleship!

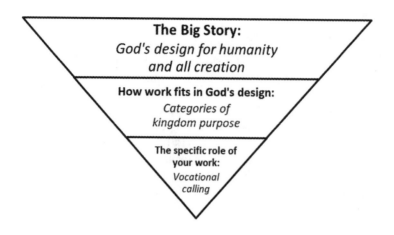

Tent-Making with Kingdom Purpose

I (Tom) had the opportunity to teach in Egypt. There, I met a Christian man in the business of providing tents for special events. I was drawn to learn more about his profession, as it reminded me of the work of the apostle Paul, the tentmaker.

Americans tend to associate tents with camping. But in the Middle East, where many public events are held outside, large tents are found at almost every community gathering—weddings, funerals, sporting events. And if you think about it, this is true for many social gatherings in the United States as well, though we may call it a canopy, pavilion, or booth.

The man I met loved his job. He helped me understand that putting up tents is a vital part of what it means to have a caring, well-run community. He told me, "I have the honor of being engaged with families and businesses and community leaders at the most intimate times of their lives." He provided a service that met their need for social connection. And he noted that it often gave him—like the apostle Paul—the opportunity to share the gospel, because it put him in people's paths at times of great emotion and meaning in their lives.

What story will the people you disciple tell about the kingdom purpose served by their work?

RESOURCE

Kingdom Purpose Affirmations

What happens when disciples realize they are called to work with kingdom purpose?

Often it brings a tremendous sense of relief and joy, as well as a mantle of responsibility, to know that what they do at work matters to God. Some may be challenged to reexamine their attitude and performance on the job. Some might even be spurred to question their choice of vocation. At the very least, this discovery is likely to reorient and reinvigorate the sense of meaning that people find in their working life.

Help people process this shift toward kingdom purpose in their work by reviewing the following affirmations. What does each statement mean to this person? Can they point to a specific application or incident in their workplace that illustrates this affirmation? What is the Spirit leading them to change as a result of this affirmation? What passages of Scripture or teachings of their church come to mind in connection with these statements?

- "I collaborate with God through my work."

- "I honor and glorify God when I use the skills and qualities he has given me to be effective in doing my job."

- "The job I do is valuable because it brings about what God wants to see done."

- "It is important for me to be productive so I can be more fruitful in bringing about what God desires."

- "I don't just serve God *at* my work; I serve God *by doing* my work."

- "I am called to full-time ministry, because my ministry is how I advance God's kingdom purpose through my full-time work."

- "I can sense how my work pleases God, which motivates me to do my best."

- "I am convicted to repent when I do not work in a way that honors God or accomplishes his purposes."

- "Knowing how my work is my ministry gives me clarity and focus."

- "I support other workers in how they are serving God's purposes, even if they're not aware of it yet."

- "I invite others to discover how they can collaborate with God through their work."

10

THE FOUR-CHAPTER GOSPEL: HELP PEOPLE TO KNOW THE BIG STORY

Case Study

At a denominational retreat for Christian women, Eileen prepared the breakout room for her afternoon workshop on "Faith in the Workplace." As was her custom, she prayed that God would help her to strengthen the ministry of everyone who walked through the door.

As the workshop began, Eileen asked everyone in the small circle of attendees to share their name, where they worked, and how they connected their faith with their job.

After a college professor and a coffee shop owner, a petite woman introduced herself. "My name is Helen. I'm an epidemiologist." Helen could see several people giving her blank looks, so she explained: "My lab works on tracking and controlling outbreaks of infectious diseases. Like COVID-19." A murmur went around the circle.

"You must find many meaningful ways to live out your faith in your line of work," Eileen commented.

"Not really," Helen responded. "It's a government office. I wear a cross so people will know I'm a Christian and I have my Bible out on my desk, but I'm not supposed to talk about my faith."

"Working in an epidemiology lab, you don't see any other connections with the gospel story?" As Eileen asked, her mind overflowed with thoughts about the medicinal plants that God designed at creation, the link between germs and the curse of sin, the provisions for public health in the law of Israel, the many stories of healings by Jesus and the disciples, and the leaves of the tree of life in the New Jerusalem that will put a final end to all disease.

"Well," Helen began, "I've started praying every day for each of my coworkers to be saved. No one else there is a Christian. That's why I'm here, because I'm hoping you can give me some new ideas about how to share the gospel."

Yes, thought Eileen, I think we can do that—but I suspect it will go beyond what Helen has in mind.

Disciplers Share the Big Story

I (Heidi) never learned to enjoy football. My eyes gloss over whenever my husband watches a televised game. I get the general idea that the offense is trying to score touchdowns while the defense is trying to stop them. But I just can't track the action taking place on the screen, unless someone bothers to explain to me what's going on. It just seems like a random string of plays, until suddenly the game is over.

My husband—who is a big Kansas City Chiefs fan—insisted that I join him for at least one live game at the stadium. Based on my experiences with football at home, I prepared myself (I confess) for several hours of boredom. But the live game was nothing like watching it on a small screen! There were no close-ups, no cuts between plays—just the entire field laid out below us. I was able to follow the whole unbroken story of the game, from beginning to end. For the first time, I really understood, and felt connected.

Understanding the "Big Story" told by the Bible is essential for people to connect meaningfully with their vocational calling. Hugh Whelchel argues,

> Christians do not fully comprehend the biblical concepts of work, calling, and vocation because we have lost a vision of the grand metanarrative told by the Bible. This metanarrative encompasses creation, fall, redemption, and restoration. It is sometimes called the four-chapter gospel.[1]

Michael Metzger offers this perspective:

> Tragically, two hundred years ago the story was edited to two chapters; the fall and redemption. . . . The new starting line was Genesis Three. It reminds people that they are fallen sinners. . . . The four-chapter gospel elevates our worth as image-bearers of God. The two-chapter story focuses on our deficiency. The four-chapter story reminds us of our dignity.[2]

Many use the biblical term *shalom* to capture the unifying thread of God's purpose in the four-chapter gospel: "*Shalom* bookends human existence. It characterizes the garden (the way it was supposed to be) and the eternal city (the way it is going to be) and so provides a vision for our existence in between."[3]

We leave it to others to more fully flesh out this Big Story and the inadequacies of the two-chapter gospel.[4] The main point we want to emphasize is the vital role of vocational disciplers in making sure that Christians grasp this "metanarrative," this top-of-the-stadium view of the whole arena of God's involvement with humankind. Only in this glorious context can people fully appreciate the kingdom purpose of their work.

Necessary Correctives

Discipling people in the Big Story often entails helping churchgoers connect the dots between the snippets of Bible stories and teachings that they have collected without recognizing how they fit meaningfully together.

This was modeled by the risen Jesus, when he accompanied a mournful group of disciples on the road to Emmaus. After hearing their version of the events of the Passion Week, Jesus told them they had been missing the point. "Beginning with Moses and all the prophets, he interpreted to them the things about himself in all the scriptures." They likely had heard all these stories before, but they had not realized how Jesus was the thread weaving them together. Finally, "their eyes were opened," and the course of their lives was radically changed (Luke 24:13–35).

Discipleship also fills in the gospel story when believers have an incomplete picture. An illustration is how Priscilla and Aquila discipled Apollos:

> He [Apollos] was an eloquent man, well-versed in the scriptures. He had been instructed in the Way of the Lord; and he spoke with burning enthusiasm and taught accurately the things concerning Jesus, though he knew only the baptism of John. . . . When Priscilla and Aquila heard him, they took him aside and explained the Way of God to him more accurately. (Acts 18:24–26)

Like Apollo, many people have a perception of the gospel that is true in part—but incomplete. In particular, the church has tended to focus on the message that we are sinners, saved by the grace of Jesus, but without adequately anchoring this in the beginning and end of the story. As Whelchel puts it, "Many in the church . . . have narrowed the gospel to two chapters rather than the biblical four-chapter Gospel. They have focused on personal salvation (as important as that is) and neglected our purpose in creation and our destiny in a new heaven and new earth."[5]

A key theme running through this book is that vocational discipleship is needed to shift Christians from a church-centric perspective to an image-bearer lens. Sometimes the biblical narrative is narrowed to a story about the church, rather than a story about and to image-bearers, some of whom have accepted the invitation of redemption through Christ.

Another way the Big Story is sometimes skewed is when it's framed as a spiritual drama about individual souls in relationship with a non-corporeal God. The physical world is a temporary stage setting, which will be removed from the picture at the grand finale. Vocational disciplers have the task of showing how the physicality of the world is an integral part of the story, from the dawn of creation into the new creation.

Work in the Four-Chapter Gospel

If we start the story of the gospel with the fall and its personal implications (that is, we are all sinners in need of salvation), we naturally think our work primarily has purpose in getting to redemption (to pray for and witness to people at work, fund missionaries, and so on). We are saved from this fallen world and the physical nature of our sin-bound mortal bodies, freeing us to enjoy unending spiritual life in heaven.

Telling the whole story lets people see how God's kingdom purpose, and the role of human work in this purpose, has not changed, from creation to the church age to eternal life in heaven. They gain a renewed sense of dignity and significance in their work when they see how it is an integral part of the whole picture of God's plan for restoration, and how it will have a place in eternity. They will have more motivation for doing excellent work.

Here is how a businessman in Tom's Kingdom Purpose Workshop told the story from a vocational perspective:

At creation, God begins with a garden. At the re-creation of the new heaven and new earth, God establishes a city. In this grand narrative from Genesis to Revelation we see the idea of progress, increase, or improvement upon what God has created—which is the work of His image-bearers. With this being our created state and our future fully re-created state, we see continuity and conclude that the redeemed children of God should have a concern for their work and its eternal significance for the kingdom and glory of God.[6]

This four-chapter story not only helps to teach people a more complete theology of work, but it also supplies a framework for applying this theology to address practical issues in the workplace.

A pastor shared how he used this model in discipleship:

A manager of a health provider spoke of the complexity she faced at work in managing people and projects. It seemed challenging to integrate faith and work with so many different issues happening, but she was thankful for the way the arcs of the biblical story—creation, fall, redemption—provided a lens to make sense of any issue. She could hold any problem up and ask, "What's good? What's wrong? How does the gospel speak about this? What could it look like in God's future?" This theology is a way for our congregations to make sense of redundancies, frustrating emails, and impossible deadlines—and have hope to overcome them.[7]

How would those whom you disciple tell and apply the Big Story?

RESOURCE

Talking Points: Work in the Four-Chapter Gospel

This outline for disciplers focuses on the main ideas of how work connects with each chapter of the Big Story—creation, fall, redemption, and restoration. Much more could be said about the four-chapter gospel (and has been well said elsewhere). Here, we focus on highlighting only a few key points relating to work that often have often been absent or misunderstood.

Creation

- God is introduced as a worker, who makes humanity in his image and immediately gives them work to do (the creation mandate).

- God makes humans out of physical substances and places them in a physical world, which is declared very good.

- God does not create finished products, but sustainable potential. God assigns and empowers image-bearers to cultivate the abundance of his creation through their labor.

- There is a direct connection between inputs (work in the Garden of Eden) and outputs (an abundance of food). Work is rewarding.

- Work is an integral part of paradise, as it honors God and blesses people—it is not a distraction, punishment, or necessary evil.

- God's interactions with the first humans are centered on their work. God builds a relationship with his image-bearers around creative, physical labor.

- When Adam was working alone in the garden, God said, "I will make him a helper as his partner" (Gen. 2:18). The first human relationship is described as a partnership of image-bearing workers.

Fall

- The act of disobedience took place in the Garden, where humans were supposed to be working.

- Adam and Eve were created *in the likeness* of God, yet they were tempted into sin by the false promise, "You will be *like* God." They rebelled against their identity as image-bearers.

- When Adam and Eve sinned and were ejected from the Garden (see Gen. 3:23), they were cut off from their idyllic workplace, but not from their mandate to work. The consequences of sin do not negate our status and calling as image-bearers.

- In the description of the curse, the implications for work are underscored: work becomes toil, associated with pain, futility, and frustration. Image-bearing work is no longer rewarding in the way God designed.

- God's first act after proclaiming the curse is to do work that mitigates its effects: God makes them clothing to cover their newly discovered nakedness (Gen. 3:21).

- The breakdown of relationships is interconnected with the curse on our work. Note that the first murder occurred in Abel's field—in the workplace (Gen. 4:1–12)!

- Work continues to expose and amplify our sinfulness: defiance of God's mandate and rejection of his image, alienation from and hurtfulness toward others, and selfish destruction of creation.

Redemption

- Only a relationship with Jesus can transform the fallenness we bring into our work and renew us to know and do God's will.

- As the imprint of God's being, Jesus is a worker: as God the Son, Jesus is co-creator with God the Father and God the Holy Spirit, he "holds together" all things, he reconciles and rules over all things, *and* he worked on earth as a carpenter!

- Jesus, the beloved Son and perfect image of his Father, redeems us to fulfill our capacity as beloved image-bearers.

- "Redemption" means "to buy back." Redemption is not the goal of the story. Rather, it takes us back to God's original purpose. Because of Jesus, image-bearers can get back to the work they were initially placed in the Garden to do.

- Redemption is not just a change of status that takes place on a disembodied spiritual plane. We are redeemed to "work out our salvation" and "do good work" (see Phil. 2:12–13), which includes labor in the physical world that furthers God's good plans for the world.

- The Spirit commissions us for the work of rebuilding that which sin has ruined. For example, see Isaiah 61:1–4, "They will rebuild the ancient ruins and restore the places long devastated." Redemption leads to restorative work.

Restoration

- God did not create us to be redeemed; he redeemed us to be restored to the purpose for which we were originally created.

- In Revelation 21–22, God gives us a picture of our ultimate destination: the city of God where God lives with people. This is described as a physical place, with gates, buildings, streets, and a garden at the center.

- Humanity was created to live with God in the new heaven and new earth, with all the physicality that God declared "good" in creation. Our physicality will be changed, but we will not be disembodied spirits.

- Redeemed humankind will rule in this heavenly city. It will take work to manage and cultivate its potential. As image-bearers of the eternal God, we will be co-creators with him for eternity.

- The description in Revelation indicates that the best of what we create is found in the heavenly city. The value of our good work on earth has everlasting significance.

- Jesus taught us to pray, "Your kingdom come, on earth as it is in heaven" (see Matt. 6:9–13). Working with kingdom purpose anticipates heaven. We are dedicated to our earthly work not in spite of but in light of our home with God in eternity.

- The blessing of heaven is not that we won't have to work, but that we will finally get to work as God intended, with no sin and no curse! We will see our work contribute to the full flourishing of the new heaven and new earth, to the glory of God.

11

DISCIPLERS ASK: HOW DOES YOUR WORK REFLECT LOVE OF GOD AND OTHERS?

CASE STUDY

"What a great day I had!" Ezra crowed to the other church council members gathering for their monthly meeting, as he poured himself a cup of coffee in the church's fellowship hall.

Someone of course asked Ezra about this, and he was happy to explain. "I've been trying to convince my boss for weeks that I deserve to head up the project division. And today I got the position!"

There was a round of congratulations. "So, what finally tipped things in your favor?" asked Naomi, the church's director of Christian Education.

For a moment, Ezra looked a tad less triumphant. "Well . . . with the consolidation, the company had to eliminate a few positions, including the guy who was my main competition. But they wouldn't have cut him if I wasn't the better person for the job, right?"

"So, did they find him a new position in the company?" Naomi asked.

Ezra appeared surprised by the question. "I doubt it. There's been a company-wide cutback in services. Even more reason to praise God that I got promoted! What a blessing!"

Naomi appreciated Ezra's attitude of thankfulness, but she made a mental note to have a conversation with him on the topic of "blessing"—after he came down from his cloud. She wondered how God might speak to him through Philippians 2:3-4: "Do nothing from selfish ambition or conceit. . . . Let each of you look not to your own interests, but to the interests of others."

Getting in the Game: Work with Kingdom Purpose

The previous chapter presented the analogy that appreciating the whole sweep of the biblical story is like watching a football game from a perspective that takes in the whole field. But this analogy is flawed in at least one important respect: We are not merely spectators of the Big Story. We are called to have an active role in it.

As disciplers, we help people claim their role in the biblical story. They have been redeemed from the curse to be collaborators with the Creator whose image they bear, for the restoration and flourishing of image-bearers and all creation, to the glory of God. The priorities of their Creator shape their motivation, attitude, and actions in relation to the tasks of each day, including and especially their work.

Following up on the four categories of kingdom purpose outlined in chapter 9, this chapter focuses on helping Christians grasp the first two purposes of work: *glorifying God* and *blessing people*.

Kingdom Purpose for Work #1: Glorify God

As the Westminster Catechism famously puts it, our first purpose in life is "to glorify God, and to enjoy him forever." Say "glorify God" and what pops into the minds of most Christians is singing spiritual songs, speaking words of praise to God, and lifting up prayers. In other words, what many Christians assume we were created for is a church-centered activity set apart from our "regular" life. Andy Crouch captures this mindset:

> More than once I've heard a worship leader say, "Worship is the only eternal thing we will do." . . . Without a doubt our original purpose and eventual destination is to love God with our whole heart, mind, soul and strength. But it is a great misreading of both Genesis and Revelation to suppose that the only way we will ultimately love God wholeheartedly will be through something like what happens in church on Sunday morning.[1]

One of the most important aims of vocational discipleship is to help image-bearers offer their work as worship. The standard is set in 1 Corinthians 10:31—"Whatever you do, do everything for the glory of God." This passage directs Christians to give their best effort in their workplace as an expression of love and honor for their Lord. Significantly, the Hebrew word *avodah* is translated both "work" and "worship" (thus we refer to a worship *service*)!

Never let image-bearers forget: God is their boss. "Whatever your task, put yourselves into it, as done for the Lord" (Col. 3:23). Disciples are to offer their gifts and talents to God at work with the same "reverence and awe" they would bring to a gift laid on the church altar, knowing that their daily work serves God's unshakable kingdom (Heb. 12:28).

Since our work on earth honors God, we can expect heavenly worship also to be expressed in our work—but without sin and freed from the curse. Disciples thus glorify God by doing work that will be meaningful throughout eternity. Revelation 21:22–26 links the glory of God's presence with the glory of the products that God's people bring into the city:

> The city has no need of sun or moon to shine on it, for the glory of God is its light, and its lamp is the Lamb. The nations will walk by its light, and the kings of the earth will bring their glory into it. . . . People will bring into it the glory and the honor of the nations.

Andy Crouch concludes, "In the new city our work will be praise."[2] This merger of work and praise is the aim of disciples "on earth as it is in heaven."

Kingdom Purpose for Work #2: Bless People

The next kingdom purpose to present to disciples is that work provides what is needed for people to be healthy and prosperous. This starts with the worker and their household, and then radiates outward to coworkers, clients, and other individuals impacted by their labor.

God's "Plan A" to meet people's needs and make the world a very good place is through the dignity of image-bearing work.[3] Not only does work meet *financial needs*, it meets *psychological and social needs* as well. Since humans are made in the image of a creative God, humanity is driven to create, expand our abilities, and leave an imprint on the world around us. Deep satisfaction comes from reaping the benefits of good work done well: "You shall eat the fruit of the labor of your hands; you shall be happy, and it shall go well with you" (Ps. 128:2).

Our work can also bless us with a *sense of community*. Some of our most significant relationships come from the experience of working together to accomplish an objective. In work environments where there is trust and mutual respect, employees bring out the image of God in one another. When people are able to support their household by doing meaningful work along-side people who spur them on to do their best, it brings delight to both themselves and their Maker.

Disciples also need to understand the vital role of their work in *meeting others' needs*. As Ephesians 4:28 instructs, "Thieves must give up stealing; rather let them labor and work honestly with their own hands, so as to have something to share with the needy." In God's economy, one of the purposes of earning an income is to share with those unable to support themselves, whether this is due to a temporary hardship or a permanent condition. Encourage disciples to share generously from their earnings, products, skills, time, connections, and influence. (Chapter 18 explores options for generosity.)

Most Christians (and non-Christians) understand the importance of being generous with the resources generated from work. However, it may be a new concept to explore how to *bless others to work*. This is rooted in the core principle of the inherent goodness of work with dignity. Disciples bless their coworkers simply by respecting each person's contribution. They also serve this kingdom purpose to the extent that they are able to cultivate a healthy, supportive work environment, pay sustaining salaries, place people in jobs, and create new jobs.

We also serve God's purpose of blessing others by investing in their capacity as workers. Those who raise and teach children bless them by instructing them in how to work well. Experienced workers can mentor, coach, train, and encourage others in their field. Employers can give people opportunities to develop their skills and advance in their fields. Employers can also change lives by giving people the chance to work who might not otherwise be hired. An example of this blessing is Boaz, offering Ruth his protection while enabling her to feed herself and her mother-in-law by gleaning in his field (see Ruth 2).

Dave Pritchard was a business owner in my (Tom's) Convene group, a small group that meets regularly for developing leadership in faith and work. He told us the story of making a hiring decision for a warehouse position. One of his guys brought him an applicant who seemed to raise a battalion of red flags. He had a Satan tattoo on his arm and smoked like a chimney—and he had failed a drug test. My first thought was, frankly: "Why are we even considering this hire?"

But an employee Dave trusted had recommended him, and Dave recalled how our Convene group had been talking about the blessing of work. When he prayed about it, he sensed God was telling him to hire the man with the Satan tattoo. They put some safeguards into place, like random drug testing, and gave him a chance.

Fast-forward several years. This employee turned out to be a solid worker who served Dave's company well. He became a Christian and married a delightful Christian woman. Eventually, with the experience and good references he had gained, he left for a better job. At our Convene group, David read aloud the letter this man had written him, expressing gratitude for believing in him. It brought tears to our eyes.

Kingdom Purpose and the Great Commandment

Asked which commandment was the greatest, Jesus answered:

> "The first is, 'Hear, O Israel: the Lord our God, the Lord is one; you shall love the Lord your God with all your heart, and with all your soul, and with all your mind, and with all your strength.' The second is this, 'You shall love your neighbor as yourself.' There is no other commandment greater than these." (Mark 12:28–31)

Love God and love others as you love yourself—everything we do to fulfill God's will is encompassed by this statement.

In the dualistic, church-centric worldview, work is conceived as being distinct from both worshipping God and loving neighbors. Worship is what you do at church or in your heart. Loving neighbors is what you do through acts of compassion and ministries of charity. If anything, work competes with God for our heart, mind, and strength; work saps time and resources that we could devote to our neighbors. But from a kingdom purpose perspective, we love and honor God through our work, and we bless and provide for our neighbors through our work.

In Matthew 25:31–46, Jesus tells a story about "when the Son of Man comes in his glory." In his parable, the king tells one group, "Come, you that are blessed by my Father, inherit the kingdom prepared for you from the foundation of the world." What qualified this group for their eternal inheritance? "I was hungry and you gave me food, I was thirsty and you gave me something to drink, I was a stranger and you welcomed me, I was naked and you gave me clothing." The group responds with surprise: "Lord, when was it that we saw you hungry and gave you food, or thirsty and gave you something to drink?" The king answers with a twist: "Just as you did it to one of the least of these who are members of my family, you did it to me."

Typically, this passage is interpreted to encourage people toward acts of service and compassion for those in need, such as donating food or volunteering at a homeless shelter. This is indeed a valid, crucial application. But when the founder of a microenterprise training program reflected on this passage, he was struck by an additional interpretation.

What jobs are required to feed people? *Farming, distribution, grocers, restaurants.* To clothe people? *Textile manufacturing, tailoring, retail, laundry.* At every point in the process, each worker contributes to meeting the needs of people they will likely never meet. Microenterprise makes it possible for people to participate in a chain of labor that leads to the care of the king of heaven himself.

Then I (Tom) heard this microenterprise leader share this interpretation at a conference, and I had my own *aha!* moment. At that time my business employed eighteen hundred people worldwide. Because they had good jobs, these workers were able to feed, clothe and house themselves and their families. It struck me that the parable in Matthew 25 calls for not just provision of aid to those in need but also for provision of decent-paying work that can lift and keep people out of hardship.

Tom Nelson writes, "Productive work that adds value to others matters not only to God but also to our neighbors. . . . For-profit business enterprises are essential for the flourishing of all people of a community, particularly the most vulnerable."[4] As disciples in the workplace compensate employees, meet customer needs, and contribute to the well-being of the community, especially the most vulnerable, they do it to Jesus. And if they neglect or harm others in the way they manage their work, Jesus is affected personally as well.

Of course, this passage is still a call to give and serve generously to meet needs. But we can also make disciples aware of how they bless others, and ultimately serve the King of kings in his glory, through their faithful work.

RESOURCE

Kingdom Purpose Discipleship Questions:
Glorify God, Bless People

Below are questions and exercises that disciplers can use with people to help them grasp the first two categories of kingdom purpose for their work.

1. Say aloud, "I fulfill my kingdom purpose as an image-bearer at work when I glorify God." What does this mean to you? What reaction does this spark in you?

2. Walk through a "typical day" at work, and identify opportunities to be intentional about honoring God:

   ✓ For every task, dedicate the effort to God's glory.

   ✓ For each person encountered, be mindful that this individual bears God's image and has been redeemed by Christ's sacrifice.

   ✓ For every resource used, be grateful to God as Creator and Provider.

   ✓ For every plan made, recognize its connection with God's good design and redemptive plan in the broader gospel story.

3. "Whatever you do, do everything for the glory of God" (1 Cor. 10:31). Name at least four specific things you do in your vocation that bring God delight.

4. The next time you head to work, tell yourself, "I'm going to worship now."

5. Say aloud, "I fulfill my kingdom purpose as an image-bearer as my work is a blessing to myself and others."

   ✓ What does this mean to you? What reaction does this spark in you?

   ✓ How do you pursue this kingdom purpose in your work?

✓ What hinders or distracts from this purpose in your work?

✓ What could you do to strengthen this kingdom purpose?

6. How has work provided for your personal/household needs, as well as your financial, psychological, and social needs? What is your prayer regarding needs that have not been met?

7. What opportunities do you have in your work for practicing generosity and compassion?

8. What opportunities do you have for investing in the potential of other image-bearers?

9. The next time you earn a paycheck, receive it with gratitude as a spiritual blessing, not just a financial transaction.

10. Jesus said, "Love your neighbor as yourself" (Mark 12:31). What does fulfilling this command this look like at your job? Be as specific as possible.

12

DISCIPLERS ASK: HOW DOES YOUR WORK DRAW PEOPLE TO CHRIST?

CASE STUDY

Lee glanced up as the man in a business suit settled into seat 2C, curious what manner of person would be sitting next to him for the flight to New York. He groaned inwardly when he glimpsed a Bible among the papers in the man's briefcase. "If he asks me if I know where my soul would go if the plane crashes," Lee thought, "I'll probably punch him."

But Dean, as the man introduced himself, seemed to prefer talking about work. As it turned out, they both worked in human resources, though in different industries. Lee shared about a challenge he was facing with an employee, and Dean told him about a relevant policy that had worked at his company.

"We might need to try that," Lee mused. "Where did you come up with that idea?"

Dean hesitated before he said, "From Jesus."

Lee's eyebrows rose. But he couldn't help being interested.

Dean described the gospel story that had been the source of inspiration for his company's policy. This led Lee to ask more questions about Jesus' teachings and their applicability to business principles.

As the captain announced the start of their descent, Lee shared with Dean about how he had learned about Jesus as a child but had drifted from church after college. He had gotten absorbed in starting a family and a business and never really saw the relevance of faith to either. For the first time in many years, he actually felt curious about what the Bible might have to say to him.

Dean recommended a few resources on faith and work for Lee to check out. He also wrote down the name of his own Christian leadership coach.

"So, I guess you've built your career by flying all over the place telling people about Jesus' management strategies," Lee joked as they unbuckled their seatbelts and gathered their things.

"Not really." Dean grinned. "I became a Christian only a few years ago. But I've learned a lot from my coach."

Dean thought back to the times his coach had told him that his work served the purpose of making Jesus attractive to others. But this was the first time he felt he had truly understood—and engaged—this kingdom purpose.

Kingdom Purpose for Work #3: Draw People to Jesus

Disciples make disciples. Those who have been transformed by Christ can share their experiences of forgiveness, healing, hope, joy, and peace with others. Redeemed image-bearers attract other image-bearers to Christ to be redeemed, so they too can live and work with kingdom purpose.

Since work is where people not only spend most of their time but are the most likely to interact with unbelievers, discipleship leads people to see their workplace as their primary mission field. How do Christians attract people to Jesus in the workplace? While unpacking this with those you disciple calls for in-depth study,[1] here is an overview of some key ways.

How Redeemed Image-Bearers Draw Others to Jesus at Work

The first strategy that may come to mind for many is *being invitational.* Explore ways to communicate with others about their faith and to invite them to learn more about Jesus. Note with those you disciple that this is not limited to church-centric options. While inviting people to church services is good, consider also meeting with coworkers at lunch to discuss the relevance of biblical teachings to workplace challenges.

Many Christians look for evangelistic openings when nonbelievers become aware of their need for salvation—when they feel most acutely the effects of the fall. A four-chapter gospel approach looks additionally for openings to share with people about who they are as image-bearers, created by God for good. When we express to nonbelievers that God cares about the work they do, this draws their attention in an uplifting way. It naturally opens doors for them to want to learn more.

A related strategy is to *point people to the source of meaning of work.* As believers take their work seriously as a calling from the Creator, others may also come to see their work as having spiritual significance and be drawn to learn more about the source.[2]

As James Smith points out, "Instead of nagging questions about God or the afterlife, your neighbors are oriented by all sorts of longings and 'projects' and quests for significance." What meets this longing is "not to have an argument about the data or 'evidences' but rather to offer an alternative story that offers a more robust, complex understanding of the Christian faith."[3] Disciples can help others make sense of their "quest for significance" by showing them how their work has a place in God's Big Story.

A third strategy for making Christ attractive to colleagues is *modeling Christ-likeness at work.* Every human being is made in the image of God, but followers of Jesus are intentional about reflecting godliness in their attitude and actions. This is particularly critical in settings predisposed to be unwelcoming to the Christian faith (see 1 Pet. 2:12). Doug Sherman says our workplaces need "Christians whose lifestyle and work style are so unique and so distinctive that coworkers will want to know why."[4]

Disciples need to be warned that talking about Christ is ineffective, or even counterproductive, unless they also model Christ. I (Tom) have been cheated five times (that I know of) by other businessmen. All five who cheated me presented themselves as Christians. Bad behavior will always shout louder than any evangelistic message.

Last, but certainly not least, emphasize to disciples that they make faith attractive by *doing great work*. Disciples are to enter their workplace with the mindset of making God's glory visible, even to unbelievers. "Let your light shine before others, so that they may see your good works and give glory to your Father in heaven" (Matt. 5:16). Workers display the image of God by doing work that is "very good." Conversely, work done poorly, or with a poor attitude, discredits the gospel (1 Tim. 6:1). Quality service and products, offered to the glory of God, are effective advertisements for God's design.

Years of experience in the business world confirm that evangelism is far more effective when Christians attract others because of the way they're doing their work, than when they use various tactics to slip in the gospel message detached from the context of their work.

The *Theology of Work Bible Commentary* summarizes the connection between sharing the gospel and being devoted to "good works" in Titus 2–3:

> Paul is not talking about giving speeches, passing out tracts, or telling people about Jesus. He is talking about good works in the ordinary sense of doing things that others recognize will meet people's needs. In workplace terms, we could say he means something such as helping new co-workers come up to speed on the job, more so than inviting them to join a Bible study....

> Godly behavior is encouraged for Christians, "so that in everything they may be an ornament to the doctrine of God our Savior" (Titus 2:10). Right doctrine leads to good works, and good works make the truth of God attractive to others. That is the aim behind Christian workers' devotion to good works at their jobs—to live out by their actions the truth they proclaim with their lips. This may prove a powerful witness both to defuse antipathy toward Christians and to appeal to nonbelievers to follow Christ themselves.[5]

Encouraging Readiness

If disciples are to work in such a way that they inspire people to notice the difference and ask for an explanation, then they need to be prepared to know what to do next! "Always be prepared to give an answer to everyone who asks you to give the reason for the hope that you have" (1 Pet. 3:15). When a nonbeliever asks what a believer's secret is to making leadership decisions, or how they stay peaceful in the midst of a turbulent economy, or how they consistently deliver such high-quality products, how will the believer respond?

This is where your role as a discipler is especially vital. If Christians lack the ability to integrate their own faith with their employment, they will be hard-pressed to present their faith with conviction to coworkers. As you equip disciples in how their work connects with the gospel story, you also equip them to share this with others.

A final point to make to those you disciple is that every effort to make Christ attractive should be accompanied by the work of prayer. Ultimately, it is the Spirit who draws people to their Creator. "Our message of the gospel came to you not in word only, but also in power and in the Holy Spirit and with full conviction; just as you know what kind of persons we proved to be among you for your sake" (1 Thess. 1:5).

"You Showed God to Me"

I (Tom) helped start a company with Christian partners who shared my belief that God cared deeply about our work. As owners we had an unwritten rule: We never initiated conversations about faith with employees. We never evangelized a person unless they approached us first. We never wanted anyone to come to church with us or claim to be a Christian out of a desire to curry our favor. We were, however, intentional about modeling Christ in the way we conducted our business and treated clients and employees. And we shared openly with anyone who wanted to know more about what we believed.

Over the years we saw many of our staff come to Christ. We didn't keep track of specific numbers, but I would estimate that about half of our employees became believers after coming to work with us.

Eventually, I left the company. Then one day, out of the blue, about a decade after I left, my former administrative assistant called to tell me about an employee who was facing a really tough situation. "You were always ready to help out the people here, so I thought you would want to know," she said. I told her I would reach out and see what I could do.

As I worked with the employee on his problem, I had several phone conversations with my former assistant. In one of these calls, she began reflecting on her experiences working for me. Her words brought me joy: "I never told you this before, but when I worked for you, you showed God to me."

She still had many questions about faith. I offered to send her a book written by my pastor that answered some of her questions, and she said she would like to have it.

One Sunday, about a month later, she again surprised me with a call. "You might be glad to know that this morning I was baptized and joined the church!" She expressed her gratitude for giving her hope and pointing her in the right direction.

Kingdom Purpose and the Great Commission

Jeff Norris came to Tom's Kingdom Purpose Workshop with thirteen years of campus ministry experience. In a course assignment, he shared the shift in his understanding of the Great Commission from an image-bearer perspective:

> *Matthew 28:19-20 has been a key verse in my life. It fueled why I went on staff with Cru. . . . However, I most often only applied the command of the verse, to make disciples, within a ministry context. Therefore, the types of disciples I most often made . . . only understood disciple making in the context of small group Bible study, evangelism, prayer and structured discipleship.*
>
> *Although I still believe in these things whole-heartedly and see them as my personal life calling, I failed to make disciples who understood that part of "teaching them to observe all that I have commanded" includes a proper theology of work and a more robust understanding of the story of redemption that God has been writing from the beginning. In other words, God's redemptive narrative doesn't just include the salvation of man's heart and life, but the redemption, renewal, and restoration of all created things through redeemed mankind.*[6]

The vision for the people you disciple is that they will draw people to Christ and make disciples in the context of the ministry of their vocation. These new disciples can then engage others in the whole gospel story, for the "redemption, renewal, and restoration of all created things." Your role as vocational discipler can be the launching point for this vision.

RESOURCE

Kingdom Purpose Discipleship Questions: Draw People to Christ

Below are questions and exercises for disciplers to ask to help people grasp the kingdom purpose of attracting people to Jesus:

1. State aloud: "I am fulfilling my kingdom purpose as an image-bearer at work when I draw people to Christ."

   ✓ What does this mean to you? What reaction does this spark in you?

   ✓ How do you pursue this kingdom purpose in your work?

   ✓ What hinders or distracts from this purpose in your work?

   ✓ What could you do to strengthen this kingdom purpose?

2. People at your workplace are watching you. How do you hope they see Christ reflected in you?

3. Disciples have several strategies for drawing people to Jesus: being invitational, pointing people to the source of meaningful work, modeling Christ-likeness, and doing quality work. Which are you best positioned to pursue at this time and how? Do any other strategies come to mind?

4. Jesus said, "The harvest is plentiful, but the laborers are few; therefore ask the Lord of the harvest to send out laborers into his harvest" (Luke 10:2). Evangelism is not an end in itself but a quest to recruit more image-bearers to collaborate in God's work of restoration. How does this make a difference in the way you approach people with the gospel?

5. Colossians 4:6 says, "Let your speech always be gracious, seasoned with salt, so that you may know how you ought to answer everyone." Write out three questions you hope people might be prompted to ask you in connection with your work and how you might answer.

13

DISCIPLERS ASK: HOW DOES YOUR WORK ENABLE GOD'S WORLD TO FLOURISH?

Kingdom Purpose for Work #4: Contribute to the Flourishing of the World

Discipleship for this kingdom purpose begins by helping people realize that God's original creation mandate still applies to them! The unbroken theme from Genesis on is that image-bearers "share a common vocation to care not only for our own flourishing, but for the flourishing of the world."[1]

This kingdom purpose is linked with the purpose of work to bless people, as discussed earlier. However, it is distinct in that it focuses on the ways that the outcomes of labor—that is, the stuff that gets done because it's someone's job to do it—shape the world in ways that delight God by bringing out the goodness inherent in his creation.

To convey God's intentions for a flourishing world, look at Isaiah 65:17–25. This passage paints a picture of a community that brings delight to its Creator: health, longevity, sufficiency, stable intergenerational relationships, peace, security, and intimacy with God. God invites his people to "be glad and rejoice forever in what I am creating!" (v. 18). This state of holistic well-being is captured in the Hebrew word *shalom*, which appears 550 times in various forms in the Bible.

It's also clear that this thriving community is built on human work: "They shall build houses and inhabit them; they shall plant vineyards and eat their fruit. . . . My chosen shall long enjoy the work of their hands. They shall not labor in vain" (vv. 21–23). Our kingdom purpose is to be co-creators with God of a world that all can enjoy.

God therefore appointed image-bearers to make God's world flourish through their work.[2] Under this broad heading, we can identify three subcategories that correspond with the creation mandate (as laid out in chapter 7): (1) Build abundant community: "fill the earth"; (2) Bring order: "subdue it"; and (3) Cultivate potential: "have dominion." These activities must be carried out in a myriad of interwoven ways to create and sustain *shalom*. Keller and Alsdorf write,

> We are continuing God's work of forming, filling, and subduing. Whenever we bring order out of chaos, whenever we draw out creative potential, whenever we elaborate and unfold creation beyond where it was when we found it, we are following God's pattern of creative cultural development.[3]

But we also work in a world shaped by the self-centeredness of sin, rebellion against God's kingdom, and the curse—all of which unravels *shalom*. Thus the creation mandate is intertwined with a fourth strand of this kingdom purpose: *Restore brokenness*.

As redeemed image-bearers, we join Christ in "our calling to reweave *shalom*,"[4] anticipating the last eternal chapter in the gospel story. All redeemed image-bearers must resist evil and seek healing and liberation wherever "the whole creation has been groaning" (Rom. 8:22); but for some, this is at the heart of their vocation.

Helping Disciples See Where They Fit in

Every individual image-bearer is gifted and positioned to contribute to *shalom* in distinct ways. Though the four types of work for flourishing overlap, people generally gravitate to one subcategory more than the others. For example, some vocations specialize in bringing order and others in extracting potential. Disciplers help people discover which of these four areas aligns best with their work.

It's actually not necessary to believe in God to serve his kingdom purpose. A person can be a skilled welder without giving the Creator the credit for the metals and the skill to fashion it. Even Christians are often unaware of how their work connects with the broader gospel story. It may never occur to the follower of Jesus who mops floors and cleans toilets at a hospital how they are imitating Jesus in overcoming the curse of disease.

As a discipler, you can help Christians become more aware of how their vocation fulfills their kingdom purpose. When they see how their work contributes to the flourishing of the world, they can affirm, "My work is my ministry." You also encourage Christians to nudge nonbelieving image-bearers to discover how they have, unknowingly, been agents of God's plans for *shalom*.

Below we offer highlights for each strand of this category of kingdom purpose to help disciples recognize how their work fulfills this purpose.

Build Abundant Community

This kingdom purpose centers on fostering strong, caring families in vibrant communities, characterized by just and stable social relationships and a rich culture reflecting God's truth and beauty. Examples of vocations fulfilling this purpose include: childcare and education, senior care, communications, arts and entertainment, sports and recreational activities, neighborhood/city planning, homemaking, history and the humanities, household finances and estate planning, marriage and family counselors, cultural centers, and governance.

EXAMPLE

Larry Witherspoon founded the Automotive Training Center (ATC) in Atlanta, with the vision "to mold every young man into a thriving leader in their community by embodying the values of confidence, work ethic, and a passion for learning." Witherspoon learned the power of investing in young people from his father, who was a teacher, coach, and youth mentor. Here is Larry's description of their approach:

> *The majority of our students are at-risk, from low-income neighborhoods where unemployment and high school dropout rates are high. ATC was founded on the principle that all of its students have untapped potential that has not developed because of their life circumstances. ATC gives students opportunities to grow the technical and entrepreneurial skills they already possess. . . . ATC's training produces graduates that are more likely to maintain stable employment, become business owners, and have stable family lives.*

First Presbyterian Church in Atlanta chose the training center for its Epiphany venture fund for social entrepreneurs, making a $65,000 investment to enable the company to expand its programs. "The more students we are able to help, it's a win-win for society to get them back in the job field," Witherspoon said, summarizing the link between training, work and abundant community.[5]

Bring Order to the World

This kingdom purpose involves restraining and harnessing the wild powers of creation and maintaining the infrastructure and systems that enable our society to function well. Examples of vocations fulfilling this purpose include: scientific research and exploration, heating/air conditioning, pest control, water and sanitation systems, road maintenance, traffic control, judicial system, regulating commerce, insurance, landscaping, firefighting, food safety inspectors, and conservation.

EXAMPLE

Dan, an elder at Perimeter Church in Atlanta, became project leader for a team of developers developing a mobile banking phone app. About two billion people in poverty worldwide have cell phones but don't have access to a bank. Dan's project would give millions of people in India and Pakistan, most earning less than three dollars a day, the ability to do their banking on their phone.

Ever since Dan became exposed to faith and work principles, he had been praying for a vision for how his expertise in technology-related businesses could contribute to the flourishing of shalom. His team began doing more than writing code. They began developing a system of mobile banking that could fundamentally improve the lives of some the poorest people on the planet.

Develop the Potential of Creation

Rather than create finished products, God gave image-bearers an abundance of raw materials and the capacity to draw out the countless possibilities embedded in his creation. Thus "an engineer who designs a bridge or a sewage treatment plant actually accomplishes God's work of providing for humanity's needs."[6]

Vocations that cultivate, reshape, and redistribute the potential of creation to enable life to thrive include: business enterprise, information technology, machinists, agriculture, animal husbandry, food service, mining, manufacturing/textiles, handicrafts/artisans, retail, engineering, transportation, and human resources.

EXAMPLE

Barranco Beverage is a service company for beverage machines at gas stations and convenience stores. I (Tom) coached Barranco's owner, who was questioning the value of his work from the perspective of his faith. I asked him a simple question: "Can you imagine a world in which no one had morning coffee?" If you're a coffee drinker, then you know this is not a pretty picture!

We unpacked how God created the bitter coffee bean and image-bearers ingeniously developed its potential to become one of the most popular beverages in the world. Barranco is one link in a long chain of development that enhances the lives of morning commuters, late-night workers, and highway travelers who rely on their cup of joe. Sustainable coffee production also provides livelihood for millions around the world.

After gaining a new appreciation for the kingdom purpose of his company, the owner learned to talk with his employees in a new way about the value of their work. They too began to see the connection between their jobs and the well-being of their community. Morale and engagement improved.[7]

Restore Brokenness

When sin and death entered the world, God's intended abundance went awry. Instead of abundant community, humanity suffers from broken relationships and scarcity. Instead of bringing order to the world, we are devastated by natural disasters and disease. Instead of developing the potential of creation, we corrupt creation by our greed.

"We see that God is on the move, doing his work of restoring all things. Such a vision should provoke our awed worship: how amazing a Savior is our God, who is conquering all evil and is about the work of re-creating paradise!"[8] Some of us are called to partner with God in this restorative kingdom purpose: to bring healing and compassion where there is brokenness, to reverse the effects of the curse in nature, and to confront and restrain expressions of sin.

Examples of vocations that relieve, redress, protect, and restore include: health care, humanitarian aid, morticians, homeless shelter, policing/prison system, firefighters, justice advocacy, military, disaster response, divorce court, addiction recovery, foster care, and grief counselors.

As disciplers, we can note that this final kingdom purpose will *not* continue into heaven—because in heaven "no longer will there be any curse" (Rev. 22:3 NIV). So when we pray, "Your kingdom come on earth as it is in heaven," we're praying for the time when anyone whose vocation falls into this category will have to find a new line of work!

Example

When it comes to favorite public employees, TSA agents rarely make the top of anyone's list. TSA workers often get an earful from harried travelers. One would hope that Christians coming through security checkpoints would treat TSA agents better, but as a frequent traveler, I (Tom) have not observed a difference among my fellow passengers. Too often the person berating the screener for holding up their luggage has a Bible in their carryon bag.

It might make a difference if we viewed our interaction with TSA agents beyond the virtues of being patient and kind to those who annoy us (though that too would be a welcome change). We need to apply the lens of kingdom purpose. TSA agents serve God's purpose of restraining evil (Rom. 13:4–5). They serve God by keeping his precious image-bearers safe from those who would disrupt and destroy.

Whenever I travel, I therefore make a point of looking a TSA agent in the eye and saying, "Thank you for doing the job you do. God bless you."

Discipling Makers of *Shalom*

Vocational discipleship invites people to fresh awareness and a deeper commitment to their role in God's intended *shalom*: that is, how their work is their ministry.

> Shalom is the stuff of the Kingdom. It's what the Kingdom of God looks like in context. . . . Shalom is a vision of a Kingdom that provides for all. It is a vision of abundance, of God's presence wiping away fear. It is also a vision of just and healthy interdependent relationships—a vision of respect for the image of God present in all humanity and the call and capacity of all humanity to exercise dominion. What's more, it is a vision of the self-existent, supreme God present and active in the muck with humanity.[9]

Every task that aligns with God's purpose in creation and restoration, no matter how humble, is a step toward this *shalom*. If people truly can't see how their work enables *shalom* in a meaningful way, then discipleship might entail helping them reevaluate their job and discover a new vocational calling.

The goal of seeking *shalom* can carry into how disciples manage their daily tasks. Each workday brings opportunities to cultivate abundant community, to promote order, and to develop the potential of creation to meet the needs of the world, as well as to lift up God's glory, be a blessing, and show others the likeness of Christ. Sometimes this means reprioritizing tasks based on what's most important to promote flourishing. Or it might mean going above and beyond their regular workload. For example, during the COVID-19 crisis, many health-care providers spent their vacations volunteering in hard-hit communities. Their dedication to their purpose of overcoming disease extended beyond their job.

Working for *shalom* also brings fresh perspective on what people are already doing. Nathan, a student in Tom's class, offered this commentary on 2 Corinthians 10:5 ("We take every thought captive to obey Christ"):

> Take thoughts captive like, "I have to do these stupid reimbursements so I can get to what God really cares about." This can become thoughts like, "Doing these reimbursements well and in a productive manner will bless the accounting department as well as the flourishing of our family's finances." This transforms the task, and there is energy and motivation to glorify God now while doing the task.[10]

Note that being a *shalom*-maker at work shouldn't come at the expense of shalom at home. God's design is work that blesses and strengthens families. Discuss with disciples how their job may be taking a toll on the peace and well-being of their household. If you are discipling business owners, explore how they are taking the shalom of their employees' families into consideration.

The Disciple Maker's Handbook reminds us, "Discipleship and disciple making are simply forming our lives around Jesus and helping others to do the same."[11] At a foundational level, equipping people for *shalom* means pointing them to Jesus as the one who reconciles people to God and to one another, who restores wholeness and calls people to a new way of life. Only Jesus forgives and frees people from the sin that stands as a barrier to *shalom* and emboldens followers to confront the forces that are destroyers of *shalom*. As we invite people to the forgiving, restorative work of Jesus, we also call them to be followers of the ways he engaged with people in the context of their work.[12]

RESOURCE

Kingdom Purpose Discipleship Questions: Enable the World to Flourish

Help disciples connect with the four ways in which their work contributes to the flourishing of the world:

1. Build community
2. Bring order
3. Cultivate potential
4. Restore brokenness

Everyone should be able to identify (with pride!) the particular ways their work advances what God wants to see done in the world. A starting point is to ask them the following questions:

- *What do you imagine shalom or God's intended flourishing looks like for your workplace? For your family, your community, and for your global neighbors?*

- *What goods or services are produced by your workplace? How does this help the world to flourish?*

- *How does your specific job contribute to the goodness of that outcome?*

- *What can you do this week to accomplish that purpose well?*

- *Which of the four subcategories (build community, bring order, culti-vate potential, restore brokenness) best fit that description for your job and for the agency as a whole?*

If someone has a difficult time pinpointing the way their job leads to flourishing, read Isaiah 65:17–25 and Revelation 21–22 for a picture of a fulfilled community. Can they imagine doing the work they do in such a setting? What aspects of what they do bring relief or delight?

A powerful way to help people affirm their kingdom purpose is to ask the question: *What would the world be like if no one did the work you do?*

For some jobs—such as trash collection—the answer is obvious. Others, however, will need the help of disciplers to do some probing. For example, someone who works for a plant that manufactures metal fasteners might feel like an insignificant cog. But then comes the question: "What might the world be like if no one ever made fasteners?" Then they can imagine desks coming apart, shelves collapsing, and planes falling out of the sky! It quickly becomes apparent how their job contributes to the kingdom purpose of developing potential.

Another question to discover kingdom purpose is: Where do you see God doing something similar to what you do? For example:

- ✓ *Manufacturing:* God the Creator shaped Adam out of the dirt
- ✓ *Life guard:* Jesus rescued Peter from drowning
- ✓ *Job trainer:* "The Holy Spirit, whom the Father will send in my name, will teach you all things" (John 14:26)

In the example of the fastener manufacturer, the disciple could cite Colossians 1:17. By making metal fasteners, this employee reflects the image of a God who holds "all things together"!

Finally, help the person you're discipling bring it all together by drafting a personal statement about their work: *My work serves the kingdom purpose of enabling God's world to flourish by . . .*

14

HELP PEOPLE DISCOVER THEIR PERSONAL CALLING WITH KINGDOM PURPOSE

Dave, an executive with a large banking software company, took Tom's Kingdom Purpose Workshop. This is his story of finding his sense of calling.[1]

DAVE'S STORY

Most of my gifts are around leadership, and I found myself consistently being asked to take leadership responsibilities at church and at work. But I never had an overarching narrative for how those things fit together. There was my spiritual calling, and then there was my job; they didn't really have much to do with each other.

One of our pastors gave a sermon on shalom, *and something really resonated in me. I already knew I was responsible to be faithful in my job, to work hard, to be generous with my salary. But participating with God in* shalom, *in the restoration of the world—that was a completely new concept. Then I read* Why Business Matters to God, *and I really started to feel that my work is critical to what God has created me for.*

Now, I have a much better understanding of why my job matters to God. In the past, I would have said, "God doesn't care about financial services technology." I had thought of my corporate job as a necessary evil, which God redeems because I'm able to provide for my family and tithe and give money to support a kid in Africa. Then I learned about places in the world where financial services don't exist. All sorts of bad things come in. It's painful, it's ugly, it's corrupt—it's the opposite of flourishing. So, God cares about financial services technology.

As I better understand my calling, there's less guilt about saying no to other things. For example, I don't feel bad about not being on a worship and arts team. I have some musical gifts, but that's not my calling. Instead, I can help a staff member at church charged with leading cultural transformation and crafting a new leadership institute. I'm going to have much greater kingdom impact spending three hours on the leadership institute than in a choir rehearsal.

Kingdom Purpose, Personal Calling, and Jobs

Kingdom purpose, as defined earlier, refers to the ways that work fulfills God's plans for his creation. Image-bearers fulfill their kingdom purpose by doing what God wants to get done. *Calling* is where God's broad aims meet an individual's design. "Calling is not a job description or a gut feeling; it goes beyond occupation and integrates what we do (our purpose) with who we are (our identity)."[2] Every image-bearer has a kingdom purpose they are uniquely gifted, positioned, and summoned to fulfill.

A key verse for understanding calling is Ephesians 2:10: "We are what he has made us, created in Christ Jesus for good works, which God prepared beforehand to be our way of life." Our calling is the "good work" God has specifically prepared each of us to do. "Calling" is from the Latin root *vocare*, to summon. *Vocation* is the occupational path that channels our gifts and energies toward the fulfillment of our calling. Our vocation turns our calling into a "way of life."

As a vocational discipler, you help people discover their calling and sort out where their job or career fits in. Workers often are unaware of how their work advances a kingdom purpose. For example, a graphic designer who lays out packaging for a soap company may not think about how their work serves the kingdom purpose of controlling the curse of disease. Leading people to connect their current job with kingdom purpose is one step. Another step is to help people discern their calling (see the resource at the end of this chapter) and then explore jobs that align with that purpose. It often requires intentional effort to pursue work that fulfills a calling.

Some pursue a career without considering whether it's their calling. They may be encouraged to reflect on what factors influence their career choice, such as salary, others' expectations, or simple inertia. Others, by necessity, work in jobs that are outside their calling. They may face barriers (such as discrimination, poverty, or lack of connections) that stand in the way of realizing their God-given potential and passion. Feeling stuck in work that does not fulfill a calling can lead to soul-crushing dissatisfaction. In addition to offering encouragement as people seek to overcome the obstacles to their sense of calling, disciplers can also help affirm the dignity and value of whatever work they find themselves doing. By exploring kingdom purpose, people may discover that the job they happen to be in has more elements of their calling than they thought.

I (Heidi) had a friend in seminary who, after graduating, struggled to find a church position. Financial necessity led him to accept the only job available to him in his rural town—fast food. When I later checked in to see how he was doing, he said, "It was hard at first. But then I thought about how what I do is feeding people, and how Jesus also fed people in his ministry. I'm still getting to care for people, just in a different way than I had planned."

Teaching People about Calling

Below are six points to share with disciples about their personal calling.

1. Your Calling Requires Cultivation

Just as God created the world with potential needing cultivation, God also creates each image-bearer with the potential to be shaped into their calling. In order to develop the goodness that God implanted in the world, we must first develop the potential that God implants within each of us.

Disciplers help people with the charge laid out in Ephesians 4:1: "Live a life worthy of the calling you have received" (NIV). Cultivating a calling is a sacred responsibility. Image-bearers are accountable for the stewardship of their talents, passions, knowledge, skills, experience, and influence.[3] Help those you disciple to build up the self-discipline, confidence and initiative to support the development of these gifts.

Another we can help people to be "worthy of your calling" is by encouraging them to direct their gifts toward a kingdom purpose. It's grievous to see talented people working counter to the glory of God or the flourishing of the world. In the movie *The Remains of the Day,* a distinguished butler serves an aristocratic family with superlative dedication. He is so devoted to his calling that he overlooks the growing anti-Semitism of his employer, but realizes later with deep regret how he contributed to supporting the Nazi cause. Disciplers help people see what's at stake in the development of their calling and offer guidance and accountability.

2. Your Calling Is Seamless across Multiple Areas of Life

In my Kingdom Purpose Workshops, I (Tom) have seen a hunger for integration of purpose across the various roles that people play in their daily lives. Shawn, the CEO of a software development company, remarked that what people want is "not to be different in each role; it's to be the same person in that calling in all their roles. It's not compartmentalizing."[4]

A calling can stitch together the various facets of family, work, church, and play. Who each person is created to be is always consistent, though it may have different expressions across the various sectors of their life. As you help people confirm their calling, this integration can bring a greater sense of clarity and unity to their complex lives.

3. Your Calling Is Interdependent with Many Others

Each person's work is a piece of a vast mosaic. One independent piece can't do much good without being part of the bigger picture. Each disciple's calling contributes to, and depends on, many others effectively following their callings as well.

There are different kinds of gifts, but the same Spirit distributes them. There are different kinds of service, but the same Lord. There are different kinds of working, but in all of them and in everyone it is the same God at work. Now to each one the manifestation of the Spirit is given for the common good. (1 Cor. 12:4–7 NIV)

Is this only about the church? Or does this wisdom about "different kinds of working" refer to the many callings that must be exercised together in order for God's purposes for the flourishing of the world (the "common good") to be accomplished?

Discipleship leads individuals to approach their calling with confidence (because their work is important) and humility (because everyone else's work is important). Each individual's unique gifts must join with others to accomplish kingdom purpose.

4. Calling Is Not Just for High-Status Positions

In 1 Corinthians 12:21–25 (NIV), Paul develops the metaphor of one body with many parts, all deserving of honor. "Those parts of the body that seem to be weaker are indispensable. . . . There should be no division in the body, but that its parts should have equal concern for each other." People tend to judge the importance of jobs by their skill, status, or pay; God cares about their function.

In Exodus 31:1–6, as God is preparing Moses to manage a major building project, he announces his choice to lead the design work: "I have called by name Bezalel . . . and I have filled him with divine spirit, with ability, intelligence, and knowledge in every kind of craft." Then God continues his instruction: "Moreover, I have appointed Oholiab . . . to help him." Both positions—the leader and the assistant—are equally divine appointments. We are made in the image of God's Spirit, who is also described as a helper (e.g., John 14:16–17). Being part of a team helping those with specialized skills is also a calling from God.

The story goes that when President Kennedy visited NASA, he asked a man what his job was. This man, who happened to be a janitor, answered the president, "To help put a man on the moon." Disciplers help people in jobs considered lower status to hold fast to the larger kingdom vision of their work as ministry.

5. There Are No "Higher Callings"

The language of calling has been steeped in church-centric thinking, which presumes that only people who do "spiritual" work are called in a special way.

The desire for our life's work to be an investment in something we believe to be lasting, even ultimate, is rooted deeply in our spirituality. That is why this idea of "special calling" appeals to many of us. We almost always hear about this kind of "calling" when "ministers" and those training for full-time ministry tell their stories and talk about their work. . . . God has called a chosen few to serve by focusing on eternal, lasting matters, while He has called others to serve by focusing on earthly, less ultimately important, matters.[5]

But there are no second-class employees in God's kingdom, just as there are no second-class image-bearers. *Every* worker is called to serve God and minister to the world.

There is also sometimes an assumed hierarchy between those who are called to volunteer or do nonprofit work and those whose callings are in the marketplace. One student in Tom's Kingdom Purpose Workshop initially associated the "good works" in Ephesians 2:10 only with charitable service: "If I went on a mission trip, was involved in an outreach to feed the homeless, or gave money to clothe people in Jesus's name." But this changed after he learned about his kingdom calling:

> I see this differently now. When I invest time in subordinates at work, listen to a supervisor who is having family problems, or demonstrate concern for a peer who is sick, I am walking in the good works that God has prepared for me.[6]

As a discipler, be attuned to respond to those who feel they are "settling" on their calling. Many Christians go about their daily work believing deep in their souls that God is disappointed with or disengaged from their vocation. Review passages such as Ephesians 2:10 to assure them that God gave them the skills and ability for that work and appointed them to do it.

6. A Calling Has Heavenly Significance

Revelation 21:24–26 says that "the glory and the honor of the nations" will be brought into the New Jerusalem. God's very good design for his creation will be fulfilled in paradise. In some fashion, all the work people do that contributes to human flourishing will be incorporated into our heavenly existence. Vocational callings have an eternal reach.[7] Thus there is no hierarchy between callings that address "eternal, lasting matters" and those focused on "earthly, less ultimately important, matters."

As we have seen, however, some callings will *not* be found in heaven. Those working for the kingdom purpose of overcoming the curse will have to redefine their vocation, because there will no longer be any curse!

Helping Disciples Discover Their Calling

According to Michael Novak, a calling has four characteristics: it is unique to the individual; it requires talent and passion; it is accompanied by a sense of enjoyment, satisfaction, and renewed energy; and it is not always easy to discover.[8] God occasionally uses extraordinary measures to light the way, but "for the vast majority of Christians God's callings are discerned quietly, when the heart of faith joins opportunities and gifts with the needs of others."[9]

Disciplers can play an invaluable role in walking alongside people as they examine their calling. Discerning one's calling is not a one-time decision, but a process. It takes life experience, self-reflection, feedback from others, and spiritual discernment.

For someone who already has a career, exploring their calling can bring excitement but also vulnerability, because it may lead to changing course or taking new risks. It may also reaffirm what someone is already doing, with a reinvigorated awareness of kingdom purpose.

For example, Mark Wells is a divorce attorney who struggled with his sense of calling. How could God have called him to help people to get a divorce? Should he be looking for another line of work? As the facilitator of his discipleship group, I (Tom) helped him wrestle with this question. Then one day, Mark walked into the group with a grin: "God told me my role is to be a protector." Reframing his job as a calling brought a tremendous sense of peace and purpose.[10]

What can disciplers do to help someone discern their calling?

- Provide a solid foundation for this process, by reviewing the core principles of image-bearing work and the categories of kingdom purpose.

- Ask questions to draw out insights (see the questions on the resource page).

- Help identify how their calling contributes to a specific kingdom purpose.

- Review how they have been a steward of their gifts and passions.

- Facilitate connections with mature Christians in their vocation (2 Thess. 3:6–9), who can share about their calling and how they engage their work as a ministry.

- Pray for/with them.

- Refer them to good books and other resources for exploring their calling.

Disciplers can also consider helping people put together a "life plan" that builds on their calling to integrate consistent kingdom purpose into every role in their life (see Appendix A).

The Voice version of Ephesians 2:10 brings out the artistry of our God-given callings: "For we are the product of His hand, heaven's poetry etched on lives, created in the Anointed, Jesus, to accomplish the good works God arranged long ago." Each person you disciple has been lovingly, deliberately crafted by their Maker. Help them fully engage their unique potential to get kingdom work done.

RESOURCE

Guiding Image-Bearers to Explore Their Design for Vocation

A calling is where God's broad kingdom purpose meets an image-bearer's design. Olympic runner Eric Liddell was famously quoted in the movie *Chariots of Fire*: "God made me fast. And when I run, I feel his pleasure." Help each person you disciple to make a similar declaration, adapted to their own unique calling: *"God made me _____. When I _____, I feel his pleasure."*

Use the following questions to help people explore their design for vocation. These questions draw on 1 Corinthians 12:4–6, which says that people have varieties of gifts (*charismata*), service (*diakonia*), and workings (*energemata*), but they all come from God to achieve his intentions. Ask people to assess themselves and also seek input from others who know them well. Use the chart below to record notes and visualize connections.

Satisfaction: Work That Feels Like a Gift

Consider your dreams and goals related to work. What do you love and aspire to do? What kinds of activity give you energy, fulfillment, inspiration, and deep joy? When do you feel most motivated? (Also consider the opposite: What are you least motivated to do? What drains your energy? What kinds of work "fit" you, and what work simply gives you fits?)[11]

Strengths: Work That Engages Abilities

Take stock of your talents, skills, qualities, capacities, and experiences, especially those that enable you to contribute to the flourishing of the world. What do you have a natural knack for, or what have you learned to do well? What work are you qualified to do? When do you feel most competent? (Consider using a spiritual gift inventory, talent inventory, or other assessment tool.)

Service: Work That Meets a Need

Reflect on your passion connected with an opportunity you want to develop, a problem you want to solve, or an element of the status quo you yearn to help change. When you listen to the "groaning" of the world (Rom. 8:22–23), what compels your attention? What is the difference you hope to make in the world? Where could you be most useful?

Work That Supports the Well-being of Your Household

Take note of the needs of your household for income as well as for benefits, scheduling, and vacation/sick time. Do you need more income, or more flexibility? Financial sufficiency is important, but so is mental and relational health.

Chart the "Sweet Spot" of Vocational Calling[12]

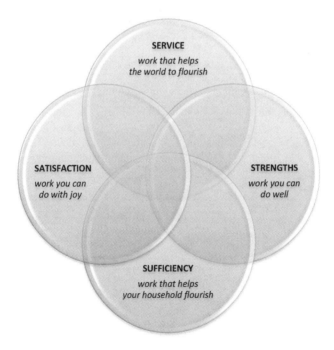

Reflect

- Is a picture emerging of your sense of vocational calling or "sweet spot" where these elements are aligned?

- How does this alignment relate to your current employment?

- How does this alignment relate to your unpaid work in other areas of your life (family, church, community, and culture)?

- How has God positioned you to follow through on this "sweet spot"? What opportunities or influence might you have?

- What might bring you closer to your "sweet spot" in your job and other areas?

PART FOUR

DISCIPLESHIP CORE QUESTION #3: HOW WILL YOU FULFILL YOUR PURPOSE?

(Helping People to Faithfully and Fruitfully Live out Their Calling)

15

DISCIPLESHIP LEADS PEOPLE TO DEMONSTRATE "I AM PRODUCTIVE IN GOD'S KINGDOM!"

CASE STUDY

"How are things at work?" Esteban asked his young friend Tyler, as the waiter left their table after taking their lunch order. *The two had gotten to know one another in the men's Bible study at church. They had been meeting monthly since the retired Esteban had felt the Holy Spirit nudge him to ask Tyler if he would consider having him as a mentor.*

Esteban's question set off a firestorm of complaints. As a new hire at a big insurance company, Tyler felt unnoticed and unappreciated. Everything that went wrong was somehow his fault; but when things went well, someone else took the credit. He had started out full of energy and ideas—but instead of being pleased, his supervisor seemed to feel threatened by Tyler's initiative, while the other low-level employees in his department resented him for making them look bad.

"I'm at the point of saying, why bother? Why should I put anything on the line if I just get slapped down for trying? I might as well just show up, check off my assignments, and play on my phone the rest of the day, like everyone else does."

"I can understand your frustration," Esteban responded. *"Now, let me ask you a few questions. What kingdom purpose do you serve in your vocation?"*

Tyler remembered this well from a previous conversation with Esteban. He had taken this purpose to heart. *"Insurance protects people from damage related to the fallenness of people and nature. It helps to bring order to the world by stewarding resources to restore families and businesses after a crisis."*

Esteban nodded. *"And as someone who has had to file a claim, I can tell you that it's truly a blessing to have a kind, efficient agent working with you on your case."* He took a sip of his lemonade and then asked, *"So, why wouldn't that purpose deserve your very best, every day?"*

Discipleship is about being, knowing, and doing. Formed to bear the image of our Creator, redeemed by Christ, and called to fulfill God's kingdom purpose, we know why we get up and go to work each day. These biblical truths impel and guide our actions. "Now that you know these things, you will be blessed if you do them!" (John 13:17).

This section supports disciplers in supporting fellow Christians in walking through the grind of workday activity in a way that's both faithful and productive. It's not enough for people to know they are image-bearers called to a purpose; they also have to be able to make demonstrable progress toward that purpose through their efforts!

Kingdom Productivity

From creation onward, work has been key to God's plan for the flourishing of the world. Thus discipleship must include helping people be productive in that work. "If God's purpose for your job is that you serve the human community, then the way to serve God best is to do the job as well as it can be done."[1]

In the context of vocational discipleship, we propose this definition of productivity: *When work makes progress toward achieving its kingdom purpose of making God's world flourish.* Productivity is always linked with the creation mandate. We can measure aspects of productivity quantitatively, such as how many tables were produced, but the ultimate question is how labor contributes to God's goals for the world he created, such as cultivating the potential of natural resources in a useful and sustainable way, and supporting vibrant human community.

Examples of kingdom productivity include the following:

- After a rowdy start to the school year, a first-grade teacher trained her students to enter the classroom quietly in the morning, ready to learn (most of the time!).

- A city planning administrator worked with the zoning board to simplify the permit process for residents starting a home-based business.

- A shift manager at a fast-food restaurant began checking in personally with all employees every week, to see how they were doing and help resolve practical challenges like transportation, resulting in a decline in absenteeism.

- A worker at a textile plant discovered a way of handling the equipment that resulted in less waste of materials, which management then instituted factory wide.

- After a year of gathering evidence, an investigator filed a suit against a company that paid female staff significantly less than its male employees.

In the eyes of the world, productivity is often synonymous with "more"—increased output, better results, higher profits. As a discipler, your role is to encourage people to invest themselves fully in whatever way they're positioned to have an impact, regardless of the status or the scale.

Colossians 3:23 is a key passage to study with those wrestling with what it means to be productive as a faithful disciple: "Whatever you do, work at it with all your heart, as working for the Lord, not for human masters." This passage helps disciples refocus their motivation for productivity. There's nothing wrong with being rewarded for meritorious work, but Christians need to understand that productivity is *not* guaranteed to bring wealth, success, or recognition from others. In fact, kingdom productivity may even trigger the opposite results. Instead of honoring a worker's achievements, colleagues may be jealous and even steal the honors for their own (see the biblical story of Joseph). Many accomplishments by people in low-status positions or occupations go unsung. And entrepreneurs often invest their own resources into growth plans, with little guarantee of financial return.

In such contexts, disciplers can remind people that they work "for the Lord," who is pleased and glorified by their contribution to his kingdom. We also remind people that they cannot earn God's favor through productivity. God pronounced the first humans "very good" before they had done a thing. "The power behind our productivity comes from realizing that, through faith in the gospel, we are accepted by God in Christ apart from what we do. This puts wind in our sails and unleashes the power of the Spirit in our lives (Gal. 3:5)."[2] Growth in spiritual maturity entails increasingly rooting kingdom productivity in one's identity and relationship with God as a redeemed image-bearer.

Efficacy, Efficiency, Growth

What does productivity with kingdom purpose look like? Workers tend to feel productive when they "get stuff done." Connecting productivity with kingdom purpose, however, requires helping workers be more precise in how they assess the fruitfulness of their labor. It's not always easy to tell if one's work is actually "making progress toward achieving its kingdom purpose of making God's world flourish."

The value of productivity is a consistent theme in Scripture. In the Gospel of Matthew, for example, Jesus frequently uses productive imagery to teach about the kingdom in contrast to unproductive things. While these passages are typically interpreted on the "spiritual" plane as a metaphor for intangible aspects of our relationship with God, vocational discipleship also looks to these passages for guidance about productivity in the work of image-bearers in the world. Biblical wisdom suggests three productivity indicators to look for as measures of progress: *efficacy*, *efficiency*, and *growth*.

Efficacy (or Usefulness)

Work is productive when it leads to its intended result. Consider Jesus' words in Matthew 5:13–16:

> "You are the salt of the earth. But if the salt loses its saltiness, how can it be made salty again? . . . You are the light of the world. A town built on a hill cannot be hidden. . . . Let your light shine before others, that they may see your good deeds and glorify your Father in heaven."

Salt is meant to season. Light is meant to illuminate. Workers need to know what impact their efforts are meant to have in the world and whether their actions lead to that effect—both in the big picture of their job as a whole, and on the smaller scale of accomplishing daily tasks.

Note too Jesus' warnings against the wrong kind of productivity: being effective at doing work that goes against God's purpose. See Matthew 23:15, where Jesus cries "Woe!" to false religious leaders who go to great lengths in their efforts to make converts, yet, he says, "when you have succeeded, you make them twice as much a child of hell as you are." Productivity is not value-neutral. In other words, it matters a lot what "stuff" is getting done.

Efficiency (or Stewardship)

Work is productive when it makes wise use of resources, since workers bear the image of the Creator of all resources. Efficiency is also associated with timeliness: doing things at the right time, and taking the right amount of time. Being efficient requires intentional, thoughtful readiness. Productivity and preparedness go hand in hand.

Matthew 25 has rich content to review with a disciple regarding efficiency. First, the parable of the wise and foolish wedding guests (vv. 1–13) has a lesson on preparing ahead in the use of resources and staying focused on what's most important. This is followed by the parable of the talents (vv. 14–30), in which those who wisely invest the resources entrusted to them are rewarded.

In their drive to be efficient with economic and material resources to maximize profit, producers throughout history have often misused human resources. Scripture emphasizes that image-bearers are to be considered the most precious resource of all. This is illustrated by the directive in Deuteronomy 24:14–15:

You shall not withhold the wages of poor and needy laborers. . . . You shall pay them their wages daily before sunset, because they are poor and their livelihood depends on them; otherwise they might cry to the Lord against you, and you would incur guilt.

Paying wages daily may be less efficient for the employer, but it respects the needs of employees.

Growth

Purposeful multiplication is another key dynamic in God's kingdom. Jesus shows his divinity through miracles of productivity, such as the multiplication of loaves and fishes in Matthew 14. The pursuit of growth is one way that image-bearers reflect their Maker. In the parable of the talents in Matthew 25, the wise servants invest the coins given to them and gain more. The net amount was not what earned them their "well done!" from their master, but the multiplication of resources to serve their master's purposes.

Growth multiplies value. Where many workers get tripped up is in letting the world's standards define what has value. Resources have value—if they are used for kingdom purpose. Profit loses its value, however, if it comes at the expense of one's soul (Luke 12:13–21). The highest value belongs to people created in God's image. Productive work always in some way improves the well-being of image-bearers and expands their potential.

Matthew 13 is a good chapter to study together to explore the principle of kingdom growth. Here, Jesus describes ordinary workers (a farmer, hired laborer, cook, merchant, fisherman) using resources to produce more of what has value. These parables also suggest that growth for its own sake can be toxic. Jesus warns against weeds that choke out other life and bad trees that multiply bad fruit (Matt. 7:16–20; 12:33). This study can spark meaningful conversation about what values are multiplied in the disciple's line of work.

Is Being Productive "Spiritual"?

The things workers do to be productive—completing inventory reports, debugging code, taking accurate orders, maintaining equipment, establishing a filing system, resolving supply issues, updating protocols, improving office communications, researching best practices—may not seem very "spiritual" to people as they are doing them. Christians steeped in church-centric thinking may assume that biblical fruitfulness applies primarily to winning coworkers to Christ or encouraging others to join in devotional activities like prayer on the job. While these are vital, they don't fully define spiritual maturity in the workplace.

God's first very first command to humanity—"Be fruitful and multiply"—makes it clear that productivity is God's plan. Good results are spiritual in nature, because God cares about the outcomes of our work for the sake of this world, and because our work has eternal significance. Being unproductive, or producing the wrong kind of results, is an affront to God's design. When followers of Christ practice kingdom productivity, not only do they eventually reap a reward but other image-bearers also benefit; the world gets a little better, and God is glorified.

RESOURCE

Discipleship Questions for Productivity

Here are some questions to ask to help people grasp what it means to be productive in God's kingdom:

- Say out loud, "I am productive in God's kingdom." What does this mean to you? What reaction does this spark in you?

- What have you been taught about "being productive"? How does the Bible inform your perspective?

- Is there a difference in your field of work between *being productive* and *being productive in God's kingdom*? If so, how do you resolve that difference?

- How can you tell if your work is *effective*? What fruits are you seeing from your work? What tells you if your efforts lead to intended results that advance your kingdom purpose?

- How can you tell if your work is *efficient*? What are the resources God has entrusted to you to use in your work—including time, your own gifts, and other human resources? What can you do to maximize the wise investment of these resources toward kingdom purpose?

- What does fruitful *growth* look like in your vocation? How does your job contribute to this growth? How do you assess whether your efforts are multiplying "good fruit" from a kingdom perspective?

- "Whatever you do, work at it with all your heart, as working for the Lord." Imagine sitting down with God for a performance review. What feedback might you expect?

- What is the impact of your work on image-bearers in your sphere of influence?

- What can you look for as a sign of growth in multiplying value to image-bearers?

- How are the biblical teachings on productivity inspiring and guiding you to become more productive? What specific actions can you take? What resistance might you expect from others (or yourself), and what will sustain you in following this course?

- What is the spiritual nature of being productive in your work?

16

FRUITFULNESS, PRODUCTIVITY, AND PROSPERITY

CASE STUDY

"It's not fair," Rose thought as she collected the used linens from the discharged patient's room and gathered up the trash. "Here I am working in a hospital, and I can't even afford decent health insurance!"

"It's not fair," Imelda thought as she updated the vitals on a patient's chart before quickly moving on to the next exam room. "Here I am working for a doctor who makes more than three times as much as I do, even though nurses work just as hard!"

"It's not fair," Lexie thought as she wrote up a prescription. "Here I am a respected doctor and still up to my ears in debt—if only I had gone into a higher-paying specialty!"

As a disciple-maker, what would you say to these three workers?

God wants *every* enterprise to be productive. God wants *every* worker to prosper. Yet in a sinful, fallen world, the lines connecting productivity and prosperity get tangled. Disciplers can help workers sort out the relationship between work and wealth.[1] The purpose of this chapter is to give an overview of a few key issues from a discipleship perspective.

How Can Disciples Stay Faithful and Fruitful, Despite Not Prospering?

Regardless of income level, most people go through life feeling like they don't have enough. So we start by looking at prosperity from the perspective of a perceived lack of it.

In the biblical model, *fruitfulness* is a test of *faithfulness*, and fruitful work yields a reward. In God's plan, there is a direct correlation between being faithful to God's purpose and material well-being: "If you fully obey . . . all these blessings will come upon you" (Deut. 28:1–14). The abundance of Eden was meant to be enjoyed by those who worked the garden.

Yet we know full well that in a fallen world, faithfulness does not universally lead to the blessing of material prosperity (e.g., Prov. 13:23). Injustice, greed, human error, and natural disasters disrupt God's plan. All around the world there are good, hardworking people unable to earn enough to meet their family's basic needs. And there are many who reject God and mistreat others, yet live in ease and abundance.

At some point, every disciple is likely to wrestle with this seeming paradox, as this psalmist was:

> As for me, my feet had almost slipped;
>   I had nearly lost my foothold.
> For I envied the arrogant
>   when I saw the prosperity of the wicked. . . .
>
> Surely in vain I have kept my heart pure
>   and have washed my hands in innocence. . . .
>
> When I tried to understand all this,
>   it troubled me deeply.
>   (Ps. 73:2–3, 13, 16 NIV)

This psalm illustrates the complex emotions that swirl around these issues of work and wealth: anxiety, envy, resentment, aspiration, doubt. Going through financial struggles, especially in contrast to others' apparent success, can test people's faith to the core.

Thorny questions about the correlation between work and material blessing arise not only with low-wage jobs but also for essential work that is not paid—for example, those who labor outside the marketplace raising children or caring for elderly parents. Because such work is not financially rewarded, it often feels less valued. In what sense is work blessed if it doesn't produce income that makes ends meet? Is higher income a sufficient reason to make a job change?[2]

The role of the discipler is not to quash these questions but to help people view their situation from a different perspective. We must keep reminding people of *who they are* as image-bearers and *what kingdom purpose* they are called to serve. That is the groundwork for what it means to remain faithful in this calling. Following this path, the first priority of Christians is to be fruitful in their work as image-bearers with a kingdom purpose. We can walk with them to view productivity through this lens. As the author of Psalm 73 concludes:

> My flesh and my heart may fail,
>   but God is the strength of my heart
>   and my portion forever. (v. 26)

Despite their current circumstances, followers of Jesus can trust that God will be faithful to those who work faithfully for him. The story of Joseph, who continued to use his gifts whether he was imprisoned unjustly or elevated to high office, is a good illustration to encourage people questioning the ultimate value of their work. It also reminds Christians to exert their influence to reinforce God's design for the connection between doing good work and making a good living—whether advocating for their own fair compensation or for others.

How Can Disciples Stay Faithful and Fruitful When They Are Prospering?

Discipleship is also needed to help people maintain perspective when they prosper in their work.

First, we can reaffirm that prospering is a good and godly thing. Both the original garden and the heavenly city are places of great material (as well as relational and spiritual) abundance. Wealth, honestly gained, is a gift and reward from God (see Gen. 24:34–35; Deut. 8:10–18; Josh. 22:6–9). In and of itself, wealth is not something we should criticize others for having or shy away from ourselves. Although God does not judge us for what we have, he *does* hold us accountable for how we got it and what we do with it!

While prosperity should be a blessing, becoming wealthy is one of the most dangerous places to be spiritually, especially if you have wrong ideas about why you have wealth and what it's for. Scripture rings with warnings about the dangers of wealth (Isa. 44:1–21; Jer. 2:13; 9:23–24; Hos. 12:8; Matt. 13:22; 19:16–30; 1 Tim. 6:9–10). Again and again, the prophets, Jesus, and the apostles confronted people (especially those in positions of influence) about their idolatry of greed, which usually went hand in hand with maltreatment of fellow image-bearers.

When the context warrants it, disciplers must be bold to share Jesus' warning: "Watch out! Be on your guard against all kinds of greed; life does not consist in an abundance of possessions" (Luke 12:15). Yet we must do this with loving compassion, the way Jesus did in speaking with the rich young man (Mark 10:17–22). The goal is not to shame people for having (or wanting) wealth, but to hold them to high standards of faithfulness, because "from everyone who has been given much, much will be demanded; and from the one who has been entrusted with much, much more will be asked" (Luke 12:48).

One of my (Tom's) favorite movies is *Braveheart*. In this historically based story, the Scottish folk hero William Wallace rebukes the new king of Scotland for allying himself with the oppressive English regime: "You think the people of this country exist to provide you with position. I think your position exists to provide those people with freedom!" Keep reminding people that they serve God's kingdom purpose, which will guide how they use the resources entrusted to them.

Our work is meant to bless us *and* to be a blessing. Our jobs exist because there is work to be done for the functioning of God's creation. The people of Israel got into trouble when they became prosperous and used their wealth only to reinforce their own power and position, rather than expand the reign of God's blessing. Ask: *What are you building with your resources? Are you using wealth to build your own kingdom or stewarding it to serve God's kingdom?*

What Claims Does a Prosperity Mindset Make That Might Not Be True?

In the parable of the sower of seeds in Mark 4, Jesus warns that "the worries of this life, the deceitfulness of wealth and the desires for other things come in and choke the word, making it unfruitful" (v. 19). Prosperity, as a blessing received gratefully and used wisely, is good. The prosperity mindset—a consuming focus on profit and wealth—is deceitful. It distracts people's attention from what is vital, life-giving, and eternal, and pulls toward what is small-minded and short-lived. It tempts people to pursue affluence at the expense of fruitfulness.

Disciplers challenge false assumptions about wealth, including:

- Wealth is always a sign of God's blessing.

- Poverty is always a sign of God's judgment.

- I deserve financial success because I have worked hard or sacrificed to achieve it.

- The purpose of work is to seek profit (or, the goal of work is to become wealthy).

- God wants us to use our wealth for our own enjoyment.

- God frowns on using our wealth for our own enjoyment.

- My (or your) worth as a human is linked with my (or your) profitability.

Each of these false statements can be unpacked and refuted at length, using curriculum such as *Provision and Wealth*, a Bible study from the Theology of Work Project.[3] Aim to help workers replace these falsehoods with biblical affirmations, such as:

- We offer ourselves to God, not to the pursuit of profit.

- The identity and worth of each person are rooted equally and indelibly in being created as an image-bearer, not in what they earn or possess.

- Hard work may be productive without being profitable.

- Wealth may follow productivity, but it's not the purpose of productivity.

- All we have belongs to God to be used for his purpose and pleasure.

- God delights when we enjoy the fruits of productivity and share it with others.

In our acquisition-oriented culture, it is easy to succumb to dependence on wealth for security and self-worth. Wealth can become a fortress keeping us from God, rather than a tool used to serve God. There is a big difference between having wealth versus relying on it, between regarding profits as a blessing entrusted to you versus a reward due to you, between viewing income as a fruit of your labor versus as an extension of your identity. Ultimately, the prosperity mindset is idolatrous, because it leads people to put their trust in what they earn or possess rather than trusting in God.

As a discipler, it's your responsibility to warn people against the idolatry of wealth. Jesus is our role model when he declares to his followers: "Watch out! Be on your guard against all kinds of greed; life does not consist in an abundance of possessions" (Luke 12:15).

What Is Prosperity For?

Addressing financial issues often leads to ethical questions such as: "How much should . . . ?" or "Is it wrong if . . . ?" or "When is it okay to . . . ?" Any discussion about money should lead back to the root question: What is the *purpose* of wealth?

Vocational discipleship takes as its starting point the principle that says: *We are image-bearers redeemed by Christ, called to fulfill kingdom purpose through fruitful work.* From that starting block, the purpose of wealth is the same as the kingdom purpose of work: glorifying God, blessing people (including a person's own household), drawing people to Christ, and enabling the world to flourish.

Within a business, profits are what allow the company to carry out its creation mandate—whether building abundant community, bringing order to the world, or developing potential from natural resources. Wealth is also to be used for the purpose of overcoming the curse. It takes significant investment of financial resources to repair damage, alleviate suffering, confront injustice, and restore the goodness of creation. Prosperity is intended to fuel productivity that multiplies good fruit.

As a discipler, you can help people explore how they are using whatever wealth God has entrusted to them—whether it's considered to be a little or a lot. Every financial question that comes up is thus an opportunity to explore kingdom purpose.

One test reveals the state of a person's heart: Does learning about the kingdom purpose for their wealth bring them relief or anxiety? When Jesus told the rich young would-be follower "Sell your possessions and give the money to the poor," the man went away "grieving" because his wealth was a barrier between him and abundant life (Matt. 19:16–22). On the other hand, when Zacchaeus encountered Jesus, he was eager to use his wealth to bless others and make amends, because his heart yearned to be restored as an image-bearer with a good purpose.

Helping people navigate the purpose of prosperity without falling into its lure is quite difficult—but thankfully, "for God all things are possible" (Matt. 19:26).

How Much Is Enough?

If people lose track of the biblical purpose of productivity, it's easy start focusing on prosperity as a goal in itself. Once they start seeking wealth for its own sake, they may have to learn this painful lesson from Habakkuk 2:5: "Wealth is treacherous; the arrogant do not endure. . . . Like Death they never have enough."

An example of a biblical lesson to consider together is the parable in Luke 12:16–21 of the "rich fool," who tore down his barns to build even bigger barns to accommodate his crops. Ask the person you are discipling what made this man foolish. If the response is *greed*, then point out that productivity and growth are part of God's design—more crops mean more food to feed people, and more barns means more jobs for carpenters. Suggest instead that the problem was his belief that having *more* would mean finally having enough to satisfy his soul (see v. 19). His attitude exemplifies the motto of endless acquisition: *How much is enough? Just a little bit more!*

Counsel people that if they build a bigger barn, they should do it because it enables them to be more fruitful in their kingdom purpose—not because they think it will mean they can finally enjoy life, be less anxious about the future, make their family love them more, or feel better about themselves when they look in the mirror. Red flags should go up any time you hear someone's drive toward profits linked with the idea, "If I just get . . . then I'll be able to . . ." This path leads only to disillusionment.

Another point to emphasize is that the rich fool thinks only of himself: "Then *I'll . . .*" Self-centered people never feel satisfied with their work or its fruits. True contentment comes only from working to satisfy God's calling on one's life, which is never just about accumulating good things for oneself. Kingdom productivity is always rooted in God's bigger plan for the flourishing of the world. Discontent greases the temptation to enlarge one's barns at others' expense.

People sometimes run the other direction and believe that happiness comes from *not* building barns—that the answer to the question of *how much is enough?* lies in simply making less. As John Wesley so famously admonished, before you "give all you can," you must "earn all you can." While a Christian may have good reasons to choose a job with a lower salary, such as pursuing a calling or having more time with family, there is nothing inherently spiritual about earning less money. Regardless of salary, the goal is to keep focused on the kingdom purpose of the work, as messy as that may be to sort out sometimes.

For disciples struggling with "enough," there are many biblical passages to study on the principle of contentment, such as Hebrews 13:5: "Keep your lives free from the love of money, and be content with what you have; for he has said, 'I will never leave you or forsake you'" (see also Luke 3:14; Phil. 4:11–12; 1 Tim. 6:6–8). At the same time, be mindful of how these passages have sometimes been abused in the past to keep people from speaking out against unfair compensation or advocating for better wages.

Talking about Money

Anything having to do with money is a difficult topic to broach in our culture, and you may face a number of hurdles in discipling people in this area. For individuals who have been taught that money is a private matter, it may be helpful to shift the focus from *how much they make* to *how they are using what they make.* Keep emphasizing the link between prosperity and biblical productivity. You can invite people to examine their attitude in relation to prosperity (or the lack of it), and offer a new path toward faithfully pursuing God's kingdom purpose.

This chapter barely scratches the surface of this topic. A Bible study or theological curriculum on money may open up discipling conversations about personal finances. If you are discipling an employer, you can expand your focus to consider a spiritual perspective on business (for example, *Business for the Common Good* by Kenman Wong and Scott Rae). You may also find it useful to dive into a broader theological framework for economics (such as Tom Nelson's *The Economics of Neighborly Love*).

When it comes to sensitive topics such as money, people will pay as much (or more) attention to how you live your own life as to your words.

If you have the resources, time, and education to read this book, then on a global scale, you are probably among the most privileged on the planet. If you are modeling biblical fruitfulness as best you can and being transparent about the ways you still need to grow, then your words will likely have more weight with those whom God has led you to disciple.

RESOURCE

Asking Tough Questions about Prosperity

Each person is responsible for themselves—yet each person's choices impact others in far-reaching ways. Do those you disciple recognize their responsibility for the consequences of their actions (or inactions) in the workplace? Discuss the following principles with them. Do they recognize any aspect of their situation in the examples? This can lead to a tough but impactful conversation. "Speaking the truth in love" is essential for spiritual growth (Eph. 4:15).

Your prosperity should be linked with biblical productivity (see Ps. 62:10). Examples:

- A broker gets rich by manipulating the market rather than investing others' money for growth.
- A sales manager tops the commission list by using pressure tactics with older customers who don't really need the product.
- A company survives mainly by making political donations that assure contracts without much oversight.
- Line workers make an item designed to break easily so consumers will have to replace it.

    Discipleship Question: Are you making money without doing work that meaningfully advances God's kingdom purpose?

Your prosperity must not come at the expense of others' ability to be productive and prosperous, even as an unintentional byproduct (see Exod. 22:26–27). Examples:

- A manager refuses to upgrade employees' equipment, costing them commissions and leading to injuries.
- A title loan company profits from repossessing customers' vehicles after imposing conditions that make loans difficult to repay.

- A factory cuts costs by using cheaper materials that release more air pollution, causing higher asthma rates in the community.

- A spa owner prefers white applicants for staffing, in order not to lose customers who are racially prejudiced.

  Discipleship Questions: Is your income linked to actions that make others less safe, healthy, or capable of doing their work? Does your company's quest for profits go beyond healthy competition to undermining the flourishing of a community?

Your prosperity must not come by taking the fruits of others' labor (see Deut. 24:15). Examples:

- A CEO issues senior staff huge bonuses after a profitable year, while front-line workers get no raises.

- A supplier deals in materials produced by overseas sweatshops that pay workers barely enough to survive.

- An executive gets promoted by taking personal credit for the work of subordinates.

- A manager underpays small contract laborers, who lack the resources to mount a legal challenge.

  Discipleship Question: Does the profit you earn depend on breaking the link between labor and its just reward for other workers, while inflating the worth of your own contribution?

If someone you disciple has been taking what they did not earn, cheating others of what they are due, cutting corners, or sacrificing the well-being of other image-bearers in their work, Scripture makes it very clear what they are to do: "Thieves must give up stealing; rather let them labor and work honestly with their own hands, so as to have something to share with the needy" (Eph. 4:28). In this world, the relationship between productivity and prosperity will always be tainted by the temptation to sin. So keep affirming the perspective of God's eternal kingdom:

> The final hope of Christians is to participate in the abundant, blessed life promised when the world is fully restored upon Christ's return. In the new earth there will be plenty for all. No one will lack provision. Justice will reign. Wealth will be experienced by everyone, without corrupting any person or anything. All will be as God always intended it to be.[4]

17

SPUR PEOPLE ON TO DO GOOD WORK IN A GOOD WAY

Tom's Story

Years ago, I helped to start a company that provided a service to businesses active in the commercial construction market. In those early days, cash was always tight, so we were particularly aware of delinquent accounts and made every effort to collect on invoices when they were due.

As I was paying close attention to the budget, I began to look for patterns in the accounts that were overdue. Much to my surprise, I discovered that over half of them were people who openly presented themselves as Christians when we opened their account. This led us to create an unwritten policy regarding new accounts, which went like this: "If you see a Bible on their desk, ask for a check in advance!"

Kalon Work

Hebrews 10:24 speaks directly to our role as disciplers: "Let us consider how we may spur one another on toward love and good deeds" (NIV). Here we encounter again the Greek word *ergon*, often translated "works." In chapter 2, we showed how *ergon* can be taken to literally mean "work" in the sense of tasks undertaken for a job.

The full phrase in this verse is *kalon ergon*, "good work." When we say "Good job!" to someone, this usually refers to the quality of the work, which—as discussed in the chapter on productivity—is crucial. But the Greek term *kalon* carries the sense of having "moral beauty." Christians motivate one another to do *kalon ergon*—valuable, virtuous, worthy work. "Good work" refers both to what people get done and how they do it.

In Matthew 7:17, Jesus affirms, "Every good tree bears good [*kalous*] fruit." Doing good work is rooted in *who we are* as the image-bearers of a good God. If people are living out of that core identity, then their work will reflect and reveal God's nature to the world (1 Pet. 3:15; Eph. 5:1; Luke 18:19). Jesus also warned against having a "Christian identity" that is contradicted by one's actual behavior (Luke 6:46). After all, the word *Christian* comes from the Greek word *christianos*, "little Christ." To be a follower of Christ in the workplace means to adopt the mind of Christ and to conduct oneself in a way that shows people what Christ is like (Phil. 2:1–5).

Here again, we see the critical role of vocational discipleship: To "spur" people to keep growing in their discovery of the nature of God revealed in Christ, and to continue following in his footsteps as they walk through their workday. This path leads to *kalon ergon*.

In this chapter, we suggest three key standards for "morally beautiful" work, where a good mindset meets good actions, which leads to good outcomes. Each of these is an area where disciple-makers can "spur on" growth toward doing jobs that advance God's kingdom in a way that reflects God's character:

1. Work with excellence: God is great (Deut. 7:21)

2. Work with integrity: God is true (John 3:33)

3. Work with fairness: God is just and righteous (Isa. 5:16)

These qualities of good work are by no means exhaustive; for example, we could add "Work with reverence: God is Lord," "Work with wisdom: God is the way," "Work with innovation: God is creator," and "Work with contentment: God is sufficient." In fact, a good discipleship exercise might be coming up with a list of God's attributes and how they should be reflected in our work.

Good Work Is Excellent: Image-Bearers Reflect God's Greatness

"Serve wholeheartedly, as if you were serving the Lord, not people." (Eph. 6:7 NIV)

God's creations of paradise in Genesis and the heavenly city in Revelation are both described with superlatives. This is the model image-bearers are to emulate. God wants people to be good at what they do! Dorothy Sayers underscored this simple yet profound teaching:

> The Church's approach to an intelligent carpenter is usually confined to exhorting him not to be drunk and disorderly in his leisure hours, and to come to church on Sundays. What the Church should be telling him is this: that the very first demand that his religion makes upon him is that he should make good tables.[1]

The standard of excellence for disciples encompasses both *competence* and *diligence*. William Diehl affirms "the ministry of competency" as the bedrock of a society where people can rely on one another.[2] Encourage disciples to recognize how being good at what they do is essential in fulfilling their kingdom purpose.

Earlier we introduced the discipleship question, "What would happen if no one did your job?" A follow-up question to illuminate the stakes of excellent work is to ask, "What would happen if no one did your job *well*?" Paving crews need to believe that God's city deserves good roads. Someone who creates jewelry should respect that God put the raw materials in the ground to be extracted and shaped with good artistry. A legal clerk should understand why good recordkeeping is essential for an orderly community.

Diligence also matters. Lack of diligence shows disrespect for God's directive to "till and keep" his creation. God's greatness is revealed not just in raw talent but how it is developed and applied through hard work.

There is a rich theological tradition behind the precept of a work ethic to explore with someone who struggles with diligence. Consider 2 Thessalonians 3:10, "Anyone unwilling to work should not eat." This is more than a warning against laziness. The context for this directive was that a group of believers had stopped working in order to focus on waiting for Jesus to return. They didn't want to be doing something "unspiritual" like physical labor when Christ came back. If Jesus comes tomorrow, then we will rejoice—but today, we keep working![3]

Pursuing excellence requires a continual process of growth, which disciplers can support by helping identify practical steps toward developing competency and their diligence. Such steps might include professional training, finding a mentor, improving time management, minimizing personal distractions, and getting sufficient rest and exercise. Help workers stay focused on the spiritual nature of these activities as ways of offering their gifts of time and skill to God "with reverence and awe" (Heb. 12:28).

> The work we do on earth—to the extent we do it according to the ways of Christ—survives into eternity. . . . To the degree that our work is done in excellence, by his gifts and grace, it will become part of God's eternal kingdom. That should motivate us—even more than our employer's approval or our paycheck—to do as good a job as we possibly can.[4]

Good Work Has Integrity: Image-Bearers Model God's Purity

"God is light; and in him there is no darkness at all. . . . Walk in the light."
(1 John 1:5, 7)

Working with integrity means demonstrating Christ's character in the workplace. As a disciple-making exercise, consider four scenarios:

1. The first test of integrity is how people act when they believe no one is watching. Few people swipe supplies in plain sight of their boss, but would you "borrow" a stapler if you were alone in the office?

2. The second test is how people act when others expect you to do something that violates your conscience. For example, a coworker may lean hard on you to "be a friend" and overlook her errors when you file your quality control report.

3. The third test is how people act when they believe no one cares. If most of your coworkers pad their billable hours, why not do the same?

4. The fourth test is how people act when choosing integrity comes with a cost—such as keeping your marriage vows despite a strong attraction to a coworker, or reporting fraud despite the risk of losing your job.

As a discipler, remind workers that the real test is how they act with the awareness that God is their boss, God desires purity and truth, and God is always watching. "We have renounced secret and shameful ways. . . . By setting forth the truth plainly we commend ourselves to everyone's conscience in the sight of God" (2 Cor. 4:2).

Help disciples identify practical applications of walking in the light while on the job, including:

- ✓ Tell the truth to coworkers, supervisors, customers, stakeholders (Col. 3:9).

- ✓ Keep your word, honor commitments, deliver on promises (Matt. 5:37).

- ✓ Maintain honest measurements and accounts (Lev. 19:36).

- ✓ Don't represent yourself, your company, or your competition falsely (Exod. 23:1).

- ✓ Don't take what isn't yours, whether objects or payment (Exod. 20:15).

- ✓ Don't give or accept bribes (Exod. 23:8).

- ✓ Follow the law and the spirit of the law (Rom. 13:1–4).

Encourage disciples who are business owners to think through the implications of these basic principles at an organizational level (for example, don't use misleading advertising, pay invoices fully and promptly, provide promised employee benefits, maintain honest tax records). For faithfulness on a still wider scale, God may stir Christians to work toward greater integrity in their vocational field (for example, greater industry-wide transparency and accountability regarding safety standards, connections with child labor or forced labor, disposal of toxic waste, or bribery and other forms of corruption). Andy Crouch explains why discipleship extends beyond individual behavior to the systems in which Christians participate:

> Very often, the church has taught its members that their main Christian responsibility at work is to act ethically. But what if we are not in the world just to maintain ethical systems, but to repair systems that have become corrupt? ... To think this way is to shift from individual choices to systemic responsibility, and it's also to shift from thinking ethically to thinking redemptively. Redemptive thinking goes beyond honest individuals to the kinds of actions that actually could restore trust in whole systems. ... Once you start looking at the world redemptively rather than just ethically, you realize how far we've fallen. But you also set a new standard for the flourishing we are meant to pursue.[5]

Credibility enhances a disciple's ability to carry out the kingdom purpose of their work, because they are more likely to be entrusted with important tasks. An organization with honest, reliable employees and straightforward business practices can function more productively. Steven Covey coined the phrase, "Working at the speed of trust." Cultivating trust is key to the social capital that is the bedrock of a successful business and a flourishing community.

On the other hand, we need to prepare disciples that while that honesty is the best policy, it is not always the most *profitable* policy. In fact, a life of integrity may be costly to Christians in the workplace. Draw on passages like 1 Peter 4:4 that sympathize with those who suffer for doing good, when those who don't follow Jesus "are surprised that you do not join them in their reckless, wild living, and they heap abuse on you." For a business owner, a commitment to integrity can seem like a handicap in a field that's rife with deception, underhanded tactics, and broken promises. In situations like these, assure faithful Christians that Jesus calls them blessed when they are reviled for following in his footsteps (Luke 6:22).

When workers are tempted to cut corners, remind them that not only is their own reputation at stake but also the authenticity of their witness to Christ. Standing in the truth, especially when it comes at a cost, models the fear of the Lord. A good verse to reflect on together is 1 Peter 2:12: "Conduct yourselves honorably among the Gentiles, so that, though they malign you as evildoers, they may see your honorable deeds and glorify God when he comes to judge."

Walking in integrity includes a willingness to admit mistakes and make amends. "If we say that we have no sin, we deceive ourselves, and the truth is not in us" (1 John 1:8). Vocational discipleship calls people to "walk in the light" by being transparent about their shortcomings and failures on the job, and then turning to Jesus to "purify us from all sin" (1 John 1:7).

Good Work Treats People Fairly: Image-Bearers Seek God's Justice and Righteousness

"He will judge the world with righteousness, and
the peoples with equity." (Ps. 98:9)

In both Hebrew (*tzedakah*) and Greek (*dikaiosune*), the same root word may be translated as either "justice" or "righteousness." Righteousness tends to be associated with personal holiness, while justice has more legal or systemic connotations. It's worth diving into further study of these complex terms in the context of vocational discipleship.[6] The broader principle is that godliness means practicing right relationships on the job, particularly with regard to those who are most vulnerable to being mistreated or neglected. The Bible has a lot to say about treating people fairly, without holding prejudice, showing favoritism, or taking advantage. Jesus summed it up: "In everything do to others as you would have them do to you" (Matt. 7:12).

Spurring on people to pursue justice at work begins with promoting a culture of respect for every individual based on their equal and inestimable value as God's image-bearers. Explore with disciples how these principles of "right relationship" apply in their work setting:

✓ Respect every image-bearer as a valued equal (1 Pet. 2:17).

✓ Don't show favoritism (James 2:9).

✓ Reject any form of racism and prejudice (Deut. 16:19).

✓ Don't hurt anyone with your words or actions (Rom. 13:10).

✓ Don't abuse your power or take advantage of people who are weaker than you (Prov. 22:16).

✓ Don't condone wrongdoing by others (Eph. 5:11).

✓ Take responsibility for what you do wrong (even if you could get away with it) and make amends (Lev. 6:2–7).

Examples of how someone may act unjustly or violate of fair treatment on the job:

- A manager gives the best shift assignments to staff who are willing to go out drinking after work.

- A server is rude to customers who don't speak fluent English.

- An executive pressures new female employees to go out with him.

- An employee is laid off for vague reasons soon after reporting a safety violation.

- A secretary "accidentally" leaves the only Black employee out of group emails.

- A relative of the CEO makes a mistake, but someone else gets blamed instead.

- Staff spread humiliating rumors about a coworker who has unpopular political views.

At the organizational level, injustice may be ingrained into company practices or culture. Examples:

- The HR department repeatedly shelves sexual harassment claims against senior staff.

- Whenever someone gets hurt on the job, management routinely blames it on the incompetence of the worker.

- Résumés with Arabic-sounding names are commonly moved to the bottom of the applicant list.

- A memo to sales clerks tells them to keep a close watch on anyone who looks "undesirable" or "out of place" in the store.

- Racist jokes and memes frequently circulate on company email; anyone who complains is told to "get over it or go work somewhere else."

- Older employees are passed over for promotions and choice assignments in favor of younger staff, who are closer in age to their bosses.

- It is hinted to new hires that people who make it known they are Christian won't go far in the company.

- It is hinted to new hires that people who make it known they are Christian are more likely to advance in the company.

The above examples could be used as case studies to help people explore biblical responses, as well as spark conversation about what they themselves may have experienced (or perpetrated). As you connect with people in their real, day-to-day work life, it's inevitable you'll deal with scenarios such as these. These may be difficult to talk about, but they shouldn't be swept under the rug. If not dealt with, many workers end up hating their jobs, losing their jobs, or even experiencing health problems due to the stress of unfair and hurtful treatment. And this is costly to the company and its kingdom purpose as well.[7] Here are some questions in a discipleship context to help draw out their experiences:

- Are you experiencing unjust treatment at work? If so, what do you need to take care of yourself? How might you advocate for yourself, or who might be able to intervene on your behalf? (As a discipler, consider whether you might be willing to be called on to play this supportive role!)

- Is there anyone you've treated unfairly or disrespectfully at work? Examine yourself for prejudice or favoritism. Have you used your authority or influence in ways that have hurt people? If so, how will you make it right? (See Matt. 5:23–24)

- Do you see anyone being treated unfairly at work? If so, what can you do to show care to these persons? How could you use your authority or influence to confront wrongdoing and promote change? (See Prov. 31:8–9)

- What will it take to work fruitfully as a redeemed image-bearer with kingdom purpose in the midst of this situation?

As a discipler, it's important to listen to people's concerns about fair treatment on the job and take them seriously, even if you've never had a similar experience—and to encourage the person you are discipling to do the same for others.

Whenever image-bearers are treated unjustly, the Bible calls us to speak up and step in, to stop the mistreatment and do what is possible to restore those who have been hurt by it (see Prov. 31:8–9; Lev. 6:2–7).[8] When the person you are discipling needs to confront injustices at work, the first step is for them to seek personal reconciliation (Matt. 18:15–17). Other steps to discuss include putting their concerns in writing to supervisors, speaking out in staff meetings, meeting with a mediator, inviting public scrutiny, and organizing interventions. Disciplers can help people examine their options, count the cost, and seek the wisdom and strength of the Spirit.

Leadership for Good Work

If you're discipling business owners and executives, help them be mindful that "everyone to whom much has been given, much will be required"

(Luke 12:48). Leaders who follow Christ are accountable for setting standards of integrity and excellence. They bear a special responsibility to ensure that their workplaces (and as much as possible, any organizations with which they partner) are free from discrimination, harassment, bullying, favoritism, exploitation, degradation, and manipulation.[9] A business may be a success by worldly standards of profit and productivity even if it's not being led competently, honestly, and equitably. But it cannot serve God's good (*kalon*) kingdom purpose.

Leaders may need this reminder from Ephesians 6:7–9 (MSG): "No matter who happens to be giving the orders, you're really serving God. . . . You and your servants [employees] are both under the same Master in heaven. He makes no distinction between you and them." Do the executives you disciple recognize each individual in their organization as their equal in God's eyes, regardless of pay or authority? Are image-bearers valued for their uniqueness as God's employees, or are human resources viewed simply as a commodity?

John Lennon once said, "Being honest may not get you a lot of friends, but it'll always get you the right ones." Insisting on leading good work done in a good way can set up Christians against powerful interests. It can be intimidating and lonely. If you're discipling someone seeking to persist in *kalon ergon*, your encouragement can help them stay the course.

Corruption and injustice are so deeply engrained in our fallen systems that Christians may feel that all their efforts to foster change are like trying to plant a garden in a dust storm. At the very least, disciples must abstain from participating in or appearing to approve of unworthy conduct. Encourage workers to do what they can, even in small ways, to build up a culture of integrity, honesty, fairness, and respect in their work environment. Mustard seeds of goodness can grow to make a difference.

RESOURCE

Ethical Decision-Making

Vocational discipleship is vital in helping workers sort out the ethical questions that inevitably arise in the context of doing their jobs. *If I catch a coworker padding their hours to increase their pay, should I report it, even if I know the family is in need and would be devastated to lose a job? What is our company's responsibility if we discover that a long-time supplier sells goods made by child labor? How should we handle a regular customer who makes rude comments about immigrants—in the presence of immigrant staff? Is it okay to go public with information about a personal scandal involving our main competitor?*

ave bearing on the situation.

Making good work decisions requires balancing multiple interests and values that may seem at first to be incompatible, such as being generous and being efficient. Here, we offer some stepping-stones to disciplers as they wade with other Christians through muddy ethical waters.

Focus on Process

In their book *Business for the Common Good*, Scott Rae and Kenman Wong describe a process for ethical decision-making at work:

1. Gather the facts
2. Identify the ethical issue (the parties involved and their conflicting interests)
3. Clarify ethical values at stake (specific biblical principles, broad moral values)
4. Brainstorm alternatives, looking for win-win solutions
5. Weigh the significance of relevant values
6. Consider the consequences[10]

Focus on Framework

The *Ethics at Work* study guide from The Theology of Work Project presents a decision model for moral dilemmas. This model synthesizes three key ethical frameworks, each representing a different way of looking at the question:

1. *Command:* What do the rules say is the right way to act?
2. *Consequences:* What actions are most likely to bring about the best outcome?
3. *Character:* What kind of moral person do I want to be or become?

Before making a tough decision, determine the relevant rules (from the Bible and other sources) and how they apply (*commands*), consider potential results of various courses of action and discern which is best (*consequences*), and practice being the kind of person who will follow through on doing the right thing (*character*).

This guide also acknowledges the relevance of three other C's: *context, confirmation bias,* and *community*. Understanding *context* means considering how factors like culture and history may have bearing on the situation. Be aware also of *confirmation bias*, the tendency to steer a discernment process (maybe subconsciously) toward a preferred decision. Because of this, people should not try to make tough ethical decisions all on their own, but in *community* with others they trust and respect (like a discipler!). "Ask for help from others in your community who know you and the situation; this will help you avoid self-deception and paying too much attention to your particular biases."[11]

Focus on Purpose

The vocational discipleship perspective adds a "four-chapter gospel" point of view to ethical decision-making. What options reflect the purpose for which God created image-bearers to work in a very good world? How does this situation show the effect of or temptation to sin? What does it look like to imitate Christ and live worthy of his redemptive sacrifice? What options are most consistent with, or give a foretaste of, what heaven will be like? "Our favorite question will not be 'Is this justifiable?' but 'Is this how things will be done when God's kingdom comes?'"[12]

It would be simple to say, "The Bible is your guidebook for ethics. Just do what Scripture says." But we need to acknowledge the gap between the words of the Bible and its meaning for contemporary dilemmas. Subjectivity is inevitably present in the selection, interpretation, and application of Scripture passages. As Keller and Alsdorf point out in *Every Good Endeavor*, "Wisdom is more than just obeying God's ethical norms; it is knowing the right thing to do in the 80 percent of life's situations in which the moral rules don't provide the clear answer."[13]

On the other hand, complexity can become an excuse for avoiding what someone deep down knows to be right. Jesus declared that the greatest commandment is to love God and love your neighbor as yourself. When a lawyer challenged him with a "loophole question" ("Who is my neighbor?"), Jesus didn't let him get away with it (Luke 10:25–37). Sometimes your job as a discipler is to cut to the chase and tell them directly, "You know the right choice. Go and do it."

18

INSTRUCT DISCIPLES TO BE GENEROUS IN THEIR WORK

CASE STUDY

When Julie, a store manager, first grasped the idea that God cared about the work she did and how she did it, it felt like a jolt of lightning. To learn more, she started a faith and work book study with Vicki and Mei, two friends from church who were also retail managers. Then Ellen, another manager at her workplace, asked to join. She wasn't a religious person, Ellen said, but she was curious to see what had improved Julie's attitude on the job.

One day, the chapter their group was discussing included a reflection on King David's prayer: "But who am I, and who are my people, that we should be able to give as generously as this? Everything comes from you, and we have given you only what comes from your hand" (1 Chron. 29:14). The book suggested making a list of everything related to their work that they could receive as a gift from God, and then consider how these gifts could be shared with others.

Their list began with "salary, benefits, and skills"—"and friends," Vicki added with a smile. After a little discussion they added "knowledge, time, connections, and managerial status."

Then began the second part of the exercise: Ways to be generous with these gifts.

Again, they started with the obvious—donate to churches and nonprofits; help people at work with needs, like a coworker whose son needed an operation. They could be generous with possessions provided by their salaries, such as offering coworkers rides when needed, and opening their guest room to a visiting missionary or international student. They came up with lots of ideas for sharing their time off, from volunteer work, to visiting a lonely elderly neighbor, to spending a vacation on a service project trip.

Looking at "skills" and "knowledge" led to a discussion about mentoring newer employees. Julie had heard about a job training program for domestic violence survivors that was looking for instructors. Mei brought up the thrift store their church helped sponsor. "It's so disorganized!" she said. "I wonder if they'd let me consult with them on floor layout and managing stock."

The group jumped on that idea. Ellen pulled in "connections," suggesting that they all ask their bosses to donate retail stock to the thrift store. They also came up with the names of a few retired managers they could ask to volunteer. Then Julie, thinking of the job training program, wondered about sponsoring participants to work at the thrift store to build up their résumés and references.

The last item on their list, "managerial status," had them stumped. Being store manager brought authority and a measure of respect from their employees, but how could they share that?

Mei and Vicki exchanged a glance and then looked at Julie.

"What?" she asked.

"Well," said Mei hesitantly. "You could be more generous with your praise."

Once again, Julie felt that jolt that told her God's Spirit was speaking to her. She had to admit being stingy with encouragement and positive feedback. That could change, with her friends' and God's help, starting today.

Multiplying Goodness

Generosity is another key feature of *kalon ergon*—work that multiplies the goodness of God's kingdom. The purpose of productivity is always linked not only to meeting one's own needs but also to sharing the gospel and helping others, particularly those who are vulnerable or impoverished (Deut. 15:7–11; 2 Cor. 9:6–11; Eph. 4:28; Titus 3:14). Image-bearers are generous because this displays God's nature: "Every generous act of giving, with every perfect gift is from above, coming down from the Father of lights" (James 1:17).

First Timothy 6:17–19 gives directions for discipling those with wealth:

As for those who in the present age are rich, command them not to be haughty, or to set their hopes on the uncertainty of riches, but rather on God who richly provides us with everything for our enjoyment. They are to do good, to be rich in good works, generous, and ready to share, thus storing up for themselves the treasure of a good foundation for the future, so that they may take hold of the life that really is life.

Most American workers, even those not considered wealthy, have enough to be "ready to share."[1]

When my (Heidi's) children were little, I had a saying to help them guide their choices: "God wants us to make the meanness smaller, and the love and goodness bigger." As adults, most of our time is spent at work, so that's where we must make the goodness bigger! The previous chapter focused on what image-bearers must do to make the meanness smaller: don't cheat, confront prejudice, protect those who are mistreated. This chapter considers the positive actions disciples can take to enlarge the ways in which work can be a blessing. In *God at Work*, Ken Costa puts it simply: "The life of a Christian at work is a leaning toward goodness."[2]

Influencing Generosity

Most people have been told since early childhood, "It's nice to share." As a discipler, however, simply repeating the virtue of sharing may not move people to become more generous in practice. How might you have an influence?

First, note the ways they are already demonstrating generosity. Affirming a behavior is a good way to see more of it! Next, discern potential barriers to generosity. Here are a few possibilities, based on 1 Timothy 6:17–19:

- Dependence "on the uncertainty of riches" for security, instead of trusting God to provide "everything for our enjoyment."

- The prosperity mindset that prioritizes having more now over laying up treasure in the kingdom of God.

- Fear that sharing resources will put their own business or household at risk.

- Assuming that people who have wealth deserve it and don't have to share it.

- Regarding wealth as an end in itself, instead of a gift "for our enjoyment," and not realizing that tight-fistedness is a shadow of "the life that is truly life."

- A misreading of Jesus' words, "You always have the poor with you" (Matt. 26:11), not realizing that Jesus was quoting Deuteronomy 15:11, which reads in full: "Since there will never cease to be some in need on the earth, I therefore command you, 'Open your hand to the poor and needy neighbor in your land.'"

- Looking only at their bank account and not recognizing the full extent of how God has gifted them in and through their work.

Spiritual formation to align values and motivations with God's kingdom, "to be transformed by the renewing of your mind" (Rom. 12:2), is the ongoing project of discipleship.

Another barrier may be lack of awareness of the scope of need. Amy Sherman comments on what "loving your neighbor" means in the context of vocational faithfulness:

Some of those neighbors may be people within their workplaces, such as the nighttime janitor who's struggling to make it as a single mom with three kids and two minimum wage jobs. Other times neighbors in need may be people affected by the . . . employer (such as families living close to a company factory that is polluting the environment or poor people in the developing world who are hired by the firm at unfair wages). . . . The righteous educate themselves about the conditions of the vulnerable. They ask questions about the firm's engagements abroad; they are informed of their local community's news; they make a point of knowing the names of the service workers in their companies. They provide some mental and emotional space for their neighbors' realities.[3]

Learning the real stories of those who struggle and making a personal connection can provoke generosity more than generic obligation.

Lack of vision can also be a barrier to a generous way of working. What the word *generosity* typically brings to mind is donating to churches or charities, volunteering for community service, or personally helping individuals in need. But that's only the leading edge of opportunities for generosity linked with vocation. Just as Christ poured out all he had for us, Christ-followers can be inspired to use whatever God has given them to generously bless others (1 Pet. 4:10). This includes the resources, connections, skills, and influence associated with their work. (See "Stewardship of Vocational Power" at the end of chapter 20.) So, if you are discipling someone who works in social media marketing, generosity might lead them to design a campaign for an international mission agency's health initiative.

Brainstorming together is a valuable discipleship skill. Here are some questions you can ask:

- What is something you get paid to do that you would enjoy doing pro bono for those who really need it?

- What is a job skill you would enjoy teaching to others?

- What is something you produce or own in your work that could be shared to bless others?

- Name the most influential people you know—who can you imagine introducing them to that could benefit from the connection?

- What is your dream for contributing your talents to innovate solutions to tough problems?

As ideas emerge, encourage people to pray and listen to the Spirit, and then support them in stepping toward this vision.

Opportunities for Generosity

Here we walk through ways people might be encouraged to be "rich in good works." Examples are provided in the table on the resource page.

For Every Worker

Dedicating financial support from a salary to a church or nonprofit is one expression of the kingdom purpose of work. Mosaic law established the pattern that the productive work of God's people would sustain those who served in their religious institution (see Num. 18:21–24), and Jesus and Paul relied on financial backers (see Luke 8:1–3; Rom. 16:1–2).[4] Encourage disciples to be faithful patrons of gospel movements in their church and around the world, as well as nonprofit work that restores brokenness and cultivates *shalom*.

Beyond financial giving, generosity also looks like offering coworkers and customers encouraging words, caring gestures, a listening ear, thoughtful gifts, or practical aid given discretely. Disciples can be generous with their time in helping coworkers succeed, listening to others' input, and helping new employees fit in. They can amply share the credit for success with team members and collaborators. "Let each of you look not to your own interests, but to the interests of others" (Phil. 2:4) has a myriad of applications that entail acts of self-sacrifice on behalf of others.

For Company Decision-Makers

Good work is God's "Plan A" for meeting household needs. So, the most foundational way employers can reflect God's generosity is by hiring people who need jobs and paying generous wages and benefits.[5] Explore with disciples the role of generosity in decision-making about company policies such as paid sick days, family leave, or flex time. Advocate a gracious approach to working with employees when crises and needs arise that might lead to the loss of income.

Since the product of good work is foundational to a thriving community, the baseline for corporate generosity is providing quality, affordable, accessible goods and services. Encourage disciples in leadership positions to go a step further in generosity. A basic opportunity is donating or discounting products to promote flourishing in the community and around the world. When I (Heidi) worked for a nonprofit that assisted families, we were quite grateful for all the donated pizzas! A business can lend use of its facilities to the community—for example, hosting arts events or blood drives. Companies can sponsor local groups such as Little League teams and youth entrepreneur programs, or child sponsorship overseas. Also suggest ways to promote volunteerism as an organization, such as providing time off for community service.[6]

Another avenue to explore, particularly with innovative leaders, is social entrepreneurship.[7] Check out examples of how leaders have leveraged the tangible and intangible resources of their organization, often in collaboration with others, to develop economic growth initiatives.[8] Companies can also be generous with their visibility and economic influence to raise awareness, advocate change, and move the needle on entrenched social issues.

The Privilege of Giving

We suggest studying 2 Corinthians 8–9 together to envision giving as a privilege. The overflowing generosity of these Christians in "extreme poverty" sets a high bar for disciples today!

This passage suggests that godly generosity is an extension of the creation mandate, embedded in God's design for work and productivity. "He who supplies seed to the sower and bread for food will supply and multiply your seed for sowing and increase the harvest of your righteousness" (2 Cor. 9:10). God's plan is that work generates abundance to be shared for mutual enrichment. It might help those you disciple to reframe generosity as an investment in kingdom blessing rather than a one-way transaction.

Consider how Paul encourages his disciples in Acts 20:34–35. Referring to his vocation as a tentmaker, by which he supported himself and his companions, Paul said, "In all this I have given you an example that by such work we must support the weak, remembering the words of the Lord Jesus, for he himself said, 'It is more blessed to give than to receive.'" This echoes the promise in Deuteronomy 15:10: "Give liberally and be ungrudging when you do so, for on this account the LORD your God will bless you in all your work and in all that you undertake."

Reviewing these affirmations will help disciples come to see generosity as a good economic decision as well as simply the right thing to do.

RESOURCE

Generosity Grid

Galatians 6:10 urges, "Whenever we have an opportunity, let us work for the good of all, and especially for those of the family of faith." Use this worksheet to help people brainstorm options for generosity related to work. See other examples in Amy Sherman's *Kingdom Calling* (esp. chs. 10–13.)

How Could You Be Generous with Your . . .			
Vocational skills	Vocational connections	Organizational resources	Organizational policies & practices
Toward flourishing in and through your church:			
Offer consulting to the church to launch a new nonprofit or social enterprise (e.g., day care or coffee house)	Organize several churches to start a Christian vocational discipleship group in your profession (e.g., engineers)	Donate products or services to church ministries (e.g., donate food left over from catered events to meal program)	Pay for church staff to attend professional trainings alongside company staff (e.g., HR best practices)
Toward flourishing in and through your workplace:			
Serve as a mentor to a younger professional in your vocation	Arrange interviews and letters of reference to help talented but disadvantaged coworkers advance their career	Organize a mutual aid emergency fund to help coworkers facing a crisis	Encourage employees to be generous (e.g., matching donations, volunteer leave, hosting food drives or blood drives)
Toward the flourishing of your local community:			
Offer services through nonprofits—as a beautician, give haircuts at a homeless shelter; as an accountant, work with refugee families on their household budget	Engage business leaders in your network to invest in a program to develop youth leadership and business skills	Share assets—give a community theater access to the office copier; let a support group meet in the conference room on weekends	Purchase supplies from locally owned businesses rather than mass retailers (though it costs more)
Toward the flourishing of the global community:			
Offer pro bono services (e.g., IT) to help an international ministry program function more effectively	Partner with an overseas missions agency and showcase artists from their region in your office spaces as a fundraiser	Dedicate a product line or income stream to fund a global development ministry	Hire a fair-trade consultant to direct business deals to companies that empower rather than exploit international communities

19

SPIRITUAL PRACTICES FOR FRUITFULNESS: FAITH FORMATION AT WORK

Mark Wells, a divorce attorney, participated in Tom's Kingdom Purpose discipleship group. This is his story of spiritual transformation.[1]

MARK'S STORY

I used to look at my work as a necessary evil. People can't stay together, so they will need divorce attorneys; but I'm facilitating something that God hates, therefore my work must displease God. There were moments of satisfaction in seeing my clients happy after getting them a support check, or getting them out of an abusive marriage—but the "yuck" factor was high.

Then I was shown that my thinking was erroneous. I discovered how I glorified God with my job. Yes, divorce is odious to God. But just as violence is odious, victims still need a doctor to come in and help heal them.

Now, I know that my work is my ministry. My work has intrinsic value. The idea that my work is an end in and of itself—that's been huge for me. Saying that it's an act of worship and saying it's an end in itself mean almost the same thing. God is concerned with what I do and is involved in my work. Before, I thought God just wanted me to work to get a paycheck. Because my work is a ministry, I'm much more free now to share God with others. I'm much more free to give him credit.

I used to have my devotional times exclusively at home, separate from that nasty place called work. Often I was driven to spend time with the Lord out of anxiety—I went to Christ when something was happening in the workplace, or I was afraid I would lose my job. Now, God is behind every step I make at work. I occasionally do my Bible studies at my office. I pray over my clients more, and I ask my wife and others to pray over court dates, hearings, depositions. I'm a minister throughout my day, carrying out what God has designed me to do.

I have greater joy when I understand that God is alongside me, inter-twined with my work. He's not just looking down at me holding his nose. God is pleased with my work. I bring a smile to his face when I defend people well and rid them of fear.

Discipline and Grace

Navigators Ministries defines a spiritual practice as "anything that shapes our body and soul to live the good life, as Jesus taught it."[2] The goal of spiritual practice is to form us into the likeness of Christ, the perfect reflection of God's image (2 Cor. 3:18). This is an act of God's grace. Vocational disciplers encourage disciplines that help people grow in maturity as image-bearers working with kingdom purpose.

> If we walk in the Spirit in our workplace, we can have confidence of his supernatural empowerment as well as our own spiritual formation in Christlikeness. By walking in the Spirit, we cooperate with God in the redemptive work he is doing in the world and contribute to the common good. Walking in the Spirit empowers us to live lives of vocational faithfulness and to experience seamless lives of work and worship.[3]

This chapter considers ways to encourage people to partner with the transformative work of the Spirit, leading to greater productivity in kingdom purpose. Spiritual disciplines foster growth in the fruits of the Spirit as they work—replacing selfishness with love, negativity with joy, and anxiety with peace.[4]

Spiritual Practices at Their Work

Spiritual formation and discipleship typically focus on private devotional practices (reading Scripture, praying), church-oriented practices (attending services, being part of a small group), and personal ethics (being truthful, maintaining sexual purity). These are essential elements of following Jesus.

One aspect of vocational discipleship is helping Christians pursue spiritual formation *at work*—bringing spiritual disciplines into the workplace. Integrating faith and work demands spiritual maturity and it also uniquely cultivates it. As a discipler, you help people become more intentional about connecting their time spent at work with an awareness of God's presence and openness to God's grace. Practicing spiritual formation in the workplace[5] might include:

- Starting the workday with praise and prayer
- Keeping a devotional journal of reflections and prayers related to work
- Listening to audio recordings of Scripture while preparing for or commuting to work

- Committing key faith and work Bible verses to memory (Col. 3:16)
- Meditating on a specific biblical passage or theme while at work
- Taking time to pray over work-related decisions and struggles
- Listening to spiritually encouraging music while at work
- Starting a Bible study with coworkers
- Joining an online devotional group on your lunch break
- Signing up for daily faith and work devotionals[6]
- "Pray the hours"—punctuate the day with regular times for a brief prayer and Scripture reading[7]
- Practicing mindfulness by dedicating each task to God[8]

For over two decades and across several changes in office space, I (Heidi) have had this prayer taped to the wall above my desk:

> Lord Jesus, I speak your peace, your grace, and your perfect order into the atmosphere of this office. I acknowledge your lordship over all that will be spoken, thought, decided, and accomplished within these walls. Lord Jesus, I thank you for the gifts you have deposited in me.[9]

Glimpsing this prayer out of the corner of my eye recalls me to God's presence and purpose. It reminds me that I do not work for myself, or by myself.

In your discipleship role, you can connect people with resources for Christians seeking to deepen and express their faith at work. You can help them develop a plan for incorporating spiritual disciplines into their workday and provide personal accountability for maintaining the plan. You can make yourself available to pray with them about work and to study Scriptures together related to their job. You can meet with them to process how their workplace experiences are shaping their relationship with God, and vice versa. Disciplers are companions to people learning to walk in the Spirit at work.

RESOURCE

Five-Minute Workplace Prayer and Meditation Exercises

If you can set aside just five minutes with someone, here are a few exercises that you can lead in practicing the presence of God at work.

- Read the Lord's Prayer (Matt. 6:9–13). Write your own prayer that personalizes this passage with relevance to your work. For example: "May the work I do to _____ [fill in the specific purpose of your work] be a sign of your kingdom coming."

- Spend four minutes reading verses that lead you to focus on the presence of Immanuel, "God with us" (Ps. 46:10; 91:1; Matt. 11:28–29; John 15:9; 17:26; Rom. 5:5; 8:16; 1 John 4:13). Then spend one minute repeating the phrase, "My work belongs to God." Sit, kneel, stand, or walk—whichever helps you to be present with God.

- Spend five minutes memorizing one of the following passages, reflecting on its relevance to your work: Gen. 1:27–28; Isa. 61:1–3; Micah 6:8; Matt. 25:21; John 15:5; Rom. 12:1–3; 1 Cor. 2:6–7; Phil. 2:3–5; Col. 3:23–24; Eph. 2:8–10; 1 Pet. 4:10. Say it aloud and/or write it out repeatedly until you have it memorized. Then try to say the verse while doing a mindless task (like washing out your coffee cup).

After Each Exercise, Debrief Together

✓ What was meaningful? What was challenging?

✓ How did God speak to you, or in what way did you experience God present with you?

✓ How can you envision keeping up this practice in your work? For example, consider starting work each day with this practice for the next month, or even just the next week.

20

SPIRITUAL PRACTICES FOR FRUITFULNESS: SABBATH, TITHE, AND GLEANING

Spiritual Practices for Fruitfulness

Vocational discipleship encourages an additional set of spiritual practices to foster faithfulness and productivity in kingdom purpose. These disciplines aren't just about bringing spirituality into the workplace but also recognizing how *work for kingdom purpose is in itself a spiritual activity.*

Here, we outline three specific practices with ancient roots to support growth in doing good work in a good way: Sabbath, tithing, and gleaning. Each is a rhythm of work life that helps people to more deeply experience God's grace. As a vocational discipler, you can:

- Introduce these practices

- Explain their biblical foundation, and how they connect with faith and work principles (e.g., *your work matters to God* and *your work is your ministry*)

- Explore how they support kingdom purpose (e.g., how they honor the Creator, bless people, draw people to God's ways, and help the world to flourish)

- Discuss how they relate to the disciple's spiritual journey

- Help people plan how to incorporate these practices into their work routines

- Offer to provide accountability and feedback as they go

- Be transparent about your own journey with these practices

Practice the Sabbath

Key Verse

"Six days shall work be done; but the seventh day is a Sabbath of complete rest, a holy convocation; you shall do no work." (Lev. 23:3)

Key Concept

You cannot gain by effort what God does not choose to give you by grace.

Actions and Attitudes to Practice

It may seem ironic that a primary spiritual practice for working is *not* working! But the discipline of keeping the Sabbath is inseparable from the discipline of work, because it's modeled after God's rhythms in creation (Gen. 2:2–3). From that perspective, you can present the Sabbath to image-bearers not as a break from working but as integral to the creation mandate at the foundation of all our labors.

Practically speaking, the Sabbath calls disciples to clear a twenty-four-hour period each week (preferably but not necessarily Sundays) for rest in body, mind, and spirit. "Doing no work" is not the same as "doing nothing." Resting can mean getting out to enjoy nature, doing creative activities, getting physical exercise, reading something intellectually challenging, and so on. The point is to take a regular break from the tasks of our vocations. Since everyone's life and work situation is unique, the Sabbath will look different for different people.[1]

Disciples may question whether a particular activity counts as "work." Rather than parsing technicalities, check the motivation behind the question. If what drives them is the belief that the activity is needed to achieve a work-related goal, then they're not resting. No one can be truly fruitful by working on God's day off. A central purpose of the Sabbath is to remind us to rely on God and grace alone. Encourage those with busy, stressful jobs to view the Sabbath as a way of declaring their trust in God with their time.

Guide workplace leaders in considering the broader implications of the Sabbath for their organization. Practicing the Sabbath means ensuring that workers in their care also get a true day of rest. Exodus 20:10 (NIV) insists: "On it [the Sabbath] you shall not do any work, neither you, nor your son or daughter, nor your male or female servant, nor your animals, nor any foreigner residing in your towns." Businesses also need to take planned breaks from extracting value from animals and the land (see Lev. 24:2–6; 26:34).

Walk with innovative leaders through issues such as what the Sabbath looks like in an age of automation.

In addition, help people be mindful of ways in which their Sabbath practices affect others. If someone says that "resting" for them means not cooking but ordering takeout, reflect on all the work that others must do (take orders, cook, deliver) to make this rest possible. The Sabbath is for everyone—though what this looks like is far more complicated today. As the story of Jesus healing on the Sabbath makes clear (Luke 13:10–17), the Sabbath is a break from work, but not from the kingdom purpose of promoting human flourishing.

Practice Tithes and Offering

Key Verse

"All tithes from the land, whether the seed from the ground or the fruit from the tree, are the Lord's; they are holy to the Lord. . . . All tithes of herd and flock, every tenth one that passes under the shepherd's staff, shall be holy to the Lord." (Lev. 27:30–32)

Key Concept

You cannot gain by hoarding what God does not choose to give you by grace.

Actions and Attitudes to Practice

Offering a portion of one's income from work to God has deep biblical roots—all the way back to the first human family (see Gen. 4:3–4)! Not everyone agrees whether a 10 percent rate is the goal, but you can encourage disciples to regularly earmark assets for God's kingdom, regardless of whether they call it a tithe.[2]

The discipline of tithes and offerings reminds Christians that while prosperity is the fruit of work, it still comes from God and is to be used for his purposes. Not setting aside an offering is actually considered stealing from God (Mal. 3:8–9)! Rather than viewing the tithe as a subtraction from what they earn, encourage disciples to consider it a repayment of the abundance of God's provision. Like Sabbath rest, tithing is an expression of trust—especially when resources seem limited.

In an era when most financial transactions are virtual, help those you disciple to remain mindful of the connection between tithing and work. For example, instead of basing the tithe on a paycheck, perhaps encourage people to try giving based on a tenth of their hours. Or set aside the profits from a tenth of items produced or services rendered. What's important is the regular discipline of returning the fruit of labor to God, along with a thankful and yielded heart.

As with the Sabbath, help people understand the meaning of the tithe in the context of kingdom purpose: "You don't think just in terms of giving the excess, but you're showing up in God's story, which is a story of redemption and restoration. A story that frees me from defining my life in terms of what I own, rather who owns me, which is Jesus."[3] Against the fraying forces of "the cares of the world and the lure of wealth" (Matt. 13:22), a regular practice of tithing is like stitches holding people to their kingdom purpose.

Exploring points of resistance to tithing can lead to spiritual growth. What's holding a disciple back from tithing their income? Are they worried about making ends meet? Skeptical of religious institutions? Angry at their church (or at God)? Simply wanting to keep more in the bank? Remind them of what Jesus says: "Where your treasure is, there your heart will be also" (Matt. 6:21). When they hold onto their treasure, what does this say about their hearts? How might they experience more freedom and joy in their offering?

Also encourage Christians to examine their hearts when they *do* give. Are they giving joyfully of their free will (2 Cor. 9:7)? Might they be trying to look good to others (Matt. 6:2), bribe God (Acts 8:18–22), or curry spiritual favor (Luke 18:9–14)? Some may think of the tithe like paying taxes—that once they satisfy God by giving 10 percent, the other 90 percent of their income is fully at their disposal. Or they might see it as protection money: anyone who donates generously to the church is assumed to be a good person in the rest of their business affairs. Above all, warn people never to try to cheat God (Acts 5:1–11)!

Deuteronomy 14:28–29 describes one interesting and lesser-known function of the tithe. Every third year, the tithe went not to the temple but to the local community, where a portion was used so that "the resident aliens, the orphans, and the widows in your towns may come and eat their fill so that the LORD your God may bless you in all the work that you undertake." The tithe is not just for church-centric purposes. In God's economy, the aims of maintaining religious institutions, caring for those in need, supporting a household, and enjoying the goodness of God's bounty are intertwined outcomes of the fruitfulness of labor.

Thus tithing is just one facet of the discipline of generosity. The grace that God extends to people in the form of income is to be shared regularly with others in both church and community, with a spirit of reverent, overflowing generosity, and on a scale appropriate to a person's resources (Luke 21:3–4; 2 Cor. 8:2).

Practice Gleaning

Key Verse

"When you reap the harvest of your land, you shall not reap to the very edges of your field or gather the gleanings of your harvest. You shall not strip your vineyard bare, or gather the fallen grapes of your vineyard; you shall leave them for the poor and the alien: I am the LORD your God." (Lev. 19:9–10)

Key Concept

You cannot reserve for yourself what God chooses to give to others by grace.

Actions and Attitudes to Practice

While tithing sets aside a portion of one's income, gleaning is about sharing assets and opportunity. Like tithing, gleaning is a direct expression of God's concern for those who are poor or vulnerable.

Mosaic Law instructed landowners not to squeeze their harvest to get every last drop. They were to allow those who lacked other means of support to gather up the produce left behind on the first pass.

> The basis of the law is the intention that all people are to have access to the means of production necessary to support themselves and their families. . . . God's intention is for people to receive his fruitfulness by working. Gleaning did exactly this. It provided an opportunity for productive work for those who otherwise would have to depend on begging, slavery, prostitution or other forms of degradation.[4]

While charity offers people the goodness of bread, gleaning allows people "to experience the abundance of good work."[5] One of the advantages of gleaning is that it reinforces God's design for the bond between family, work, and self-sufficiency, without perpetuating the indignity of dependency.

Gleaning, like other spiritual practices, is a practical expression of trust in God. As an act of discipleship, it entails putting the margins of productivity on the altar of faith, for the sake of other image-bearers. Andy Crouch explains,

> You might think a diligent harvester's job would be to extract the maximum amount of grain from the field. . . . Instead, the discipline the Lord required of Israel was not to do everything within their power, not to push their productivity to the limit—to intentionally leave margins that made room for others to participate in the economy.[6]

This is not the easiest discipline to help people translate into a modern context. The main question to help people explore is, "How can you use your resources and power to give others greater opportunity to support themselves through work?" Here are a few examples:

- Hire an assistant instead of working overtime
- Advocate for bonuses to be shared by all the workers
- Accept a pay freeze, or even a cut, to make room in the budget for a new position
- Invest in entrepreneurial ventures in the community
- Donate the use of company equipment to educational or job training programs
- Collaborate with probation officers to hire former offenders and help them succeed
- Create a fund to help struggling employees with car repairs, childcare costs, medical bills, or other barriers to their ability to work
- Develop a bonus system to counter the "cliff effect" disincentive for promotions[7]
- Provide gas cards or bus passes to workers picking up extra shifts
- Fund a paid summer internship program for college students
- Volunteer as a vocational mentor or jobs coach
- Help immigrant workers pay the legal fees for their work visa
- Partner with an agency to place workers who have disabilities

Disciplers can also invoke the gleaning principle to point out practices that business leaders should *not* do in order to maximize profit, such as:

- Utterly crush "Mom and Pop" competitors
- Push massive layoffs to bump share price and CEO pay
- Lay off workers without any provision to help them find new jobs
- Cut off hourly workers' schedules just short of full-time status with benefits

The gleaning principle applies in a different way to those who struggle with low job status or income—people who could benefit from being gleaners.[8] If the person you disciple doesn't get enough hours to make ends meet, do they have dreams for starting a side business? If a disciple is unemployed, how can they keep their skills fresh and make new contacts as a volunteer? How might a little extra hustle on the job—coming in a little early, staying a little late, taking on extra tasks—improve their chances for a better position?

Like other spiritual disciplines, opportunities for discipleship can be found by probing resistance. If the person you disciple has a negative reaction to the prospect of applying gleaning to their vocation, is it due to the pride of making the most profit? Unwillingness to share? Stereotypes about those who are poor? Preferring to give (or receive) handouts over opportunities for work? Uncomfortable conversations can lead to heart transformations.

A great starting point for encouraging this spiritual discipline is to read the book of Ruth together, focusing on the role of gleaning in the story. Questions to ask include, "What lessons can you take from the actions of Boaz the business owner?" and "How is God inviting you to emulate the diligence and courage of Ruth?" Note too how gleaning goes hand in hand with creating a safe environment for workers to do their jobs. Explore the connections between gleaning and the gospel story (especially noting that gleaning helped Ruth survive to become great-grandmother to Jesus!).

Spiritual Disciplines and Fruitfulness

The disciplines of keeping the Sabbath, tithing, and gleaning have a curious relationship with productivity. God commands people to work, because work is good—but every seventh day he says they must stop working. God desires to bless people with abundance in the fruit of their labor—but he asks for a tenth of it back. God directs people to multiply their fruitfulness—but he expects producers to stop short of their potential harvest. Image-bearers hold productivity in balance with "seeking first the kingdom of God" (Matt. 6:33).

These three disciplines can accelerate spiritual growth toward working with kingdom purpose. They give people a practical expression of the Great Commandment—"Love God with all your heart, soul, mind and strength, love your neighbor as yourself." They train people to trust, honor, and obey God, even at a cost. In these ways, they prevent people from making productivity an idol. These disciplines share the blessings of fruitful work with "neighbors" who have fewer resources and protect workers who are less powerful. Thus they prevent productivity at the expense of other image-bearers fulfilling their kingdom purpose. "The more our territory expands, the more we must embrace the disciplines that make room on the margins for others to also exercise their calling to image bearing."[9]

It's worth noting one other biblical practice intertwined with the Sabbath, tithing, and gleaning: feasting! Fruitfulness and feasting go hand in hand (see Deut. 16:13–15; Exod. 23:16). Spiritual disciplines aren't intended to make people pinched and dour. Rather, they're intended to lead to the enjoyment of abundance, which God intends for all image-bearers. The kingdom purpose of work leads to an eternal banquet. So, as you walk with disciples through these serious topics, make sure the rhythm of spiritual formation includes partying too! "For the LORD your God will bless you in all your harvest and in all the work of your hands, and your joy will be complete" (Deut. 16:15).

RESOURCE

Stewardship of Vocational Power

Productivity comes from the purposeful application of power. Vocational power is the capacity to effect change and create more of what helps the world to flourish through one's work.

In *Kingdom Calling: Vocational Stewardship for the Common Good*, Amy Sherman explores the important concept of "stewardship of vocational power," defined as "the intentional and strategic deployment of our vocational power . . . to advance foretastes of God's kingdom."[10] This comes in a range of forms, not just direct authority or access to resources. Sherman identifies seven forms of vocational power:

1. *Knowledge:* Expertise gleaned from formal education or on-the-job experience in a particular field.

2. *Skills:* Competencies to get things done, whether hard skills (ability to perform specific measurable tasks) or soft skills (capacities related to personal or relational qualities).

3. *Position:* Title, seniority, decision-making power, level of authority in an organization; also takes into account the positional power of the organization itself (e.g., a reporter at the *New York Times* has more positional power than the editor of a college newspaper).

4. *Networks:* Links with professional contacts (e.g., coworkers, vendors, suppliers, customers, regulators, business partners); affiliation with job-related groups (e.g., professional guild, union, alumni association, chamber of commerce).

5. *Influence:* "Capacity to cause an effect in indirect or intangible ways," not necessarily linked with position or authority.

6. *Reputation:* Recognition or fame that gives "entrée to powerbrokers, capacities for mobilizing a large following or strategic opportunities to direct wide-scale attention to a particular issue or cause."

7. *Platform:* Having the opportunity and access to communication tools to shine a spotlight on an issue or get out a message, and an audience to share it with.[11]

The people you disciple likely have greater power than they realize! Or they may not have thought deeply about how God has gifted them with this power to serve his kingdom purpose.

Discipleship Exercises

Using the chart below, help the person you're discipling to explore the following questions and discern how this may call them to action.

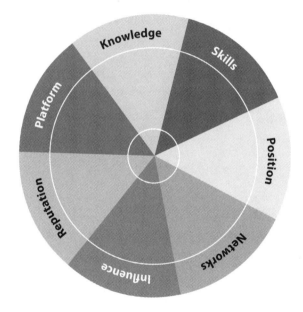

✓ Identify your vocational power: In the inner segment for each slice each of the circle, write a number from 1–5 that indicates how much power you think you have in that area, with 1 meaning "very little power" and 5 meaning "significant power."

✓ Inside each segment, jot down how you have this power (e.g., your specific skills, position, or reputation).

✓ Consider 1 Peter 4:10: "Each of you should use whatever gift you have received to serve others, as faithful stewards of God's grace in its various forms." How is power connected with stewardship of God's grace?

✓ How have you used your vocational power in service to God and others?

✓ Amy Sherman invites taking stock of power assets "and then asking, 'For whom could I deploy these?'"[12] Who are your "neighbors" in your company, community, or around the world who could benefit from the stewardship of your power?

✓ Brainstorm new opportunities to use your vocational power to glorify God, bless people, draw people to Christ, and strengthen the contribution of your work to the flourishing of your community and world.

✓ Are there ways in which you may have misused your vocational power? For example, have you used your power to advance your own interests at the expense of others? How can you change to set that right?

PART FIVE

VOCATIONAL DISCIPLESHIP THAT LEADS TO TRANSFORMATION

21

"YOU HAVE HEARD ... BUT I TELL YOU ...": TELLING A NEW STORY ABOUT WORK

Matthew Luke, a student in Tom's Leadership and Ethics class, described the impact of learning to see his ministerial role from a fresh perspective.

MATTHEW'S STORY

We in the church have drawn a major line between the higher and lower callings and created a stigma. Those who do spiritual jobs are more important than everyone else doing "common" jobs. What we do on Sundays is more important than what happens on Monday through Saturday. However, I have come to see how the Bible speaks to life as a whole. I believe now that our role as church leaders on Sunday is to help people in their Monday-through-Saturday life.

This change in thinking has greatly altered the way I view my job in ministry. I now see my purpose as equipping and helping people in their normal, everyday lives. My goal is to help them live out the cultural mandate wherever they have been called—whether as students in school, as team members in sports, as IT service workers, as parents, as husbands. My job is to listen, encourage, and support the congregation as they fulfill their kingdom purpose.

Another change has occurred in my teaching. I strive to point my students and congregation back to the fact that they are image-bearers, created to live and work in light of God's commands. We are called to reflect God to this world, and one way we are called to do that is by doing everything we do to the best of our ability. This reflects God as a beautiful, wonderful, creative, and good God.

Confronting False Stories

Disciplers are storytellers. As chapter 10 explored, the gospel story shapes an understanding of work for image-bearers redeemed by Christ. Why do many church-going Christians carry themselves at work in a way that's utterly inconsistent with this kingdom purpose?

One reason is the competing narratives that are in the picture. Mainstream American Christianity has been steeped in a church-centric culture with ancient Greco-Roman roots that is not easily unlearned.[1] The prosperity mindset, which idolizes status and material success, is also deeply ingrained in broader Western culture. In addition, each profession carries its own set of worldview assumptions and values. "All Christians live in cultures and work in vocational fields that operate by powerful master narratives that are sharply different from the gospel's account of things. But these narratives work at such a deep level that their effects on us are hard to discern."[2]

So, unless these other narratives are dealt with, trying to focus on kingdom purpose at work is like trying to listen to an orchestra that has multiple conductors leading different compositions: the narrative making the most noise tends to win out.

As you share the core principles of vocational discipleship, be aware that you're not addressing a blank slate but speaking over all the other voices that have influenced their perspective. In his Sermon on the Mount, Jesus says five times, "You have heard that it was said . . ." followed by, "But I say to you . . ." Jesus exposed faulty narratives and replaced them with his teachings. Paul also confronted old ways of thinking, although not always graciously: "You foolish Galatians!" (Gal. 3:1). And with fiery language, the prophets of Israel warned God's people against following other traditions.

Thus to disciple others in a biblical theology of faith and work, we must first break through the flawed narratives they have long carried with them. Most often these are not other faith traditions but cultural assumptions posing as biblical truths. These assumptions are hard to see because people take them for granted. We call this "pre-theology." Confronting these implicit, pre-theological ideas may require you to help people redefine terms they think they know but have never submitted to a careful biblical examination.

When most American Christians hear the word *spiritual*, they think *non-physical*. When they hear *ministry*, they think *evangelism* or *church program*. When they hear *eternal life*, they imagine *disembodied spirit*. If these assumptions are not brought to light, challenged, and transformed, then any new discipleship ideas will likely be filtered through this old, flawed lens. New wine and old wineskins are not a productive combination (Matt. 9:17).

Until recently, most churches rarely taught a theology of work or discipled people for their work. Thanks largely to a robust faith and work movement, this is slowly beginning to change.[3] As you share about vocational theology, watch for blank stares indicating that the believer is struggling to integrate these new perspectives with their poorly interrogated but comfortably familiar presuppositions. For a vocational discipler, this calls for patience and a willingness to repeat key concepts as needed, in a variety of teaching methods and contexts.

Confronting Dualism

As a vocational discipler, it is important to learn to recognize the church-centric perspective and its roots in dualism, so that whenever it appears, you can identify it and redirect people to a kingdom-centered story. *Your Work Matters to God* offers a useful summary of dualism:

> (1) God is more interested in the soul than in the body; (2) the things of eternity are more important than the things of time; (3) life divides into two categories, the sacred and the secular; and (4) because of the nature of their work, ministers and other clergy are more important to God's program than the laity.[4]

Below, we briefly unpack each of these characteristics and their implications for work. How have you seen these aspects of dualism manifested in your discipling conversations?

Disembodied Spirituality

Dualism asserts that our spiritual (higher) nature is distinct from our bodily (lower) nature: "redemption" = "saved soul." This "soul" has no physical manifestation and will ultimately be detached from our bodily existence. When we think of God, we think not of the corporeal Jesus but a disembodied, radiant being. From this perspective, being made in God's image means that the essence of what is good in us lies in this state of pure spirit.

Since God is more interested in the soul than the body, God is not terribly concerned about work that is material in nature. This perspective reinforces the individualism of our culture. Little thought is given to how one's work impacts the world, beyond the spiritual well-being of individual souls.

Heavenly-Mindedness

Dualism envisions that our eternal destiny is to exist as redeemed, disembodied beings in an ethereal heaven, freed from our flawed physical nature and thus from the need to work.

> If we believe, even subconsciously, that bodies and the earth and material things are un-spiritual, even evil, then we will inevitably reject or spiritualize any biblical revelation about our bodily resurrection or the physical characteristics of the New Earth.[5]

If "eternal reality is more real than temporal reality," then our jobs are not our "real" calling.[6] At the end of time, the physical world will be destroyed; only what is "purely spiritual" will remain. From this perspective, the work we do on earth will not last and is ultimately insignificant. Only the goal of winning souls that can live for eternity has real value.

Secular versus Sacred

Dualism divides all life into two arenas: one where God is present and pleased; the other outside the circle of God's goodness and attention. Work = secular, worldly; church = sacred, spiritual. For example, consider the words of the hymn:

> *Turn your eyes upon Jesus,*
> *Look full in his wonderful face,*
> *And the things of earth will grow strangely dim,*
> *In the light of his glory and grace.*[7]

It is assumed that the place we go to encounter Jesus is the church. Thus God cares more about what we do on Sunday than on Monday. The "sacred" activities people do in an organized religious setting—worship, prayer, Bible study—are the only ones that really matter to God. Work in the "secular" arena is a tolerated interlude, a distraction, or even a threat to our spiritual growth.

Ministry Specialization

In a dualistic framework, some believers are gifted for "full-time ministry," set apart by God for work that really matters. Only certain individuals are called to church work (and are therefore considered more spiritual); the rest have a job, not a sacred calling. "A hierarchy of callings emerges naturally enough because, deep down, many of us believe that God designed creation itself to be hierarchical."[8]

If you have to do secular work, dualism instructs good Christians not to be absorbed by it. Rather, focus your mind as much as possible on spiritual matters. As Aquinas said, "It is impossible for one to be busy with external action and at the same time give oneself to Divine contemplation."

Once you are familiar with these themes, you will begin to see them everywhere in the church.

How Churches Reinforce a Dualistic Perspective

The faith and work movement has slowly been steering churches away from dualism toward a more integrative theology. Vocational discipleship plays a key role in advancing this movement. Encourage those you disciple to be an active part of church programs that help members live out their faith in their workplace.

Yet for too many church-goers the "Sunday-Monday gap" persists, in which "their Sunday worship hour bears little to no relevance to the issues they face in their Monday workplace hours."[9] Thus it's also important to train disciples to be aware of how dualism may still be influencing their church. You can point out signposts of dualism, such as:

- Work-related themes are largely absent from sermons, worship songs, discipleship materials, and corporate prayer.

- When work is mentioned in church, it's framed as good when it provides an arena for "spiritual" activities like prayer or evange-lism, but bad when it distracts people from their eternal calling or turns their attention to "secular" matters.

- Vocation and discipleship are presented as being in competition; e.g., "Don't put your job ahead of God" or "So-and-so left work for a higher calling."

- "Ministry" is discussed solely within a church-centric framework, with phrases such as "entering the ministry," "doing full-time min-istry," or "serving with a ministry program."

In general, a dualistic mindset is present whenever a church com-municates, whether explicitly or implicitly, that "the bulk of the Christian life—time spent working—is peripheral to the heart of the faith."[10] Ironically, such church-centric thinking essentially turns Christians into "functional atheists" during their working hours.

The task of vocational discipleship often requires a touch of sensitivity. How can you confront dualism in the church a disciple attends, without appearing overly critical or offending the pastor? One option is to suggest looking together at Bible passages with an image-bearer perspective and in-vite discussion. Or you can read material together that presents a theological alternative to dualism and let people draw their own conclusions.

It may also help to realize that Jesus too had to face dualism in the reli-gious culture of his day. When he returned to his hometown of Galilee and taught in the synagogue, people were astonished: "What is this wisdom that has been given to him? What deeds of power are being done by his hands! Is not this the carpenter?" (Matt. 6:1–3; 13:54–55). They knew Jesus by his "secular" profession, and this was a barrier to receiving him as a spiritual leader. If you practice discipleship without the proper "spiritual" credentials (e.g., church title or seminary training), then you may face similar skepti-cism. But disciples will know you by your fruits (Matt. 12:33).

Confronting Idolatry

One of the consequences of dualism is that it leads toward idolatry. God designed people to worship and glorify him through good work. Yet because of the absence of vocational discipleship, Christians at work often channel their devotion elsewhere. As *Every Good Endeavor* puts it, idolatry means "turning a good thing into an ultimate thing." Work is deeply connected with our God-given identity and purpose, so naturally this is where many people look to find meaning, significance and self-worth.[11]

False gods demand more and more of our time, attention, energy, and resources, with little return. Inevitably they damage us and those around us (Exod. 20:3–6). Whatever people are willing to sacrifice for the sake of their work may identify who or what it is that they worship. If you see someone repeatedly doing harm to their health, their family, their coworkers, their community, or the natural environment in the course of doing their job, then this is a warning sign to look for an idol.

A person's motivations for work (financial security, self-fulfillment, status) can usurp the place of God as their driving force. If you ask, "What is one thing about your work that you would be devastated to give up?," their answer may reveal the idol. For example, business leader Barry Rowan describes:

> I had made achievement my god. It wasn't until the achievement went away, that I realized a part of my god also went away. . . . My soul was pierced by Jesus' words, "Any of you who does not give up everything he has cannot be my disciple." . . . Was I willing to give up any claim to my own future?[12]

Watch for signs of idolizing excellence. There is a line to walk between pursuing excellence to reflect God's greatness and pursuing excellence (their own or that of their business) to demonstrate their own greatness. It is important to help Christians understand the difference between doing great work that pleases God and doing great work to earn God's favor.

Be aware of other possible idols to confront:

> Idols of comfort and pleasure can make it impossible for a person to work as hard as is necessary to have a faithful and fruitful career. Idols of power and approval, on the other hand, can lead us to overwork or to be ruthless and unbalanced in our work practices. Idols of control take several forms—including intense worry, lack of trust, and micromanagement.[13]

Scripture especially links idolatry with greed (1 Sam. 2:29; Ps. 10:3; Eph. 5:5; Col. 3:5). The prosperity mindset is a powerful false god.

Christians are often completely unaware of their workplace idolatry, because they have not been taught to reflect spiritually on their life at work. Calling image-bearers to name their idols, relinquish them, and turn back to worship God alone through their work is one of the most important roles of a vocational discipler. Since idols always cause destruction, this process also involves seeking to reconcile and restore any harm they may have caused. As the story of Zacchaeus illustrates, a believer's willingness to make restitution powerfully demonstrates to others in their workplace the truth of the gospel!

Discipleship Model: Being, Knowing, Doing

When dismantling false narratives, it's not enough just to teach someone a new idea. We have to help them connect it with who they are as an image-bearer and what they do in the context of their job.

Listen for signs that dualistic thinking, the prosperity mindset, or another idol still has a grip on their understanding of their work (see the resource below). Look for areas where people's actual behavior doesn't line up with what they say they believe. Ask questions to bring to light their flawed assumptions about work and lead them toward the perspective and practices of a redeemed image-bearer called to fruitful kingdom work.

Although the barriers are strong, the "aha!" factor is truly rewarding. I (Tom) have taught the Kingdom Purpose Workshop to hundreds of students. In each class, there is a pattern of initial resistance, many questions, and then a turning point of openness to a new, more integrated perspective on faith and work. Here is Cheryl's story:

> When I first began seminary, it was never with the intention to work for a church. It caused some conflict within me. Was it appropriate to go to seminary if I was never going to do "church work"? I feel called to be a nurse. I always have. In 1 Corinthians 7:17 we read, "Let each person lead the life that the Lord has assigned to him, and to which God has called him." I was "assigned" to be a nurse and to serve the Lord in that capacity. I love my job. It is just as high a calling as the pastor or the teacher or the missionary.
>
> I no longer consider only the work accomplished within the walls of the church to be "ministry work." I am called to full-time ministry exactly where I work because I am an image-bearer of the One who created me and to be a nurse, and that work is very good. . . . Doing the work he has equipped and called me to do is how I live a life in worship to the Father.[14]

RESOURCE

Top Ten Flawed Background Assumptions about Work

These statements (based on conversations with actual business leaders) illustrate common attitudes about work rooted in a dualistic or church-centric worldview. How would you respond to someone who believes these ideas? How could you begin to dismantle these assumptions and replace them with a different story? It may help to revisit the core principles for image-bearing work found in chapter 8.

1. "It doesn't matter what job I do as long as I can share the gospel."
2. "Work is my punishment for not following a call to be a pastor."
3. "What does my job matter? It's only going to be burned up when the world ends anyway."
4. "If you really want to serve God, go into the ministry."
5. "I think God holds his nose when he sees me working."
6. "Only saving souls for Jesus will last."
7. "I feel guilty about not spending more time at church because of my job."
8. "God wants me to have a high-paying job so I can give regularly to missions."
9. "The only reason I work is to feed my family."
10. "After I retire I can focus more on my spiritual life."

22

READING SCRIPTURE THROUGH AN IMAGE-BEARER LENS

CASE STUDY

The adult Bible study group had been working their way through Hebrews. "Finally, we get to my favorite part," said Raul. "The hall of heroes in Hebrews 11!"

After reading through the chapter, the group discussed the roots of faith in the creation story, as image-bearers who "understand that the worlds were prepared by the word of God" (v. 3). They noted how trust in the future fulfillment of God's plan is expressed in present action, often leading to sacrifice.

"How many of you know someone who would be commended for their faith?" Raul asked. Many named parents and grandparents; others cited missionaries, Mother Teresa, their pastor, and someone even suggested their Bible study teacher, which made Raul smile.

"How many of you know a rancher who is a model of faith? Or a farmer? Or the founder of a business empire? Or a political leader? Or a military leader? Or an administrator?" No hands went up. Raul continued, "That's another way of saying Abel, Gideon, Abraham, Moses, Samson, and Joseph. I could go on. The point is, we tend to think of 'religious leaders' as role models of faith. Yet with the exception of Samuel, Hebrews gives us a list of people who did 'secular' work. They were all uniquely gifted, called and positioned to express their faith through their vocation."

Raul let that sink in and then asked, "So, who do you know is a model of faith in the working world?" There was a pause, and then someone shared the story of a college professor who had been passed over for tenure because they were known as a Christian. Another said his faith had been encouraged by the hospice worker who had prayed with his father before he died. Another told of her first summer job, where her manager's enthusiasm for serving customers in the name of Christ had inspired her to major in business.

At the end of their hour, Raul asked everyone to write out this prayer and personalize it to their vocation: "By faith, may I please you in my work, as I trust in you."

The Word of Truth for the World of Work

"The word of God is living and active . . . able to judge the thoughts and intentions of the heart" (Heb. 4:12). To confront false narratives, expose idols, and grow in new ways of being, thinking, and acting, studying Scripture together is powerful. Every book in the Bible was given in the covenant of grace to explain to people who God is, who they are, and how God intends them to live in this world.

Yet most Christians only know how to read Scripture in "church-centric mode." They see it as a book written for church people, to be studied in church settings, guiding people toward more church-centric behavior. Passages tend to be studied for their "spiritual meaning," as defined by a dualistic paradigm. Applications of the Bible to work focus on bringing church-centric behaviors into the workplace (pray for your coworkers and share the gospel) or keeping "worldly" sins out of the workplace (don't cheat on your timesheet or your spouse).

The importance of studying the Scriptures in discipleship is underscored in 2 Timothy 2:15: "Do your best to present yourself to God as one approved by him, a worker who has no need to be ashamed, rightly explaining the word of truth." To "rightly explain" God's word, the vocational discipler needs to understand how to study the Bible as a book written to image-bearers who work. We lead people to read the Bible through an image-bearer lens, to see how their kingdom work brings the gospel into life.

Please note that we are not presenting the image-bearer lens as the *only* way to read Scripture, or as a replacement for more traditional approaches to Bible study. We are asserting that this perspective needs to be emphasized as a neglected complement if we want to see the gospel gain traction in people's workday lives.

"Paul Minear once said that the Bible is . . . 'a book by workers, about workers, for workers.' . . . It is rather stunning that we are able to leaf through most of the major Bible dictionaries and find absolutely no articles on work at all!"[1] Without learning to read the Bible in an image-bearer context, Christians cannot develop spiritual maturity in the arena of their life where they spend the majority of their waking hours. Their work life will be stunted by the milk of a truncated church-centric interpretation.

On the other hand, once Christians—especially those who have been raised in a church-centric context—begin to read the Bible through an image-bearer lens, the word becomes "living and active." One business leader exclaimed, after completing a kingdom purpose biblical survey with Tom: "I'm really starting to feel that [my work] is truly critical to what God has created me for. . . . Looking at passage after passage after passage, which I had read all of those dozens of times . . . and to see them really with the light on for the first time."

Applying the Bible to the World of Work

While many general Bible study guides still miss the vocational lens, there are nevertheless excellent print and online resources available for studying themes related to work in Scripture, including Bible study guides, courses, faith and work commentaries, and devotionals.[2] Here we share a few suggestions related to methods.

Learn from Jesus' Teaching Methods

Although Jesus was well versed in Scripture and religious practices, his teachings were not centered around the synagogue but people's workaday lives. Jesus' teachings often addressed issues relevant to work (money, exploitation, offenses) in a way that would be relevant and memorable to working people. By Tom's count, 45 out of 52 parables (87 percent) take place in the context of a work setting, and 122 out of 132 appearances of Jesus (92 percent) are in the workplace.[3] We are more effective in vocational discipleship if, like Jesus, we refer to and are present at people's jobs. (See the description of the Gospel@Work Day in Appendix B.)

We can also point out that Jesus himself spent about eighteen years as a carpenter, and it was in this context that "Jesus increased in wisdom and in stature, and in divine and human favor" (Luke 2:52). He experienced the challenges common to workers—without sin. As you study the Gospels with disciples, lead them to look for how everyday workplace observations show up in Jesus's teachings.

Note the Vocational Aspects of Familiar Stories and Characters

Christians steeped in a church-centric perspective tend to view biblical characters as inherently spiritual figures called to sacred tasks. Studying biblical characters in their workplace context and identifying them with their vocation, even if it seems at first unnatural or peripheral to the story, helps people overcome the idea that somehow a secular job is inferior to a spiritual ministry. For example, we can refer to Nehemiah as a construction project manager, Moses as a political leader, Ruth as an immigrant field laborer, Paul as a tradesman, and so on. Explain how each of these characters was uniquely gifted, called, and positioned to accomplish what God wanted done through their professions.

Apply Scripture to Real Workplace Situations

Naming the vocational elements present in Bible stories will help to bring out these interpretations. For example: Abraham wrestled with conflict in a family-owned business, Jacob dealt with being underpaid for his labor, David had to survive a boss who (literally) was out to get him, Esther coped with a male-dominated culture, and Paul confronted people who were profiting from oppressing others (Acts 16:16). Of course, each situation is distinct, and so we look to these stories as guides rather than directives.

Point out Work-Related Language in Bible Texts

As you read biblical texts, pay attention to words associated with labor, such as "calling," "good works," "build," "create," "plant," and "gifts." A church-centric perspective views these as metaphors for a "spiritual" meaning, and often this interpretation is simply taken for granted. But an image-bearer perspective invites us to consider how these passages apply to literal work of disciples dedicated to God's kingdom purpose.

Pay special attention to biblical passages describing attributes and actions of God that can also be ascribed to workers as God's image-bearers. For example, in Psalm 104, you could invite the disciple to note all the verbs describing God's activity (stretch out the heavens, set the earth on its foundations, set a boundary, water the mountains). Then ask what occupations involve these types of actions, and whether the disciple has engaged in any similar tasks in their job. A follow-up question would be to identify qualities or outcomes associated with God's activity (see "The earth is satisfied with the fruit of your work"; "How manifold are your works! In wisdom you have made them all"; "May the Lord rejoice in his works"). How can image-bearers emulate these standards?

Look Out for Dualist Interpretations

As addressed in the previous chapter, biblical texts are often interpreted in a way that reinforces the separation of life into sacred (disembodied, ethereal, holy) versus secular (physical, practical, worldly) realms. As you read Scripture together in a discipleship context, take note of key terms that may have a presumed dualistic meaning. For example, when people read the word *spiritual* (as in Rom. 12:1), do they assume this means a plane of existence that transcends our physical being, or does it involve committing all of life (including their working life) to God?

Draw on Your Own Workplace Experience and Calling

Several times, Paul points to the fact that he worked a marketplace job as his main source of support: "We work hard with our own hands. . . . Imitate me" (1 Cor. 4:12–16; see also Acts 18:1–5; 20:17–35; 1 Cor. 9:1–18;

1 Thess. 2:6–10). Paul's industriousness was linked to his trustworthiness and effectiveness in leading the church and spreading the gospel. This insight should inform how we read his letters to the church. Being a tentmaker changed the way Paul taught. Like Jesus, his teachings were more relatable to people because he drew on these experiences.

I (Tom) met Estuardo on a trip to Guatemala as a "business missionary," collaborating with local churches to train entrepreneurs for microenterprise development. Estuardo loved being an auto mechanic, and felt that God had called him to launch a business. But he shared with me that he was on the verge of shutting it down, because he was getting threatening calls demanding money. In his community, businesses operated in a context of corruption. He didn't want to close down, but he knew the threats were real.

As we talked, I recalled my devotional reading that morning about the story of Nehemiah. As supervisor of a public construction project—rebuilding the wall around Jerusalem—Nehemiah was gifted and called for an important job. He kept on doing it, despite violent opposition, until he accomplished his purpose. After I shared this story with Estuardo, he decided to follow Nehemiah's example.

Reading Scripture through an Image-Bearer's Lens: Examples from Disciples

For one of the assignments in my (Tom's) Kingdom Purpose Workshop, students read various verses specifically as God's message to them as image-bearers called to work for his purpose. He then has them select three that gave them fresh understanding through this new perspective. The excerpts below from a class in 2019 illustrate how the light can begin to shine through cracks in old paradigms.

God blessed them, and God said to them, "Be fruitful and multiply, fill the earth and subdue it." (Gen. 1:28–30)

Before this class, I would normally pass by this passage and consider it almost a set-up for . . . the fall. In this I was falling victim to the two-chapter gospel—we were created to be redeemed. This understanding led me to think we work as a result of sin. Although the "toil" aspects of work are a part of the curse that resulted from the fall, God has always intended us to work and be creative, for he works and is creative. We bear his image and glorify him when we use our God-given gifts to tend the garden he has created for us . . . not just for our own survival, but for the flourishing of life in general. (Daniel DeCriscio)

The Lord spoke to Moses: "See, I have called by name Bezalel . . . and I have filled him with divine spirit, with ability, intelligence, and knowledge in every kind of craft." (Exod. 31:1–3)

This may seem to be an obscure passage, but it speaks volumes into the image-bearer context. Here we find the first person Scripture describes as being "filled with the Spirit." The interesting thing about this is that this person wasn't a prophet, or a priest, or a king. He was a craftsman, a man chosen by God to fulfill a task and gifted by God to complete that task. God called Bezalel to be a skilled laborer, a trainer of others, and a God-glorifying artist. (Jeremy Moore)

Jesus said, "If you were Abraham's children, then you would do the things Abraham did." (John 8:39)

This is what we can learn from Abraham as an image-bearer making the world a flourishing place. He possessed leadership to deliver results and was an administrator giving his nation its structure. He was a skilled mediator and peacemaker among its people. He shouldered responsibilities in establishing social welfare, promoting morality, and abolishing idolatries. The generosity of Abraham was well known among the masses. Politicians, governors, mayors, senators, kings, and presidents can make this world a better place each and every day. (Michael Cheng)

"I have brought you glory on earth by finishing the work you gave me to do." (John 17:4)

Jesus prays this as part of his high priestly prayer. He said that he finished the *ergon* work that the Father gave him to do. Jesus had fulfilled his mission on earth and was about to go to the cross. Likewise, God has given specific *ergon* for each of us to do. We bring God glory through our work, by doing it well and with integrity. We are to reflect God's character in the work that we do, whether it is running a business, being a teacher, or being a parent. (Joyce Dalrymple)

So we are ambassadors for Christ, since God is making his appeal through us; we entreat you on behalf of Christ, be reconciled to God. (2 Cor. 5:20)

We often think of this passage in terms of . . . God using us to help other people come to faith. An image-bearer lens has helped me to see in a fuller sense that in order for this to be true we must image God well. Faith comes through hearing the word (Rom. 10), but often our behavior creates barriers that cause our words to fall on deaf ears. When it comes to our vocations, our greatest testimony is not just in what we say, but also the quality of our work. If we are bad employees who execute our jobs in a careless or subpar way, we inadvertently create a wall between us and those we work with. Not only is our character called into question, but so is the God we claim to know. (John Thompson)

So let us not grow weary in doing what is right, for we will reap at harvest time, if we do not give up. So then, whenever we have an opportunity, let us work for the good of all, and especially for those of the family of faith. (Gal. 6:9–10)

I've always understood this passage as an encouragement to keep doing what's right, as opposed to what's wrong—to obey and not sin. But, when viewed in light of my calling to image God in this world, it takes on a richer significance. As an imager of God, I have responsibility and authority. When I steward well all that he has entrusted to me, I draw attention to his wisdom and power. This stewardship takes effort, intentionality, an appreciation for my high calling, and a commitment to "work for the good of all," so that "we will reap at harvest time." . . . God's kingdom continues its steady march toward its full arrival. (Ryan Carson)

He is the image of the invisible God, the firstborn of all creation. For by him all things were created, in heaven and on earth, visible and invisible. (Col. 1:15–17)

In the traditional approach to this passage, we might not realize that "visible and invisible" does not just refer to spirits and demons. It also refers to the potential within creation to produce amazing things. There is the potential for fish to feed the stomach, for wood to build homes and furniture, for sand to create glass for light or silicon chips for computers, for minerals to create power to run a city, for medical advancements to save the population from another plague. There is great potential in all of creation to build up and beautify rather than to simply consume and destroy. (Clint Fisher)

These student examples not only share meaningful insights, they illustrate the formative process that comes from introducing the basic concepts of *who we are as image-bearers*, *what is the kingdom purpose of our work*, and *how to do good work in a good way*, and then asking questions and encouraging disciples to make the discoveries. It is fairly certain that what people discern for themselves in the Scriptures will stay with them far longer than anything they hear in a class or a sermon.

God's Spirit will speak powerfully through the word of truth, if we encourage people to develop new eyes to see, new ears to hear, and a heart willing to obey in their daily life of work.

RESOURCE

Questions and Passages for Reading Scripture through an Image-Bearer Lens

Here are possible questions to include in a Bible study to help people learn to read Scripture in a way that opens them up to new insights about working with kingdom purpose.

- In what way does this passage reference vocation? For example, is it set in a workplace, or does it depict people doing work tasks? Are there work-related terms?

- What does this passage teach us about who God is and the qualities we may reflect as his image-bearers? How are these qualities present in your work?

- What is the place of this passage in the big kingdom story? What part(s) of the four-chapter gospel story does it tell? Examples:

    Creation: "The heavens are telling the glory of God." (Ps. 19:1)

    Fall: "I do not do the good I want, but the evil I do not want is what I do." (Rom. 7:19)

    Redemption: "For God so loved the world that he gave his only Son." (John 3:16)

    Restoration: "They shall beat their swords into plowshares." (Mic. 4:3)

- What does this passage say about your kingdom purpose—to glorify God, bless people, draw others to Christ, and enable the world the flourish?

- How does this passage equip you for doing productive work in a good way?

- Are there ways this passage speaks to your specific vocational calling?

- What applications can be drawn from this passage to your ministry of work?

Selected Passages

If you're looking for a place to start with Bible studies for vocational discipleship, here is a partial—very partial—list of foundational passages: *Gen. 1:26–28; 2:15–18; 3:17–19; Exod. 20:9–10; Prov. 8:22–31; Eccles. 2:24; Isa. 48:18; 65:21–22; Ezek. 16:49; 18:14–18; John 5:17; Eph. 2:10; 4:28; 6:7; Col. 1:9–10; 3:22–24; 2 Thess. 3:6–12; Titus 3:7–8; 1 Pet. 4:10; Rev. 21:22–27.* (For a more comprehensive resource, see the Bible commentary produced by the Theology of Work Project, www.theologyofwork.org.)

We also recommend that, as a vocational discipler, you personally reflect on Paul's letters to other disciple-makers—Timothy, the Thessalonians, and Titus—in an image-bearer context, as a guide to "rightly explaining the word of truth" (2 Tim. 2:15).

Also, review the examples set by prophets who spoke out to powerful business leaders and their political allies, confronting unjust workplace practices in their day. These passages include: *Isa. 1:23; Jer. 5:23, 25–31; Ezek. 22:29; Hos. 12:5–8; Amos 5:11–12; 8:4–6; and Micah 7:2–3.*

23

REVISIONING HEAVEN: WORK IN ETERNITY

CASE STUDY

The day after the funeral, Terrence visited his father, Leroy. They talked quietly about the service, about the friends who had left gifts and cards, and about how much they both missed Cora, Terrence's mother. Then Terrence mentioned that he was going back to work the next day.

Leroy sighed. "Your mother loved her job so much. Everyone in her office has been so kind. We kept talking about retirement, but she was never ready. I've never known anyone who poured as much into her work as she did."

"She's earned her rest now, Dad," Terrence said, echoing what the minister had said at the funeral.

Leroy looked up at his son. "Is that what you really believe? That your mother is just sitting around on a cloud somewhere?"

"I guess so . . . Well, maybe not a cloud—Jesus talked about a mansion with lots of rooms . . ."

"Your mother helped design airport hotels. She was proud of creating beautiful, homey spaces where people felt welcomed when they arrived in a new place. You don't think she's already up to her elbows in helping Jesus design that heavenly mansion?"

Terrence was silent, taking it in.

"Now as for you, my boy . . ." Leroy voice had a lighter tone. "I don't think there's a need for probation officers in heaven. So, when your time comes to meet Jesus, you'll have to find a new career!"

"If Heaven Is What You Think It Is, I Don't Really Want to Go There!"

One of the most powerful influences on the way people work on earth is what they believe about heaven. But many people, Christians included, have vague ideas about heaven that typically don't include meaningful, purposeful work. This is reflected in the language typically used to describe heaven: "eternal rest," "eternal reward," "afterlife." In the words of a traditional hymn,

Let us labor for the Master from the dawn till setting sun,
Let us talk of all His wondrous love and care;
Then when all of life is over, and our work on earth is done,
And the roll is called up yonder, I'll be there.[1]

Since the church-centric framework leads people to believe that God is more present with them in church than on the job, why wouldn't they assume that eternal life in God's presence means the absence of work?

This goes hand in hand with the assumption, more influenced by Greek dualism than the Bible, that we will shed our physical existence when we reach heaven. In this vision, our heavenly forms will be disembodied, more purely "spiritual." The wedding supper will be metaphoric; our praises will be sung in some ethereal manner.

"Nearly every Christian I have spoken with has some idea that eternity is an unending church service. . . . We have settled on an image of the never-ending sing-along in the sky," writes John Eldredge in *The Journey of Desire.* He also acknowledges that many are not as excited about this potential future as they feel they should be. "Our heart sinks. *Forever and ever? That's it? That's the good news?* And then we sigh and feel guilty that we are not more 'spiritual.'"[2]

We, the authors, frankly admit: If heaven is just what the old hymns say it is, we will be disappointed.

Heaven by Design

Randy Alcorn, who made an exhaustive study of the Scriptures and theological teachings on heaven, arrived at a quite different conclusion. When Jesus said, "I go to prepare a place for you," he meant a tangible place, not for disembodied spirits, but for humans with actual bodies. Those bodies will be transformed in some way, but in their essence will still be physically human. Tom's colleague Charles Hooper calls this coming "H.O.M.E.": "Heaven on Modified Earth."

What God intends people to do in this new home is a continuation of the work originally commissioned to humanity at creation.

What we are suited for—what we've been specifically designed for—is a place like the one God made for us: Earth. . . . We'll see from Scripture an exciting yet strangely neglected truth—that God never gave up on his original plan for human beings to dwell on Earth. In fact, the climax of history will be the creation of new heavens and a new Earth, a resurrected universe inhabited by resurrected people living with the resurrected Jesus (Revelation 21:1–4).[3]

Vocational discipleship helps people grasp that the end of this life is *not* the end of their kingdom purpose. No one knows for certain what God has prepared for us (1 Cor. 2:9), but we do know that heaven is an integral part of God's design—not a tacked-on epilogue or a do-over. Imagine a "new heaven and new earth" where sin and the curse have been utterly defeated, and where people can freely work to pursue God's original purpose for creation.

Talking Points for Heaven and Work

While there is much to be said on the topic of heaven (Alcorn's book is 789 pages!), here we highlight four points that can help workers "set [their] minds on things that are above" (Col. 3:2), and recognize how these heavenly realities connect with their work on earth. Vocational discipleship encourages reflection on heaven as a fulfillment of our earthly toils, rather than an escape from them.

To make this less abstract, let's follow a hypothetical example: Judith is the secretary at a furnace and air-conditioning repair business. Like many of us, Judith tends to stay focused on the day-to-day avalanche of tasks in a busy office. She tends not to spend time thinking about how answering phones, sending invoices, and filing paperwork may have eternal significance.

As a vocational discipler who encourages Judith to grow spiritually in the context of her work, how can you help her understand about heaven?

God's Kingdom Purpose for Work Is Eternal

What if heaven is a continuation of the activity commissioned by God to the first humans at creation, before humanity rebelled against their Creator? What if instead of an "afterlife," heaven is "fullness of life"? What if heaven is not the absence of work, but the fulfillment of God's design through meaningful, purposeful work?

Judith went to a seminar at her church called "Your Work Is Your Ministry," where she saw her job in a whole new light. She learned how her work contributes to the flourishing of the world by making homes and businesses more hospitable, healthful, and conducive to productive work. Now, she tries to be mindful of how she is a witness to Christ to customers, and she looks for ways to bless people—like covering the furnace repair bill for a newly widowed woman in her church. She knows that working in heating and air conditioning is her calling.

But she always assumed that her job would become irrelevant in heaven. After all, won't heaven be a perfect, climate-controlled environment? Or will people's resurrected bodies even feel sensations of hot and cold?

We find clues to our heavenly future in the last chapters of Revelation. There, we get a picture of God living with people in the midst of his creation, the new heavens and the new earth. The setting is a city: the New Jerusalem, with buildings, streets, artistry, landscaping, and infrastructure. It is a place of beauty, healing, joy, wonders, and intimate connection between God and his beloved people.

The language in these passages is poetic, not precise. Mysteries abound. Some transformed elements are beyond our comprehension—such as the implications of God being the light source, replacing the sun. But in the description of heaven as a "city," filled with diverse cultures and their products, there is a hint that the work associated with maintaining a city and human society will continue. In the references to the natural elements integral to the design of the city—minerals, water, the tree with healing leaves—there is a hint that the work associated with tending and cultivating creation will continue. Although God lives in the heavenly city, he entrusts its care to its human residents.

God's first command to humankind was to fill the earth and rule over it (Gen. 1:28). Adam and Eve were charged with the work of harnessing the abundance God had prepared for them in Eden. Scripture gives no indication that this divinely appointed mandate will be retracted for those who enter paradise. Rather, Revelation 22:5 declares, "They will rule forever." Just as God prepared a garden and put people in it to make it productive, Jesus has gone ahead to "prepare a place" (John 14:2–3) where God's people will work as caretakers of its abundance. The beginning of the story harmonizes with the final chapters.

In this vision, heaven will not be perfect, in the sense of being unchanging or complete. Our work of exercising dominion and developing potential in heaven will never be completed, because God's creation has infinite potential! Rather, heaven will be perfect in the sense that all its residents "will bring their glory into it" (Rev. 21:24). Every gift and talent will be dedicated to the flourishing of God's city, unifying its inhabitants in fulfilling their designed purpose.

A vocational discipler could help Judith explore what it means to be a reigning caretaker in the city of God. If her work brings God glory on earth, then why wouldn't her work be an expression of her worship in heaven? What will her contribution be to the fulfillment of God's design? The laws of thermodynamics are part of God's good creation, not a result of the curse, and so are human labors to learn and harness these powers for the good of all. If residents of heaven do enjoy a perfect climate—without byproducts of pollution or noxious chemicals—then it makes sense to assume that will result from people applying their God-given scientific skills, coordinated by good secretarial management.

Work on Earth as You Would in Heaven

Christianity is unique among religions in the portrayal of work as part of paradise. The blessing of heaven is not that we won't have to work, but that we will finally get to work as God intended. We will experience work without the stain of sin, without the tyranny of the curse, in the full light of justice, among people with whom we are deeply bonded. As God's beloved community, we will have different tasks but one common purpose: to worship God through the work of reigning. And with God in our midst, we will all unendingly and equally enjoy the fruits of our labor. We will finally see what is possible when we work to our fullest capacity to bring out the fullness of creation's potential.

But here on earth, Judith often gets frustrated at work. The copier breaks down, customers are late paying their bills, the repair staff gripe at her, and her manager rarely seems to appreciate all she does. Sometimes she covers up her mistakes rather than admitting responsibility. A vocational discipler might observe that she is a hard worker and ask, "What parts of your job would give you joy, if you could do them without frustrations?" For Judith, this would be taking customer requests and matching their specific need with the technician with the right skills. She likes seeing customer satisfaction after old appliances are replaced with more efficient, environmentally friendly ones. She likes keeping the wheels of the business running smoothly, so more people get helped and more income allows the business to grow.

If only she could do this kind of work without the conflicts, rivalries, worries, and errors! It's not what she might want to do for eternity—eventually she might want to learn new skills and try new jobs—but she can certainly imagine this being her calling for a millennium or so. Reflecting on this will give her more joy and help her remain peaceful the next time the copier breaks down.

The discipler might also ask, "Imagine yourself working in heaven. Are there ways you would be working differently there that would give others more perfect fulfilment and joy?" Immediately, Judith thinks of her tendency to gossip with repair staff. She wouldn't do that in heaven. She also wouldn't "lose" messages from customers who annoy her or blame the supplier for a shipment she forgot to order. Making those changes now is part of doing God's will on earth as it is in heaven.

Your Work Matters for Heaven

One day, Judith arrived at work unsettled by a program she listened to on her commute. The radio preacher was talking about the end times when "the elements will be destroyed by fire" (2 Pet. 3:10). Since every material thing will be dissolved to make way for eternity in the new heavens and the new earth, he said, the only work that really matters in this life is preparing souls for judgment. We should live for what really counts.

As Judith went through her day, she found herself wondering whether all the tasks she does are ultimately all for nothing. Perhaps she should find a vocation that will have more lasting value to God.

A discipler could propose to Judith an alternative biblical interpretation: that God's intent is not to annihilate his creation but to reclaim and transform it. Just as Jesus' resurrected body was transformed yet was still recognizable and physical, the "new heavens and the new earth" (Rev. 21:1–2) will be connected meaningfully, though mysteriously, with our present reality. As Tom Nelson explains in *Work Matters*,

> God's original creation will not be wasted, it will be purified. If we believe that the earth—everything about it and everything we do on it—is simply going to one day be abolished and disappear, then the logical conclusion is that our work is virtually meaningless. . . . But if our daily work, done for the glory of God and the common good of others, in some way carries over to the new heavens and new earth, then our present work itself is overflowing with immeasurable value and eternal significance.[4]

When people get to heaven, "God will wipe away every tear from their eyes; there shall be no more death, nor sorrow, nor crying. There shall be no more pain, for the former things have passed away" (Rev. 21:4). This is the sense in which we can understand what gets left behind. God will destroy that which destroys his good creation. It is not human enterprise that is temporary, but anything that robs it of its kingdom purpose.

The work of God's people that fulfills the creation mandate—work that tends creation, unfurls discoveries, multiplies usefulness, designs beauty, promotes wellness, fosters order, strengthens community, and governs with justice—glorifies God on earth and is contiguous with the new earth and new heaven. Work done here on earth to right wrongs—to prevent harm, heal hurts, restore brokenness, wipe away tears, and reverse injustice—follows Jesus in preparing the way for a heavenly kingdom free from sin and the curse. The value of our earthly *ergon* is not overshadowed but illuminated in the light of heaven.[5]

A vocational discipler would affirm to Judith that inviting people to know Jesus, experience his mercy, and live forever in God's presence is of the utmost importance. But they would also remind her that God did not create us in order for Jesus to redeem us. He redeemed us so that we could be restored to the original purpose of living in God's presence as faithful image-bearers entrusted with his creation. Work was part of God's plan from the beginning, and the fruits of our labor will still be part of God's plan when it reaches its fulfillment. Revelation 21:24–26 describes people bringing "the glory and the honor of the nations" into the New Jerusalem. In some fashion, all that we do here that contributes to the best of humanity will be incorporated into our heavenly existence and thus also has eternal value. That includes Judith's work of helping to make the earth more habitable for image-bearers. According to Revelation 14:13, this work (her *ergon*) will follow her.

What Are We Looking Forward to?

In Jesus' parable of the talents in Matthew 25:21, the master says to his fruitful servants: "You have been trustworthy in a few things, I will put you in charge of many things; enter into the joy of your master." This parable implies several things about the afterlife: (1) our reward for good work includes more challenging work ("I will put you in charge of many things"), (2) this work will be joyful ("Enter into the joy . . ."), and (3) God also takes joy in our work (". . . of your master").

Redeemed image-bearers will share God's joy in being able to work unhindered by sin and free from the effects of the curse. Labor will no longer be wearisome or woeful. We will finally get to see what is possible when we work to our fullest capacity to bring out the fullness of creation's potential, in loving community with others who share the same purpose. Vocational discipleship not only encourages those saved by Christ to eagerly anticipate and invite others into this heavenly future, but also to recognize how they are already called, gifted, and positioned to contribute to it in their current work. For discouraged workers, Lesslie Newbigin's words offer comfort:

> Every faithful act of service, every honest labor to make the world a better place, which seemed to have been forever lost and forgotten in the rubble of history, will be seen on that day [at the final resurrection] to have contributed to the perfect fellowship of God's kingdom.[6]

RESOURCE

Vocational Prayer Walk

Take a prayer walk with the person you are discipling to cultivate a focus on the value of work in God's plan. Prayer walking has been defined as "praying on-site with insight."[7] Choose a route that will take fifteen to twenty minutes to walk, preferably in a commercial area. You can pray silently and compare notes afterward, or pray aloud in a quiet conversational tone. Unless the Spirit moves you to interact with people you encounter, the purpose of the prayer walk is not to pray with individuals directly but to interact with God about the gifts and needs related to work in the community.

Be intentional about seeing the community through the lens of work and its kingdom purpose. Suggested prayer points with examples are given below.

Thank God for Businesses, Workers, and the Products of Their Labor

- *Thank you, God, for these beautiful flowers that someone has planted and tended with such skill!*

- *Thank you, God, for this bank and all the fruitful enterprise that it makes possible in our community.*

- *God, thank you for these dedicated childcare workers, who nurture children so their parents can work at the jobs you appointed for them.*

Ask God's Blessing on Workers

- *May God bless the healing hands of the health-care workers in this clinic.*

- *God bless the servers, the kitchen staff, and all those whose labor went into producing the meals served at this restaurant.*

- *God, please watch over these security guards and the business they protect.*

Seek God's Mercy in Relation to Work

- *God, I pray for the decisions that judges will make in this courthouse today, that they would reflect your love of justice.*

- *God, I pray for those so desperate for funds that they borrow from this payday lender. May you lead them to compassionate care and opportunities for good work with income sufficient for their needs.*

- *God, may you bring a business into this boarded-up shop that will be successful, a good employer, and an asset in the community.*

Pray for each person to discover their identity as God's precious image-bearer, to know Jesus as their redeemer, and to pursue their unique calling fruitfully through their work.

24

RESISTING COMPROMISE

CASE STUDY

During college, four years of participation in the campus ministry leads John to believe that the highest calling would be for him to become a campus minister himself. He seriously considers this, but comes to realize that he is wired for the business world. Shortly after graduation, he marries his college sweetheart and begins his career as a regional salesman with a small manufacturer.

A few months later, he is sitting across the table from what looks to be his first big deal. John, however, senses that the buyer is about to sign the contract under a slight misunderstanding of what he has in fact promised. John has a nagging feeling he should clarify this possible misunderstanding, but he can't think of a single Bible passage or sermon that would apply.

With only the slightest sense of compromise, he remains silent and the deal is struck. John heads back to his office, contract in hand, and receives an atta-boy from his boss and a small bonus in recognition of his early success. When he returns home that night, he basks in the admiration of his new bride. For the next few Sundays, still uneasy in his spirit, John listens intently to the sermons from the pulpit, the teacher in Sunday school, and the discussions in his discipleship group, but he doesn't hear anything to suggest that he acted improperly.

Fast-forward to the end of the year sales competition. John's team stands atop the leader board, with another region close on their heels. If his team wins, they will all be taken on a special vacation cruise. John's young bride really wants to go. His boss comes to him to strategize over a large pending deal that John has been negotiating, which could put their team over the top. John explains that the potential customer is hesitant because of one important feature their product lacks.

The boss winks and then instructs, "Tell the customer that feature is being added, maybe as soon as next quarter." That does not accord with the timeline John has heard. Again, he searches his memory of Christian teachings he has received, but all he can think of is the command to "obey your masters as in the Lord." He has a vague impression that you were to do whatever the boss said.

Assured that the desired feature would soon be added, the customer agrees to the deal, and John's team wins the cruise. Once again, John receives praise from his boss, coworkers, and wife. And once again, he listens intently to the sermons from the pulpit, the teacher in Sunday school, and the discussions in his discipleship group and hears nothing to suggest that he has acted improperly.

"I am saved by grace, not by works," John says to himself. "The bonus is a sign that God is blessing my work. Besides, all my success allows me to tithe and be generous to meet others' needs." Later, when a coworker is fired to placate the customer's complaints about the failed upgrade, the ethical cloud hanging over John grows larger. But no one at church talks about it, so he keeps pushing it aside.

As John continues to be promoted, he is drawn into more and more questionable practices. But John tells himself each time that he is only imitating things he sees other business leaders do (including prominent Christians), and that he is not committing any sin he has heard about at church. John continues to tithe his profits faithfully.

The leadership team at church takes note of his success and offers him a position on the elder board. In the interview process, they ask questions about his family's spiritual life, his personal sexual purity, his evangelism and discipleship practices, and his church attendance. It does not strike him until later that nothing was said about his business practices.

John soon ascends to executive management in the firm and finally to the role of CEO. He recognizes that he may have cut a few corners or walked over a few people to get there. The higher he goes the more pressure he feels to do whatever it takes to gain an advantage over the competition and increase profit. But he tells himself that he is only following what other people in his position have done. He tells himself that the company is better off with someone who identifies as a Christian at the helm. He resolves to give even more generously to the church's ministries now.

John heads back to his office, promotion in hand, and enjoys the congratulations of his peers and members of the church board. He basks in the admiration of his (now not-so-young) bride. At his first elder board meeting, he is called out for his generous gift to the building fund and his excellent track record in evangelism.

The entire church—including his wife—is shocked when John is arrested for tax evasion and fraud. No one had taught John that God cares about the kingdom purpose of his work. No one had held John accountable for doing good work in a good way.

Do Not Conform

A key passage for disciplers is Romans 12:1–2:

> I appeal to you therefore, brothers and sisters, by the mercies of God, to present your bodies as a living sacrifice, holy and acceptable to God, which is your spiritual worship. Do not be conformed to this world, but be transformed by the renewing of your minds, so that you may discern what is the will of God—what is good and acceptable and perfect.

Doing good work in a good way will involve swimming against the current in some way—whether that current is the demands of a supervisor, the expectations of clients, the standard set by competitors, or the general norms of our culture. Conforming to this world always involves a compromise of faith. Doing good work in a good way inevitably requires sacrifice. As disciplers, we hold followers of Christ accountable to offer themselves to God alone. We support the ongoing process of "the renewing of your minds" that brings transformation for fruitfulness.

Here are some strategies for helping people to be renewed, resist compromise, and stand firm in "what is good and acceptable and perfect" as they work out their calling with kingdom impact.

Hold to Purpose

For some, discovering the kingdom purpose of one's work is a life-altering moment. Like following Christ, this is more than a one-time decision—it involves the daily recommitment to focus on what matters. You, the discipler, can help by periodically reminding people of how their work serves the fulfillment of God's design for creation, the advancement of Jesus' redemptive work, and the eternal glory of God. Read the Scriptures together to help disciples grow in understanding the place of their work in the four-chapter gospel story. Ask questions like, "How are you God's representative serving his goals today? How are your work tasks this week helping God's world to flourish?"

Keep Perspective

Keep reminding image-bearers that "being renewed in your mind" is not a passive experience. It is a choice to refocus, minute by minute, on our Maker's point of view. It is reframing the present challenges from the angle of eternity (2 Cor. 4:17–18).

There is a pattern in Scripture of shifting focus from what seems lacking to seeing what is available for God to use in accomplishing kingdom purpose: a handful of flour and oil (1 Kings 17:8–16), or a few small loaves and fishes (Matt. 14:17–19). This is not simply the "power of positive thinking." Disciplers help people readjust their perspective to stay focused on the reality that a good God is Lord of all, and that this God "has given us everything needed for life and godliness" (2 Pet. 1:3). In other words, the people you disciple already have all the raw ingredients to work fruitfully.

Support this perspective by initiating conversations: "Let's think about this situation from the perspective of being God's image-bearer, called to work with kingdom purpose. What has God given you to work with? How do you think God might view this situation? What do you know to be true and important from a kingdom perspective?"

Foster an Attitude of Gratitude

"Whatever is true, whatever is honorable, whatever is just, whatever is pure, whatever is pleasing, whatever is commendable, if there is any excellence and if there is anything worthy of praise, *think about these things*" (Phil. 4:8; italics added). Help people take stock of everything about their work that is "honorable, pleasing, commendable," and so on. Lead them in exercises to acknowledge with gratitude the opportunities, resources, assets, capacities, connections, and authority God has entrusted to them in order to work with kingdom purpose.

As needed, point to the simple directive in Philippians 2:14: "Do everything without grumbling" (NIV). If someone is doing a lot of complaining, they're probably not seeing their work from a kingdom perspective.

Cultivate a Jubilee Mindset

The principle of Jubilee outlined in Leviticus 25 established that "every fiftieth year, all leased or mortgaged lands were to be returned to their original owners, and all slaves and bonded laborers were to be freed" (Lev. 25:10). This bold policy was the means of keeping families from falling into crippling debt, preventing massive concentration of wealth and power, and "ensuring that everyone has access to the means of making a living and escaping multi-generational poverty."[1] This Jubilee passage describes how business decisions should be made with this fifty-year cycle in mind.

While the practical implications of this policy today are complicated, it's clear that if people want to renew their minds to discern God's will, then they need to think inter-generationally. The person you disciple may be pressured to make business or career decisions based on short-term gains. Ask questions to get at the longer-term impact on their household, their business, and their community, as well as broader social and environmental implications. Encourage people to plan—as much as possible—for productivity that spans generations.

Emphasize Stewardship

Disciples need occasional reminders that everything they have—resources, skills, influence, and so on—was entrusted to them for the fulfillment of God's purposes. Every worker must wisely invest what God has given them to bring about the fruitfulness God desires. If a worker invests these gifts and resources productively, then they will hear, "Well done, good and faithful servant!" (Matt. 25:21 NIV). When people are distracted by fear, greed, lethargy, or other pathways to compromise, refreshing their vision of God as the primary stakeholder in their work can provide an incentive for them to keep pressing on. Encourage people to practice saying to God, "I am the Lord's servant" (Luke 1:38 NIV).

Restoration after Error

Faced with pressure to compromise, to think and act in ways that are not faithful to being God's redeemed image-bearer, even the most dedicated follower of Christ will slip up on the job. Once they take a step onto the wrong path, Christians face further temptation—to blame others (Adam), to justify their actions (Eve), to cover it up (Joseph's brothers), even to utterly sell out (Judas). It is at this juncture that discipleship is especially critical.

You may find yourself in the position of needing to confront a disciple about unbiblical perspectives or practices. "If someone is caught in a sin, you who live by the Spirit should restore that person gently. But watch yourselves, or you also may be tempted" (Gal. 6:1).

We recommend consulting discipleship resources for details on how to confront and lovingly restore someone when they have taken a wrong path. Here is what that process might look like for John, whom we met at the beginning of the chapter.

After paying a hefty fine and serving a short sentence, John hires a Christian coach to help him rebuild his reputation—and his business.

The coach helps John understand that he is called to business as his ministry as an image-bearer. He walks with John through Scriptures on work in kingdom purpose. When his coach explains the principles of biblical fruitfulness, John finally understands that he not only committed a crime, but he had failed to work with excellence and integrity, which were violations of key principles in doing good work in a good way. He had compromised his ministry for the sake of personal advancement, and he had valued the admiration of people over pleasing God.

When John was arrested, he felt disgraced. But now, he feels genuine remorse. The next time he is in church, the gospel story strikes him in a way it had never done before. He had let everyone down, had failed to honor his Creator and Lord with the business resources entrusted to him. But after the service, John slips away again, to pray to Jesus and appeal to his mercy.

The next time John is with his coach, he shares about the experience of knowing that he has received forgiveness and the gift of the Spirit to guide his next steps. "At first I thought this was God's way of telling me I should leave the business, that I should go work for a ministry instead. Then I remembered: this is my ministry! God is giving me a fresh start to use my gifts and experience to be productive in a good way, and to put the kingdom of God first this time."

At this, John's coach radiates joy. "God is pruning you, and you know what that means? As long as you remain humble and open to correction, and put on the armor of God to resist compromise, you will keep growing even more fruitful. It will be a challenge, but I'll help you every step of the way."

RESOURCE

A Process for Encouraging Accountability for Kingdom Purpose

"If someone is caught in a sin, you who live by the Spirit should restore that person gently. But watch yourselves, or you also may be tempted." (Gal. 6:1)

Discipleship includes biblical accountability to one another. The only way that people can "grow up in every way into him who is the head, into Christ" is by "speaking the truth in love" to one another (Eph. 4:15).

In a discipling relationship, when you observe unbiblical perspectives or practices, the first thing to remember is that "nothing is hidden from God. . . . He is the one to whom we are accountable" (Heb. 4:13 NLT). The people you disciple are answerable to God, not to you. So it's important not to take their shortcomings personally—as if you had failed. Other responses to avoid are judging, shaming, or bossing. You are to restore "gently."

On the other hand, if someone looks to you for spiritual guidance, you too are held accountable if you turn a blind eye to their persistent sin and fail to point them toward the way of Jesus (Ezek. 33:8). Discipling people to do "good work in a good way" means shining an intentional light on things that people often would rather keep hidden.

If you discover that someone persists in mistreating their employees, lying to their boss, cheating their customers, or taking advantage of their partners, what do you do? The following is a suggested process for addressing issues that hinder image-bearers in their calling, with a focus on restoring them to fruitful work toward kingdom purpose.

1. *Connect.* Start with the person, not the behavior. What else is going on in their job? What do they want to share about how they are doing in body, soul, and spirit?

2. *Check.* Don't tiptoe around. Lay out the actions or attitudes in question and share your interpretation of the situation. Then ask for their perspective.

3. *Inform.* Share a biblical perspective with an image-bearer lens on the situation. Identify what sources influence your understanding of these passages.

4. *Examine.* Ask questions that lead them to consider their own actions or attitudes in the light of specific biblical teachings and the general understanding of their kingdom purpose. Create space for the Holy Spirit to work.

5. *Invite.* Point the way to a different path. The aim is not to make people feel guilty but to urge them to "produce fruit in keeping with repentance" (Matt. 3:8). What practical steps could lead toward more kingdom productivity?

6. *Restore.* Encourage reconciliation with anyone they have harmed with their words or actions (Matt. 5:23–24). How can they make things right? (See Luke 19:1–9.)

7. *Reaffirm.* Reassure the person that they are, as ever, God's dearly beloved image-bearer—redeemed, called, positioned, and equipped for God's good kingdom purpose.

25

GOD EQUIPS DISCIPLE-MAKERS TO BE PRODUCTIVE

CASE STUDY

Kendra sat staring at the blank screen on her laptop. She was supposed to be preparing the homily for her midweek service at the large food manufacturing company where she served as chaplain. But her mind kept snapping back to several recent interactions with employees.

One had texted her to pray for his mother who was in intensive care, because he was worried that she might not live until the end of his shift and he wanted the chance to say goodbye. Another had stopped by her office with the news that he had just been laid off for repeated lateness (Kendra suspected his fifteen-year-old sedan was to blame). And then there was the email from a manager, asking her confidentially for a reference to a drug treatment program.

When Kendra went to the break room for a cup of coffee, a young female employee was there. She turned quickly away, but not before Kendra saw a glimpse of tear-stained eyes and a nasty bruise on one cheek. She made a note to check in with the woman later and gently ask about her relationship with her boyfriend.

Kendra's chaplaincy training had prepared her to minister to these employees and their life struggles. She really cared about them. She viewed them as her "flock" who all just happened to work at the same place. But as she returned to thinking about her homily, it crossed her mind to wonder how these stressed-out employees could stay motivated to care about processing and packing frozen vegetables.

Productivity for Vocational Disciplers

God values productivity. This is true for disciple-makers as well as disciples! God has gifted and positioned you to be effective in your good work of walking with others in their kingdom calling. This is no easy path. To keep growing in productivity, we encourage vocational disciplers to do these five things:

1. Keep growing spiritually. Be an active disciple yourself.

2. Keep growing in your craft by ongoing study of faith and work. Stay connected with other vocational disciplers to learn from one another.

3. Keep rooted in the "real world" by doing lots of listening to workers. Go to where people work and observe, ask questions, be a learner (see the Gospel@Work Day guide in Appendix B).

4. Practice self-care, especially when working in high-conflict situations. Maintain safe and healthy boundaries.

5. Be in an accountability relationship with someone worthy of respect, who can give you feedback, and confront you as needed.

To assess your productivity, it's vital to have the right unit of measurement. Vocational discipleship is ultimately not about tasks or behaviors—it's about *people*. "You yourselves are our letter . . . the result of our ministry," Paul wrote to the Corinthians (2 Cor. 3:3).

Christ-like love for the person you're nurturing in the faith is the ultimate measure of a discipler's impact (1 Cor. 13:1–3). This includes caring about the whole person, not just the time they spend at work. This doesn't mean taking on the role of a counselor or a social worker, but it does mean recognizing that the complex struggles in a person's off-work life will affect their ability to follow their kingdom calling on the job (and vice versa; workplace stress can negatively affect their personal health and family relationships).

Sometimes being a productive discipler means putting aside the prepared lesson to just listen and offer spiritual encouragement. You can't solve all their problems, but you can show you care. And by doing so, you earn more trust for your discipleship journey together.

Productive discipleship also requires accountability without judging. We can observe and ask questions, but we can't know fully what is happening in their life, or in their heart. Only one person has the right to judge, and that is Christ who died to redeem rather than condemn (Rom. 8:34). So, lean on the Spirit for discernment and urge people to turn to Jesus. "It is he whom we proclaim, warning everyone and teaching everyone in all wisdom, so that we may present everyone mature in Christ" (Col. 1:28).

Paul: A Role Model for Vocational Disciplers

As tentmaker, apostle, evangelist and church planter, Paul worked zealously "to make the word of God fully known. . . . It is [Christ] whom we proclaim, warning everyone and teaching everyone in all wisdom, so that we may present everyone mature in Christ" (Col. 4:25–29). In Philippians 3:12–16, Paul reflects on lessons learned in this calling:

Not that I have already obtained this or have already reached the goal; but I press on to make it my own, because Christ Jesus has made me his own. ... This one thing I do: forgetting what lies behind and straining forward to what lies ahead, I press on toward the goal for the prize of the heavenly call of God in Christ Jesus. Let those of us, then, who are mature be of the same mind; and if you think differently about anything, this too God will reveal to you. Only let us hold fast to what we have attained.

Below we explore the wisdom in this passage for the long road of vocational discipleship.

Keep Looking Forward

Even the master disciple-maker Paul, in his final epistle, did not claim to have arrived. Discipleship has no graduation ceremony, no retirement, no real "end." As long as people are image-bearers, they can make progress in their kingdom calling.

Never Take Growth for Granted

The path to spiritual maturity is a staircase, not an escalator! Movement comes only by intentional effort. If you are not "straining forward" with those you disciple in the workplace, then the currents of church-centric thinking or the idolatry of success will sweep them backward. Paul summarized spiritual growth in two phrases: "press on" and "hold fast."

Win Trust, Not Arguments

Note Paul's attitude toward those who disagreed with him: "If you think differently about anything, this too God will reveal to you." He didn't feel the need to insist that his followers immediately accept every word. He trusted God as the source of wisdom and illumination.

Many of the principles of vocational discipleship run contrary to people's ingrained assumptions. Don't stress out if your input is received initially with skepticism or even resistance. Let the learning process, and the Holy Spirit, do their work.

Titus: A Field Guide for Disciplers

Paul wrote to Titus, a church leader whom he called his "partner and co-worker" (2 Cor. 8:23), to instruct him in how to disciple others. In the letter's three chapters, "good work" is addressed five times. A key passage is Titus 2:11–14, where Paul says that God's grace teaches people to live in a godly way as they put their hope in Jesus, "who gave himself for us that he might redeem us from all iniquity and purify for himself a people of his own who are zealous for good deeds." In that last phrase, in other translations rendered "good work," we again meet the Greek words *kalon ergon*: getting useful work done in a way that multiplies goodness. Good work in the world is the outcome of good leadership in the church.

Following are lessons from Paul's letter to Titus to help you to be more productive as you equip others in their calling to *kalon ergon*.

Be a Role Model

"Show yourself in all respects a model of good works, and in your teaching show integrity, gravity, and sound speech that cannot be censured" (2:7–8). This doesn't mean that only perfect people get to be disciplers, because everyone is equally dependent on Jesus to be redeemed and purified (2:14). Teach with awareness that people will trust your words to the extent they see you "zealous" about the goal of putting them into practice in your own life.

A discipler must also model not being "greedy for gain" (1:7). Paul made a point of never profiting off of those whom he discipled (Acts 20:33–35; 1 Thess. 2:9–10).

Stay Focused on Your Purpose

Your calling as a vocational discipler is to equip image-bearers to work toward God's kingdom purpose. This is an urgent mission. Don't be distracted by anything trivial or counterproductive.

I desire that you insist on these things, so that those who have come to believe in God may be careful to devote themselves to good works; these things are excellent and profitable to everyone. But avoid stupid controversies, genealogies, dissensions, and quarrels about the law, for they are unprofitable and worthless. (3:8–9)

Value the People You Disciple

People will drive you crazy and will seem unteachable. Teach them anyway. Paul warns Titus about the undisputed reputation of the people he was sent to disciple: "Cretans are always liars, vicious brutes, lazy gluttons." But then he says, "For this reason rebuke them sharply, so that they may become sound in the faith" (1:12–13). There was to be no giving up on their faith, no questioning whether some people were beyond hope. The "goodness and loving kindness of God our Savior" patiently meets everyone where they are (3:4). Treat everyone as a bearer of God's image, invited by grace to be an heir of God's eternal kingdom.

Remember That Changing People Is the Holy Spirit's Job

Do the work of a discipler, and trust God to do the work of a Savior.

> When the goodness and loving kindness of God our Savior appeared, he saved us, not because of any works of righteousness that we had done, but according to his mercy, through the water of rebirth and renewal by the Holy Spirit. (3:4–5)

You can lay out a disciple's calling to kingdom work, but God's grace does not depend on how they respond to it—and neither does your favor in God's eyes.

A Coaching Framework for Discipleship

One of the most powerful productivity tools for vocational discipleship, which we also believe is compatible with Paul's model and teachings, is a coaching mindset. A coach is a dedicated helper, one who comes alongside another to build them up, in partnership with the *Paraklete* (the Greek word used for the Holy Spirit). Coaches are excellent listeners and discerners, who recognize the gifts and calling God has placed in others' lives and encourage their development. A biblical model for coaching is found in Barnabas, called the "Son of Encouragement," who affirmed Paul as a leader, believed in him, and stood by him. A coaching relationship blends affirmation and accountability, building a foundation of genuine care and investment that helps people face tough challenges with high expectations.

One of the key features of a coaching approach is that it encourages disciples to take ownership of their learning and growth toward working fruitfully with kingdom purpose. This is different from approaches that put the discipler firmly in the driver's seat. According to Christian coaching expert Keith Webb:

> There is a common tension that leaders experience. It feels easier and faster to lead from our authority, so we over-rely on advising, telling, and directing. In doing so, we do not release the gifting, calling, and creativity that God has built into the people we lead. . . . Adult learning theory tells us that people are more engaged in learning if they have a choice in the topic and can apply it right away. Coaching taps into both these motivations by asking the coachee to choose a topic that is relevant and immediately applicable.[1]

Tom and Heidi are both professional coaches who have seen the power of this approach. Over the years, I (Tom) have learned a fairly simple truth in the classes that I teach. My experience has been that people are far more likely to act on insights that they have come to themselves rather than ideas that I have laid out for them. (Interestingly enough, many of the conclusions they come to are identical to what I would have taught!) Thus, I've learned to rely on probing questions that help people come to their own conclusions. This is why we've provided a lot of sample questions in this book.

As I (Tom) prepare to meet with a disciple I incorporate a coaching mindset by doing three things:

1. I recognize that the meeting is an appointment ordained by the Lord of the kingdom.

2. I remember that my job is not necessarily to have all the brilliant answers, but to be present for the person in front of me. I prepare myself to stay focused on what is most important to them.

3. Since discipleship is their work, not just mine, I send an email to help them to prepare for our time, usually starting with a thought-provoking question. Based on past conversations, I might also suggest topics for our discussion.

I try to keep in mind that God is their boss—not me. If all I am doing is telling them how to behave in the workplace, and they don't truly grasp how their actions flow from their identity as God's image-bearer called to work fruitfully for kingdom purpose in alignment with the gospel story, then their obedience will be shallow and probably not sustainable.

We are not calling for abandoning all didactic forms of discipleship (such as preaching, teaching, or guided Bible studies), because these strategies do have an important role. But we are convinced that a coaching framework has the unique capacity to help people retrain their thinking from a church-centric to an image-centric orientation. For people who are steeped in dualism, a coaching approach is invaluable in helping them integrate a new kingdom mindset.

A coaching approach can also be particularly fruitful with long-time Christians who are generally well versed in Scripture. They know the "right" answers but perceive a gap in how their theology translates meaningfully into their daily life, especially their work. With this group, as Webb says, "The problem isn't too little information. The problem is too little application. This is where a coaching approach shines bright."[2] (See the resource page on coaching conversations below for more details.)

Called to Multiply

Growth comes from harnessing the potential inherent in creation. What vocational disciplers cultivate is the boundless capacity in image-bearers to be fruitful in their work. Patrick Choi, a student in Tom's class, shared this insight:

> The parable of the talents (Matthew 25:14–30) is one that I've read multiple times, but reading it with an image-bearer lens allows me to look into the verses a little deeper. . . . From the beginning, God ordained humans to extract value from His creation. Everything we use today, such as this laptop, was made from different parts of the earth. How can I continuously extract from the talents and gifts God has given me, so that they can be multiplied? Knowing that God has blessed every person in the world with specific gifts and talents, and that those are a reflection of God, should lead us to extract as much as we possibly can.[3]

Every Christian is called to support every other image-bearer in their calling to good work. While this book has addressed "disciplers," we don't mean to imply that this is a separate breed of Christian. Discipleship is the work of the whole body of Christ! Followers of Jesus are to be multipliers. As Randy Pope says, "Here is how we define the finish line: mature, equipped disciples who invest in the maturing, and equipping of other disciples."[4] This means that as you walk with a worker, one of the things you're preparing them for is to become a discipler to someone else, to help more people deploy their unique talents in God's kingdom work.[5]

Making Connections to Build up the Body

Ephesians 4:11–16 is a key passage for those called "to equip the saints for the work of ministry." While discipleship is often most impactful in one-on-one relationships or small groups, this passage makes it clear that the goal cannot be measured solely in individualistic terms. Rather, the intent of "speaking the truth in love" is that "the whole body, joined and knit together by every ligament with which it is equipped, as each part is working properly, promotes the body's growth in building itself up in love."

From a church-centric perspective, this passage appears to refer to a single congregation. But from an image-bearer perspective, the "whole body" also means Christians who are connected by the marketplace in a company, a community, an industry, even around the world. Believers in their various occupations are built up together in love, "as each part does its work" (v. 16 NIV).

Vocational discipleship thus has a multiplier effect in another way. You may only be able to connect with one or a few individuals at a time, but each one has the potential to connect with and uplift many others as they build on one another's kingdom contributions. The impact of vocational faithfulness has a ripple effect "until all of us come to the unity of the faith."

What does this look like? One example comes from a company that places nursing aides to provide home-based care to people incapacitated by age or disability. I (Tom) was a running buddy with the owner of the company. He and I would talk about work as we ran, in an informal discipling relationship.

One day, I could tell that something was bothering him, so I asked, "What's your struggle? What keeps you up at night?"

He shared that it was becoming difficult to find caring, capable employees, because they were not able to pay them much. He was attached to the individuals his company served and did not want to see them neglected.

Soon after that, I met a woman at church who worked with World Relief. I asked her the same question: "What's your struggle?"

She answered, "Finding jobs for refugees." A number of West African refugees had relocated to the area recently. They were good workers, but their lack of English and work experience made them a challenge to place in employment.

You can guess what came next. It was the perfect connection. I suggested my friend solve the biggest problem of his business by also solving the nonprofit's biggest problem.[6] That is the beauty of "the body's growth in building itself up in love."

RESOURCE

A Coaching Approach to Discipleship: The COACH Model®

Coaching expert Keith Webb advocates a coaching approach to Christian leadership development. Webb defines coaching as "an ongoing intentional conversation that empowers a person or group to fully live out God's calling."[7] Coaching is both a mindset and a structure for conversation.

Distinctives of a Coaching Mindset

Characteristics of a coaching approach include:

- Inviting the other person to take ownership of their learning and growth.

- Empowering the other person to define their goals for the conversation.

- Active listening—really giving the other person your attention.

- Asking powerful questions that promote new perspectives, deeper learning, and personal applications.

- Focusing not just on information but what people do with it—action oriented.

- Following up to increase learning and accountability.[8]

"Rather than prescribing, advising, or teaching the other person, coaches skillfully help the coachee to reflect more deeply, and draw out how God is guiding them."[9] The coaching approach requires trust that the Holy Spirit is already at work in the other person.

A key tool in coaching is the "powerful question."[10] This is a question that pushes the person to connect the subject material with their own experience, which may lead them to seek the guidance of the Holy Spirit. There is no single right answer. In fact, the coach likely may not know the answer either before they ask.

Overview of a Discipleship-Oriented Coaching Conversation

Below is an overview of Webb's COACH Model®, adapted for vocational discipleship. Each letter stands for a stage in the conversation.

C: Connect

Start by connecting with the person you're discipling to build rapport and trust. If applicable, follow up on action steps from a previous conversation. Here are some sample questions a vocational discipler might use:

- *Anything you want to tell me about how work and life in general is going for you?*

- *Let's check in with what you said you wanted to try after our last conversation.*

O: Outcome

Outcome is the intended result of the conversation. In a coaching approach, the discipler does not come with a preset topic; rather, the coachee determines the desired outcome and sets the agenda. Explore the outcome at the beginning of the conversation to help focus the conversation on whatever is most important and relevant to the worker.

- *What challenges or goals related to your work do you want to focus on today?*

- *Where do you sense God wanting to equip you in your work with kingdom purpose?*

A: Awareness

"Awareness is a reflective dialogue intended to produce discoveries, insights, and increased perspective for the coachee. . . . The coachee will see a greater number of options and, in the end, will make better decisions."[11] A vocational discipler might also lay out relevant Scripture passages and key faith and work principles for the coachee to consider in relation to their situation. In a coaching framework, the coach does not simply dispense information and wisdom, but guides the coachee in making the discoveries for themselves.

- *What does this Scripture passage say to you about the situation you are in at work?*
- *Which of the core faith and work principles relate to this challenge?*

C: Course

Building on these goals and insights, help the coachee determine a practical course of action. Ask questions and offer feedback but don't tell people what to do.

- *What specific spiritual discipline for work do you want to practice until our next session?*
- *What steps will you take to resolve the issue we discussed?*

H: Highlights

Highlights close the coaching session with a review of what the coachee found most meaningful in the conversation. This helps new learning or insights to "stick."

- *What insights did you gain today about how God designed you to work with kingdom purpose?*
- *What was an aha! moment for you today in reading Scripture through an image-bearer lens?*

Integrating a Coaching Approach

While professional coaches follow a specific set of guidelines in their coaching sessions, elements of a coaching approach can be integrated more informally into other forms of a discipling relationship. For example:

After studying a Bible passage, the Disciple-Maker can ask, "What will you do, based on your understanding of this passage?" Coaching a person to make specific, concrete, application is the essence of obedience (Matthew 28:20). . . . Listen and ask more questions to help the person reflect more deeply. Hold back your own stories and advice and draw out theirs. Ask the person you are meeting with to create a couple of action steps. Make it natural.[12]

Each discipler will find their own balance of teaching, asking, listening, and drawing out, based on the person and the situation. Experiment until you find the balance that works for you and the person you're discipling.

26

GROWING TOGETHER IN
SPIRITUAL MATURITY

Tom's Story

Soon after moving to Atlanta as a busy father of seven, with a growing business and church responsibilities, I received an email from someone on my church's staff asking me to meet with a church member who was seeking new employment after being laid off. I remember thinking, "I don't have time for this."

But almost immediately, I heard a voice from God that said, "If I send someone to you, I want you to meet with them." I argued back and forth. But the Lord won, and I made it a policy to respond in the affirmative whenever these requests came in the future.

After several years, my partners and I sold our business, and I migrated to my current career focus of leading Convene Christian CEO Roundtable groups. In 2012, I cut back on my consulting work in order to focus almost exclusively (with the exception of teaching at Metro Atlanta Seminary) on mentoring people who work outside the church. My wife came up with a rallying cry for this year of downsizing: "What the world needs is people with time for people!" By the end of the year, I was working half time and starting a second Christian CEO Roundtable.

On July 3 of the following year, I was heading into a long holiday weekend. A member of the Roundtable had just informed me he would be leaving the group. During the hour-long ride home from our meeting, I convinced myself that I had made a terrible mistake in downsizing. I was sure that all the members would be quitting soon, that I had put all of my eggs in a broken basket and would be left without income. Satan had gained control of my thought processes. By Sunday morning, I was literally curled up in a fetal position, certain that my world was about to come crashing down and not knowing how I was going to fix it.

That morning, I heard the Lord say to me: "All you can do is pay attention to the person I put in front of you. You need to always be present and serve that person—and I will take care of the rest."

What a burden was lifted. I realized then that when God calls, he also prepares.

By saying "yes" to God and the people he has set before me, I have gained a wealth of experiences. I have come within reach of my lifetime goal of personally impacting two thousand business leaders through discipling conversations. I have gotten to talk with a diverse array of workers, from students to CEOs to international entrepreneurs, helping them discover and apply their calling to kingdom purpose.

As a side benefit, it has created a great network for me of friendly connections. I am never wanting for people to help in my time of need. While this may sound less than altruistic, I believe that is how God intends our relationships in the body of Christ to work. As Paul explains in 2 Corinthians 8–9, the goal is mutual blessing.

You must have a clear sense of your purpose as a discipler in order to be effective in helping the people you disciple to claim their own kingdom purpose. If you're not clear in your vision, then this will be filled in for you—either by the church-centric paradigm (which measures the goal in terms of private spiritual disciplines and involvement with the church) or by the worldly success paradigm (which measures the goal in terms of career status and financial profitability). What goals are you heading toward in your ministry of vocational discipleship? And how can you tell if you are making progress?

Kingdom Purpose and Spiritual Maturity: Tom's Research

Colossians 1:28 suggests a goal for disciple-makers is "that we may present everyone fully mature in Christ." In my (Tom's) doctoral research, I explored how Christian C-level executives (department heads or senior management) experienced increased motivation to pursue spiritual maturity as a result of gaining clarity about their kingdom purpose.

For my dissertation project, I recruited six executives, all long-time Christians who served in lay leadership positions at their churches, to participate in a vocation-based discipleship group for nine months. This included developing a life plan that reflected their kingdom purpose in each area of their life, along with an operational plan to turn purpose into action. I then conducted interviews to assess the impact.

Ken, one of the participants in the study, described his view of spirituality before our discipleship group:

It was the activity matrix: How much time did I spend reading the Bible, am I doing quiet time, am I going to worship regularly, am I plugged into a Sunday school class. It was more about generically checking the boxes off . . . very dry and robotic obedience.[1]

Another participant, Bill, reflected,

> I think I was fairly typical of a lot of people who call themselves Christians. . . . A lot of us mentally separate life from work. . . . I thought of spiritual maturity and spiritual development as very disassociated from my calling.[2]

Although successful business leaders and exemplary churchgoers, these men had reached a "plateau . . . going through the motions." Each participant sensed that there was more to spiritual maturity, although they couldn't define it. They were hungry to understand how the gospel applied to the entirety of their lives, including their work.

At the end of the study, all the participants identified significant changes in how they understood their kingdom purpose, calling, and life plan. Their perspective on how God viewed their work was radically altered. Their satisfaction level and sense of full participation in God's kingdom skyrocketed. As they gained clarity on how their work mattered to God, they also gained motivation to grow in their faith. They gained a palpable sense of purpose for their work.

Daniel summarized the difference: "I want to have spiritual maturity be defined more by living out a life that is faithful to my purpose and calling." Ironically, the more these businessmen focused on God's connection to the part of their life typically perceived to be the *least* spiritual—their work—the more important their spiritual maturity became to them. As Bill put it: "Spirituality has invaded a big piece of life that it wasn't in before."[3]

New clarity around kingdom purpose leading to renewed energy for spiritual growth in every area of life, combined with a practical plan for fulfilling one's unique calling—that's the fruit of vocational discipleship. No wonder we often had the sense in this group that we were on holy ground!

Turning on the Light

After many years in church ministry, John Granada describes the shift that took place when he began to see his role in light of vocational discipleship:

> *God allowed me to be part of a church plant at a very young age. I was in a leadership role with people who spent most of their time in one full-time or sometimes two jobs. One of the greatest mistakes that as leaders I believe we made was not teaching our members about the relationship between work and their faith. I remember feeling guilty for having to work and attend undergraduate school because I didn't have enough time to be in the church building. Not only did I feel guilty myself, but inadvertently made others feel guilty and even consider leaving their jobs because it was interfering with the amount of time they could invest in the church.*

We failed to help church members see that their place of employment was as valuable of a calling as the church work. To see how they were contributing to the flourishing of the world as image-bearers, and that this was as pleasing to God as the church work. To help disciples see that if the Creator of the universe is a creative God, he has created us in his image to be creative beings also.[4]

Vocational disciplers have the privileged calling to partner with the Spirit and the Scriptures to open people's eyes to their ministry in their workplace.

What is the cost of *not* leading vocational discipleship—of continuing to let so many people work in the dark? The loss is measured in spiritual growth, in the development of gifts and calling, in authentic witness in the marketplace, and in an attitude of worship that permeates the rest of life. We must also consider the aggregate loss of the potential impact of millions of image-bearers exercising influence in their workplace and community. The tasks essential to God's design for creation do not get done.

Ultimately, the cost comes back to the body of Christ, as Barna's research report on Christians at work sums up: "The professional and spiritual stakes are high. A failure to provide vocational discipleship could be a failure to help Christians, especially younger ones, keep their faith."[5] The next generation of workers is clearly rejecting a church-centric paradigm, and vocational discipleship offers a compelling alternative vision.

The Dream

"People are hungry for vocational discipleship—even if they don't know it yet!"[6] Millions around the world are still seeking work that offers respect, safety, and enough income to support their household. Yet beyond this basic threshold, we all have an innate yearning to spend the majority of our time in productive activities that affirm our connection to God as image-bearers fulfilling our Creator's purpose. We are made for the deep satisfaction of labor that restores that which is broken and unleashes our world's potential for abundance, beauty, and wonder. Moreover, as God "has planted eternity in the human heart" (Eccl. 3:11 NLT), our souls long also for a heavenly vocation: work that is eternally meaningful, challenging, collaborative, fruitful, and delightful, bringing glory to God in the light of his loving presence—isn't that every worker's dream?

I (Tom) became animated decades ago by the vision that every Sunday, from every pulpit, every pastor would speak with relevance to the working life of church members. And they would do this because they understood that the ministry of the church does not belong only to pastors and "full-time" ministers, but to all who are called to do God's work in the world. In this vision, leaders would embrace their role to "equip [God's] people for works of service" (Eph. 4:12). A congregation eagerly gathering at church to be equipped to excel in the ministry God has called them to do throughout the week—shouldn't that be every pastor's dream?

Imagine communities functioning well due to the competence and diligence of its workforce, brimming with diverse, God-honoring culture, and teeming with entrepreneurial energy. Imagine marketplace leaders daily searching the Scriptures for wisdom to plan business strategy and resolve dilemmas. Every workplace is characterized by excellence, integrity, sustainability, equity, and kindness. Work is where talents are incubated and shared, where people find caring connections and second chances. Those who don't know Jesus yet come to see him more clearly in other image-bearers on the job. A community invested in lifting all boats in its harbor through productive, generous, meaningful employment—wouldn't that be every social change advocate's dream?

We believe that vocational discipleship is essential to filling in the gap between our current reality and this joyful vision. Sermons, books, videos, conferences, and other means of sharing content are important, but they can take us only part of the way. We must "build up each other" (1 Thess. 5:11) for faith at work. There is no substitute for discipleship that is personal, responsive and ongoing. People need someone who inspires them to step up to their calling, and who then walks alongside them, unpacking the Scriptures with them while they are "on the road" of their vocational journey (Luke 24:32). We must be equipped to guide, teach, challenge, encourage, empower, confront, restore, and celebrate one another as image-bearers working fruitfully with kingdom purpose. May the Lord grant that it be so.

RESOURCE

Assessing Growth in Vocational Discipleship

Vocational discipleship is about change and growth related to the three core questions:

1. *Who are you?* Disciples see themselves as God's image-bearers.
2. *What is your purpose?* Disciples understand the kingdom purpose of their work and the role of their individual calling.
3. *How will you fulfill your purpose?* Disciples develop their productivity in doing good work in a good way.

How can you tell if you're on track toward these goals? What changes are you seeing in those you disciple? (And are *you* also continuing to grow?)

The questions below point to the impact that should become evident as believers begin to see themselves as image-bearers and understand their work as kingdom calling.

How are they growing in working as an image-bearer?

- Do they have confidence in their identity as God's image-bearer, in work as well as in every area of their life?

- Do they view everyone else they encounter as image-bearers—and treat them accordingly?

- Do they sense a deeper connection with Jesus as "the exact imprint of [God's] being" (Heb. 1:2) and share this insight with others?

- Are they gaining and applying new insights by reading the Scriptures from an image-bearer perspective?

- Are they grasping the value and dignity of their image-bearing work as ministry that matters to God?

- Are they more motivated to grow in the spiritual dimension of the practical work that they do?

How are they growing in understanding their kingdom purpose?

- Do they know and value the contribution of their work to God's designs for his creation?

- Are they confident in their unique calling, rooted in how God has gifted and positioned them to pursue his eternal purposes?

- Are they developing a more integrated approach to their life by pursuing a seamless calling in church, work, family, and play?

- How are they working in ways that glorify God, bless people (including their family), and cause God's world to flourish?

- How is their work drawing people toward Jesus, with a growing passion for inviting others to join as co-laborers with him?

- How is their work reflecting God's "very good" plans for eternity?

How are they growing in productively doing good work in good ways?

- Are they seeking to maximize productivity that is rooted in the value of their work to God, beyond just personal gain?

- Are they practicing faith disciplines for maintaining healthy productivity, including observing the Sabbath, tithing, gleaning, stewardship, and accountability?

- Do they honor God by working with excellence, integrity, justice, and generosity, resisting compromise?

- Are they allowing God's Spirit to expose and depose idolatries associated with work, leading to greater contentment, joy, and peace?

- Are they following a life plan that builds intentionality around living with purpose in every key area of their life?

- Is their work fruitful in achieving its purpose for the flourishing of God's creation, "on earth as it is in heaven"?

APPENDICES

TOOLS FOR VOCATIONAL DISCIPLESHIP

APPENDIX A

LIFE PLAN

Vocational disciplers help image-bearers discover how God has uniquely shaped and called them to serve his kingdom purpose. A Life Plan is a valuable tool for understanding, articulating, and acting on this design. This resource helps people integrate their vocational calling with other areas of their life.

I (Tom) have used Life Planning in my coaching and discipleship work for many years. As I practice it, a Life Plan has five main components:

1. Define key statements, including:
   - Life Purpose Statement *(Why do you exist?)*
   - Core Values
   - Focus Verses/Life Quote
   - Life Vision

2. Map your key roles (e.g., spouse, parent, employee, church member):
   - Identify the main activities currently associated with each role
   - Assess how these activities relate to your Life Purpose Statement

3. In order to advance your purpose for each role, identify:
   - Broad strategies *(What path will take you in the right direction?)*
   - Specific objectives *(What goals are important right now?)*

4. Translate these objectives into specific action steps and schedule time for these steps on your calendar.

5. Create a "Dashboard" (a spreadsheet) to track this operational plan. First, prepare a cover page or header with a statement of your life purpose, core values, and life vision. Then for each of your key roles, set up a sheet with columns identifying your vision, strategies, short-term objectives, and critical action steps in that arena. Note how each role ties into your overall life purpose and vision.

For most effective use of a Dashboard, set aside time (15–20 minutes) each week to review the activity of the previous week, refresh your purpose, and schedule upcoming action steps. Preferably, do this together with your vocational discipler or a colleague.

These elements can be adapted and expanded as needed. The key is to build on a disciple's understanding of working as an image-bearer with kingdom purpose (as described in this book) with a thoughtful, candid exercise of life planning, applying their kingdom purpose to all the roles they are called to fulfill, and supplementing with a Dashboard to help them remain fruitful as they put purpose into practice.

Example from Tom Lutz's Life Plan

Life Purpose: *God has called, gifted, and positioned me to help his visionaries find, plan, and execute their unique role in his kingdom.*

Life Vision: *I will repay a significant return on my time, talents, and resources to God, who has graciously provided them. I will do so by developing businesses/ministries to serve the visionaries God has called to build his kingdom. I will maintain a strong marriage, family, and body, develop robust friendships, and invest in service to the community.*

Core strategies in my role as a businessman: *Spend my time on high-leverage activities, be patient and diligent at meetings each month.*

Sample of how this translates to specific objectives: *Eight prospect meetings per month; schedule four Kingdom Purpose Workshops; add personal coaching clients.*

Elements of an Effective Life Plan

As part of my doctoral research project, I worked with a small group of Christian business executives to facilitate a life planning process that went hand-in-hand with a curriculum exploring the purpose of their work in God's kingdom. Each of these men had previously developed a life plan, but without lasting impact. As one of them put it, "There was dust on it." By the end of our sessions, all of the group participants were interacting with their life plans in a daily or weekly rhythm.

My experiences point to several recommendations for helping others develop a Life Plan as a vital, evolving tool for vocational discipleship.

Stay Rooted in Kingdom Purpose

Our Life Planning process started with discovering how each group member was gifted, called and positioned to serve God's eternal kingdom purposes. They generated a unique Life Purpose Statement to stay anchored in this big picture. This helps people gain clarity and get "unstuck." As Bill Heaner explained, "Kingdom purpose brings all the chapters of your life together into one book. . . . Everything stems from that. My life has a direction, a destination."

Move from Purpose to Action

Executive Daniel Steere noted: "I once had a life plan, but it was a 30,000-foot view. I also had a weekly checklist of the things that I wanted to do. Those things just have never been connected." The Life Plan Dashboard offers disciples a valuable tool for bridging their higher calling with the practical action steps needed to keep moving in that direction. It also helps people discern what activities are peripheral to their kingdom purpose— providing a framework for when to say *no*.

Integrate Purpose across Life Roles

The Life Plan helps people resist compartmentalizing their calling and instead be the same person God has called them to be across the spectrum of their roles and relationships. Ken Hilburn described a sense of unifying "connection to big picture purpose, down to one-on-one time with the kids." It also challenges the dualism of having one set of values and disciplines at church and another on the job. A consistent calling helps people embrace the full use of their spiritual gifts and capacities at work.

Provide Accountability

Some in the group initially viewed accountability as producing results for goals imposed by someone else. They came to understand accountability as being responsible to God for fruitfulness in their unique kingdom purpose. The Dashboard is a tool for tracking progress toward specific objectives aligned with their calling. Here's what this looked like for Ken in his role as COO:

> *I have six things I look at every day that align with [my kingdom purpose]: to be a servant to those I work with, to be submissive and respectful to those I work for, and to be honest, passionate, and truthful. So in my devotional time I pray about those things—God, how am I going to be a servant today? It helps me have some structure and get my mind set going into the day.*

Expand and Revitalize Spiritual Life

The Life Plan process works best with people who have a foundation in the gospel, but whose spirituality is often shallow and narrowly defined. Taking ownership of their kingdom purpose often leads to a deeper movement of the Spirit in their life. Daniel testified,

> The Life Plan ties my calendar to the creation-fall-redemption-restoration metanarrative through my kingdom purpose. That makes my spiritual life so much more integrated, because otherwise my spiritual life becomes the thirty minutes I spend on personal devotions, the couple hours I spend at church on Sunday.... Now, my spiritual life is the whole thing.

Cultivate Joy

Discovering and implementing one's God-given design for kingdom purpose is energizing. A lawyer in the group shared:

> We did an exercise to match our calling with our skill set and our passions, and one of the things that jazzed me was defending people. God especially designed me to help represent people legally. So, I realized I needed to add that into my Life Plan. Now my mission statement is, "By God's grace I want to become more like him by loving, comforting, and defending those around me."

> There is a joy that comes from working out your life statement, when you know God is pleased with seeing the person that he designed, functioning the way he ought to. So, when I'm loving, comforting, and defending people with my work, there's a joy and peace that comes from that, a sense of hearing, "Well done, good and faithful servant."

Not everyone has the privilege of a job that lines up with their purpose. The Life Plan process can help people find creative ways to move in the direction of what "jazzes" them and pleases their Creator as well.

For more details and sample forms for Life Planning, contact Tom Lutz at tlutz@visionmarketdevelopment.com.

APPENDIX B

GOSPEL@WORK DAY

Overview

The Gospel@Work Day creates an opportunity for pastoral/church staff to spend time with church members *in their workplace setting*. This encounter helps church staff to better understand members' daily lives and to speak to the unique challenges of the workplace. It also gives working believers more confidence in reaching out to pastoral staff for job-related discipleship and support.

The first Gospel@Work Day was organized by Perimeter Church in Atlanta in 2014. Through a grant from the Kern Foundation, the initiative was expanded, evaluated, and developed for broader use. The program matches a pastor/church leader (the "Guest") with a church member who works outside the church (the "Host"). The pair may review a faith and work curriculum together in advance to prepare a theological foundation for their connection.

On a designated date, the Guest shadows their Host at their job site (including remote work from home), to experience as much as possible a "typical" day of work. The pair then meets to discuss their experiences, contributing to understanding each other's kingdom purpose.

For greater impact, organize a cohort of matches to prepare and follow up together. This generates more momentum for a movement of vocational discipleship in your church. In recruiting a cohort, consider surveying church members to discover the types of work they do (including unpaid work like full-time parenting). Assign pairs to represent the vocational categories present in the congregation.

Purpose Statement for the
Gospel@Work Day at Perimeter Church

1. To equip, network, and mobilize the church community to excel in their work and to collaborate in different channels of cultural influence for the glory of God and the flourishing of this city and surrounding communities ("to equip the saints for the work of ministry," Eph. 4:11–13).

2. To intentionally connect pastors and church staff to leaders and workers in various industries in order to:

   ✓ Foster dialogue and greater appreciation of the giftedness and various callings placed upon God's people.

   ✓ Grow pastoral understanding of a "day in the life" of a people in the non-church workplace.

   ✓ To integrate that increased pastoral understanding in their pastoral practice of equipping the saints for the work of the ministry in their daily work.

Kingdom Projects

Each matched pair is encouraged to strategize together on a "Kingdom Project": a problem to solve or a goal to achieve that contributes to the kingdom purpose of the Host's vocational calling. The pair collaborates for up to a year to bring this Kingdom Project to fruition, strengthening their relational connection.

For example, for Perimeter's Gospel@Work Day, a campus minister at an engineering school was matched with the owner of a mechanical engineering company. The owner commented on their goal of creating a pipeline of quality hires to ensure continued growth. Meanwhile, the campus minister shared his challenge of helping graduating students to transition into a robust life of faith at work. A natural plan emerged for the campus minister to help secure student interns for the firm and provide them with discipleship on the job.

Another striking example involved a counselor on the church staff, who had developed a suicide prevention program intended for use in hospital emergency rooms. This Guest was "randomly" assigned to pair with an emergency room nurse. The resulting project was obvious!

Impact

Comments from participants in Perimeter's Gospel@Work Day demonstrate the benefits of disciplers spending time with people in their workplace, even for just one day. Comments from pastors/church staff (Guests) showed deeper insights into their parishioner's workaday experiences:

> Getting this look into how [my Host] integrates faith and work was . . . far more educational than just reading books, because the books finally met real life. As a pastor for twenty-three years, I have allowed myself to become too removed from everyday jobs.

> I appreciate more the tensions people face. . . . "How do I model Christ and still get the sale?"

> It's important for me to remember that giving a good "gospel-centered" talk doesn't change the reality in which people live. . . . How do we teach people to reject the mindset that performance equals worth, when most of their lives are spent in places that enshrine performance and productivity as the highest values?

> I will be able to speak about workplace dynamics and the dehumanizing components with more first-hand experience. . . . [It's] less theoretical.

> Knowing what many business leaders deal with on a daily basis causes me to pray that God would give them insight and discernment in their workplace.

Many church members wondered at first what they were going to do with their pastor at work with them all day! But the experience inspired them to be more intentional about viewing their workplace as their arena for ministry and to consider the value of vocational discipleship. Comments from participants:

> The encouragement and mentorship of pastoral staff can really make a difference in my approach to work and the role I take in my workplace mission field.

> [My Guest] helped me to view each encounter with my patients and staff as an opportunity to be Christ-like, showing them God's love.

> It was a good reminder that we in the marketplace have an opportunity and responsibility to be good citizens of the kingdom.

This initiative has made me think about more what I am doing here and viewing this as a ministry opportunity.

This one visit has helped me to see the great potential value of the input of pastoral staff in discipling individuals in their workplaces.

The Gospel@Work Day also led to impactful conversations that might not have happened otherwise. One business leader, for example, reported talking with his pastor about how to better fulfill God's mission for his company, "by being more intentional about how we share the biblical view of work and . . . how our jobs affect that mission." This was not a typical topic of discussion at his church! Another church leader, whose pastoral role involved working with young adults, was matched with a business owner who was frustrated by the young adults working for him. After talking together, the business owner was better able to understand and lead his employees. He remarked that his pastoral visitor "caused me to think more about seeing the whole person working for me versus just the results they bring."

Hallowed Ground

The new conversations and changed perspectives that can come from a Gospel@Work Day help to break down the sacred/secular divide. The presence of church staff at the workplace communicates that what happens on the job is of importance to God and to the church. Some participants even reported a sense that when pastoral staff came on-site, their workplace ground became "hallowed."

In turn, church leaders may see more clearly how members' workplaces are their mission field. Pastors are more likely to bring illustrations relevant to the world of work into their preaching and teaching, in order to equip the church for this vital ministry.

For more details on how to plan a Gospel@Work Day, contact Tom Lutz at tlutz@visionmarketdevelopment.com.

APPENDIX C

RESOURCES FOR VOCATIONAL DISCIPLESHIP

Excellent resources abound for those who want to learn more about God's purpose for work. The list below suggests resources to recommend to those you are discipling, for studying together as a discipleship activity, or for learning more on your own. This is just a partial snapshot of materials in a dynamic field.

Books

Bobo, Luke. *Living Salty and Light-filled Lives in the Workplace.* Eugene, OR: Resource Publications, 2017.

Bobo, Luke, and Skye Jethani. *Discipleship with Monday in Mind: 16 Churches Connecting Faith and Work.* Overland Park, KS: Made to Flourish, 2020.

Buehring, Dave. *The Great Opportunity: Making Disciples of Jesus in Every Vocation.* New York: Morgan James Faith, 2021.

Comer, John Mark. *Garden City: Work, Rest, and the Art of Being Human.* Grand Rapids, MI: Zondervan, 2015.

Costa, Ken. *God at Work: Living Every Day with Purpose.* Nashville: W Publishing, 2013.

Daniels, Denise, and Shannon Vandewarker. *Working in the Presence of God: Spiritual Practices for Everyday Work.* Peabody, MA: Hendrickson, 2020.

Doriani, Daniel. *Work: Its Purpose, Dignity, and Transformation.* Phillipsburg, NJ: P&R, 2019.

Eldred, Ken. *The Integrated Life: Experience the Powerful Advantage of Integrating Your Faith and Work.* Montrose, CO: Manna Ventures, 2010.

Gill, David. *Workplace Discipleship 101: A Primer.* Peabody, MA: Hendrickson, 2020.

Jensen, David H. *Responsive Labor: A Theology of Work.* Louisville, KY: Westminster John Knox Press, 2006.

Kaemingk, Matthew, and Cory B. Willson. *Work and Worship: Reconnecting Our Labor and Liturgy.* Grand Rapids, MI: Baker, 2020.

Keller, Timothy, with Katherine Leary Alsdorf. *Every Good Endeavor: Connecting Your Work to God's Work*. New York: Dutton, 2012.

Mackenzie, Alistair, and Wayne Kirkland. *Where's God on Monday?* Peabody, MA: Hendrickson, 2015.

Nelson, Tom. *Work Matters: Connecting Sunday Worship to Monday Work*. Wheaton, IL: Crossway, 2011.

Okereke, Okoro Chima. *Called to Marketplace Discipleship*. Maitland, FL: Xulon Press, 2011.

Quinn, Benjamin T., and Walter R. Strickland II. *Every Waking Hour: An Introduction to Work and Vocation for Christians*. Bellingham, WA: Lexham Press, 2016.

Rae, Scott, and Kenman Wong. *Business for the Common Good*. Downers Grove, IL: IVP Academic, 2011.

Sherman, Amy L. *Kingdom Calling: Vocational Stewardship for the Common Good*. Downers Grove, IL: InterVarsity Press, 2011.

Slater, James. *Faith at Work: Workplace Testimonies of Young Christian Professionals*. Norfolk, UK: Relational Mission, 2018.

Stevens, R. Paul. *Work Matters: Lessons from Scripture*. Grand Rapids, MI: Eerdmans, 2012.

Papazov, Svetlana. *Church for Monday: Equipping Believers for Mission at Work*. Central Florida: Living Parables, 2019.

Theology of Work Project. *Theology of Work Bible Commentary*. Peabody, MA: Hendrickson, 2020.

Traeger, Sebastian, and Greg Gilbert. *The Gospel at Work: How the Gospel Gives New Purpose and Meaning to Our Jobs*. Grand Rapids, MI: Zondervan, 2018.

Van Duzer, Jeff. *Why Business Matters to God: (And What Still Needs to Be Fixed)*. Downers Grove, IL: InterVarsity Press Academic, 2010.

Whelchel, Hugh. *How Then Should We Work? Rediscovering the Biblical Doctrine of Work*. Bloomington, IN: Westbow Press, 2012.

Witherington III, Ben. *Work: A Kingdom Perspective on Labor*. Grand Rapids, MI: Eerdmans, 2011.

Faith and Work Websites

- Business as Mission: businessasmission.com
- The Center for Faith & Work: faithandwork.com
- Faith & Co: faithandco.spu.edu

- *Faith & Work* (podcast): denverinstitute.org/category/podcast
- Faith Driven Entrepreneur: faithdrivenentrepreneur.org
- God and Work: godandwork.org
- The Green Room: greenroomblog.org
- The Institute for Faith: Work, and Economics, tifwe.org
- iWork4Him: iwork4him.com
- Life Faith Out at Work Ministry: livefaithoutatwork.org
- Made to Flourish: madetoflourish.org
- Theology of Work Project: theologyofwork.org
- Vocational Stewardship: vocationalstewardship.org
- Workmatters: workmatters.org

Resource Lists

Faith & Work Ministries List (Center for Faith & Work): www.centerfor-faithandwork.com/article/faith-work-ministries-list

The Best from around the Movement (Faith Driven Entrepreneur): www.faithdrivenentrepreneur.org/best-from-the-movement

Faith and Work Resources (Nashville Institute for Faith and Work): www.nifw.org/resources

Recommended Books and Bibliographies about the Theology of Work (Theology of Work Project): www.theologyofwork.org/resources/bibliographies-and-recommended-books-about-the-theology-of-work

NOTES

Preface

1. See books coauthored by Heidi Unruh: *Churches That Make a Difference* (Baker Books, 2003); *Saving Souls, Serving Society* (Oxford University Press, 2005); *Hope for Children in Poverty* (Judson, 2007); and *Real Connections* (Judson, 2021).

2. Amy Sherman, "Why Your Church Needs to Talk about Vocation," *Flourish San Diego* (April 3, 2017), https://flourishsandiego.org/why-your-church-needs-to-talk-about-vocation.

Chapter 1

1. The stories in this chapter are hypothetical, as are the "Case Studies" at the start of each chapter, unless otherwise noted.

2. Aaron Mann, essay written for Kingdom Purpose Workshop (2019).

Chapter 2

1. Helpful books on core principles of discipleship include: Regi Campbell, *Mentor Like Jesus: His Radical Approach to Building the Church* (Atlanta: RM Press, 2017); Robby Gallaty, *Growing Up: How to Be a Disciple Who Makes Disciples* (Nashville: B&H Books, 2013); Eric Geiger, Michael Kelley, and Philip Nation, *Transformational Discipleship: How People Really Grow* (Nashville: B&H Books, 2012); Bill Hull, *The Complete Book of Discipleship: On Being and Making Followers of Christ* (Colorado Springs: NavPress, 2014); Greg Ogden, *Transforming Discipleship* (Downers Grove, IL: IVP Books, 2016); Randy Pope, *Insourcing: Bringing Discipleship Back to the Local Church* (Grand Rapids, MI: Zondervan, 2013); and Len Woods, *Rose Guide to Discipleship* (Peabody, MA: Rose, 2016). See Appendix C for resources specifically relevant to vocational discipleship.

2. Skye Jethani, "Vocational Discipleship," *WFX Network*, January 2, 2014, www.youtube.com/watch?v=jn_4ox2o3I0.

3. Jethani, "Vocational Discipleship."

4. Adapted from Kenneth Ortiz, "Before You Disciple Others: Here are the Qualifications," *Just Disciple*, October 13, 2019, https://justdisciple.com/qualifications-for-discipleship.

5. Randy Pope, *Insourcing: Bringing Discipleship Back to the Local Church* (Grand Rapids, MI: Zondervan, 2013), 128.

6. Bobby Harrington and Josh Robert Patrick, *The Disciple Maker's Handbook: Seven Elements of a Discipleship Lifestyle* (Grand Rapids, MI: Zondervan, 2017), 26.

7. Pope, *Insourcing*, 31.

8. Pope, *Insourcing*, 105.

9. Pope, *Insourcing*, 34.

Chapter 3

1. Patrick Choi, essay written for Kingdom Purpose Workshop (2019).

2. Greg Ogden, *Transforming Discipleship* (Downers Grove, IL: IVP Books, 2016), iv.

3. Kent Humphreys, *Lasting Investments: A Pastor's Guide for Equipping Workplace Leaders to Leave a Spiritual Legacy* (Colorado Springs: NavPress, 2004), 65.

4. Timothy J. Keller, *Center Church: Doing Balanced, Gospel-Centered Ministry in Your City* (Grand Rapids, MI: Zondervan, 2012), 176.

5. Tom Lutz, "Discipling Christian C-Level Business Executives" (PhD diss., Covenant Theological Seminary, 2017), 69.

6. See for example, Deb Peterson, "Five Principles for the Teachers of Adults," ThoughtCo, February 11, 2020, www.thoughtco.com/principles-for-the-teacher-of-adults-31638.

Chapter 4

1. For more theological background, see Anthony Hoekema, *Created in God's Image* (Grand Rapids, MI: Eerdmans, 1994).

Chapter 5

1. Excerpted from Mark Salcedo, essay written for the Kingdom Purpose Workshop (2019).

2. Steven Garber, *Visions of Vocation: Common Grace for the Common Good* (Downers Grove, IL: IVP Books, 2014), 155.

3. Lutz, "Discipling Christian C-Level Business Executives," 74, 76.

4. Ben Witherington III, *Work: A Kingdom Perspective on Labor* (Grand Rapids, MI: Eerdmans, 2011), 67.

5. Patrick Choi, essay written for the Kingdom Purpose Workshop (2019).

6. Lutz, "Discipling Christian C-Level Business Executives," 69.

7. Tiffani Wille, essay written for Kingdom Purpose Workshop (2019).

8. Lutz, "Discipling Christian C-Level Business Executives," 69.

9. Ryan Carson, essay written for Kingdom Purpose Workshop (2019).

10. Matt Lacey, essay written for Kingdom Purpose Workshop (2019).

12. John Granada, essay written for Kingdom Purpose Workshop (2019).

Chapter 6

1. Timothy Keller with Katherine Leary Alsdorf, *Every Good Endeavor: Connecting Your Work to God's Work* (New York: Dutton, 2012), 23, 27.

2. Matthew Kaemingk and Cory B. Willson, *Work and Worship: Reconnecting Our Labor and Liturgy* (Grand Rapids, MI: Baker, 2020), 12. See also Evan Koons, "Work: When the Journey Is Too Much," Acton Institute (September 3, 2015), www.patheos.com/blogs/oikonomia/2015/09/work-when-the-journey-is-too-much/.

3. Keller and Alsdorf, *Every Good Endeavor*, 13.

4. Michael Frost and Alan Hirsh, *The Shaping of Things to Come: Innovation and Mission for the 21st-Century Church* (Grand Rapids, MI: Baker, 2013), 159.

5. See Tom Nelson, *The Economics of Neighborly Love: Investing in Your Community's Compassion and Capacity* (Downers Grove, IL: IVP Books, 2017).

6. For example, see Libby Sander, "Nature in the workplace makes employees happier and healthier," Phys.Org (September 1, 2017); and University of Exeter, "Why plants in the office make us more productive," *ScienceDaily* (September 1, 2014).

7. "Global Estimates of Modern Slavery: Forced Labour and Forced Marriage," report from the International Labour Organization, Geneva (September 19, 2011), www.ilo.org.

8. Glenn Sullivan, "Thoughts on the Suicide Epidemic," *Psychology Today*, March 31, 2019, www.psychologytoday.com.

9. Matt Rusten, "Where Is the Church When You Lose Your Job?" *Made to Flourish* (blog), August 30, 2018, www.madetoflourish.org.

Chapter 7

1. Many of the faith and work books listed in Appendix C give a closer look at the creation mandate. For a Bible study you can walk through together, see *God's Purpose in Creation: A Study in Genesis 1*, available from the Institute for Faith, Work & Economics (www.tifwe.org).

2. Lay Commission on Catholic Social Teaching and the U.S. Economy, "Toward the Future: Catholic Social Thought and the U.S. Economy: A Lay Letter," *Crisis Magazine* (November 1, 1984), 25.

Chapter 8

1. Similar principles can be found in many faith and work resources, such as Dan Doriani, "12 Basic Principles for Faith and Work," *The Gospel Coalition* (August 15, 2017), https://www.thegospelcoalition.org/article/12-basic-principles-for-faith-and-work. Use whatever framework is the best fit for your context!

2. *Theology of Work Bible Commentary* (Peabody, MA: Hendrickson, 2016), or see "Titus: Working for Good Deeds," www.theologyofwork.org/new-testament/pastoral-epistles/titus-working-for-good-deeds.

Chapter 10

1. Hugh Whelchel, *How Then Should We Work? Rediscovering the Biblical Doctrine of Work* (Bloomington, IN: Westbow Press, 2012), 8.

2. Michael Metzger, "Back and Forth," *Clapham Institute* (blog), January 19, 2007.

3. Whelchel, *How Then Should We Work?*, 93.

4. See especially Hugh Whelchel's books, *How Then Should We Work?* and *All Things New: Rediscovering the Four-Chapter Gospel* (McLean, VA: Institute for Faith, Work & Economics, 2016); see also Lisa Sharon Harper, *The Very Good Gospel: How Everything Wrong Can Be Made Right* (New York: Water-Brook, 2016). James Choung also offers a simple, creative and compelling way for sharing this four-part gospel in *True Story: A Christianity Worth Believing In* (Downers Grove, IL: InterVarsity Press, 2009); see also www.jameschoung.net/2007/09/17/the-big-story.

5. Whelchel, *How Then Should We Work?*, xviii.

6. Garrison Young, essay written for Kingdom Purpose Workshop (2019).

7. Matt Aroney, "Three Simple Principles of Faith and Work," *Redeemer City to City* (blog), December 2, 2019, https://redeemercitytocity.com/articles-stories/three-simple-principles-of-faith-and-work.

Chapter 11

1. Andy Crouch, *Culture Making: Recovering Our Creative Calling* (Downers Grove, IL: IVP Books, 2008), 172.

2. Crouch, *Culture Making*, 174. See chapter 23 for more on the connection between work and heaven.

3. Two books that discuss the connection between the role of work and a flourishing community: Nelson, *The Economics of Neighborly Love*; and Michael Rhodes and Robby Holt, *Practicing the King's Economy: Honoring Jesus in How We Work, Earn, Spend, Save, and Give* (Grand Rapids, MI: Baker Books, 2018).

4. Nelson, *The Economics of Neighborly Love*, 173, 177.

Chapter 12

1. Suggested resources for studying workplace evangelism include: Dr. Vera R. Jackson, *Taking Jesus to Work: Learning to Release Strong Faith in the Workplace* (Grand Rapids, MI: Chosen, 2012); Bill Peel and Walt Larimore, *Workplace Grace: Becoming a Spiritual Influence at Work* (Longview, TX: LeTourneau University, 2014); Wayne Haston, "How Can I Share My Faith at Work?" *Cultivate* (blog), Good Soil Evangelism & Discipleship, November 5, 2018, www.good-soil.com/blog/how-can-i-share-my-faith-at-work; and "Evangelism—Sharing the Gospel at Work," Theology of Work Project, www.theologyofwork.org/key-topics/evangelism-sharing-the-gospel-at-work-overview.

2. Miroslav Volf, *Work in the Spirit: Toward a Theology of Work* (Oxford: Oxford University Press, 1991), 118.

3. James K. A. Smith, *How (Not) to Be Secular* (Grand Rapids, MI: Eerdmans, 2014), vii, 77.

4. Doug Sherman and William Hendricks, *Your Work Matters to God* (Colorado Springs: NavPress, 1990), 51.

5. *Theology of Work Bible Commentary*, 868.

6. Jeff Norris (currently the senior pastor of Perimeter Church in Atlanta, where Tom attends), essay written for Kingdom Purpose Workshop (2019).

Chapter 13

1. Garber, *Visions of Vocation*, 18.

2. For more on this point, see Made to Flourish (www.madetoflourish.org), a network dedicated "to empower pastors and their churches to integrate faith, work, and economic wisdom for the flourishing of their communities." See also Amy Sherman, *Kingdom Calling: Vocational Stewardship for the Common Good* (Downers Grove: IVP, 2011); Lisa Sharon Harper, *The Very Good Gospel: How Everything Wrong Can Be Made Right* (New York: WaterBrook, 2016); and Perry Yoder, *Shalom: The Bible's Word for Salvation, Justice, and Peace* (Eugene, OR: Wipf & Stock, 1997).

3. Keller with Alsdorf, *Every Good Endeavor*, 48.

4. Whelchel, *How Then Should We Work?*, 91.

5. Hayley Mason, "Church business pitch contest helps social entrepreneurs make lasting impact," CBS46 (January 3, 2020). See the Automotive Training Center website, www.automotivetrainingcenter.org.

6. Sherman and Hendricks, *Your Work Matters to God*, 55.

7. See "Work & Faith," Darryl Ford's interview with Barranco Beverage owner David Barranco (March 23, 2015), https://lifewayresearch.com/2015/03/23/work-faith-qa-with-david-barranco/#.Vi5s8xNVhBc.

8. Sherman, *Kingdom Calling*, 85.

9. Harper, *The Very Good Gospel*, 13, 43.

10. Nathan Nix, essay written for the Kingdom Purpose Workshop (2019).

11. Bobby Harrington and Josh Robert Patrick, *The Disciple Maker's Handbook: Seven Elements of a Discipleship Lifestyle* (Grand Rapids, MI: Zondervan, 2017), 22.

12. Examples include: Luke 5:1–11; 7:1–9, 36–48; 10:38–42; 19:1–10; John 4:7; 19:11.

Chapter 14

1. Compiled from quotes in Lutz, "Discipling Christian C-Level Business Executives."

2. Redeemer City to City, *The Calling of Faith and Work: A Six-Week Bible Study*, https://redeemercitytocity.com/faithworkbiblestudy.

3. For more on helping people discover and steward their calling, see Os Guinness, *The Call: Finding and Fulfilling the Central Purpose of Your Life* (Nashville: W Publishing, 2003); Deborah Koehn Loyd, *Your Vocational Credo:*

Practical Steps to Discover Your Unique Purpose (Downers Grove, IL: IVP Books, 2015); Sherman, *Kingdom Calling*; Gordon T. Smith, *Consider Your Calling: Six Questions for Discerning Your Vocation* (Downers Grove, IL: IVP Books, 2015); and Theology of Work Project, *Calling and Work*, The Bible and Your Work Study Series (Hendrickson, 2016). See also the resource at the end of chapter 20, "Stewardship of Vocational Power."

4. Lutz, "Discipling Christian C-Level Business Executives," 85.

5. Darrell Cosden, *The Heavenly Good of Earthly Work* (Peabody, MA: Hendrickson, 2006), 18.

6. David Konigsburg, excerpt from essay written for Kingdom Purpose Workshop (2019).

7. Chapter 23 explores the connection between work and heaven in more detail.

8. Michael Novak, *Business as a Calling: Work and the Examined Life* (New York: Simon & Schuster, 1996).

9. Douglas James Schuurman, *Vocation: Discerning Our Callings in Life* (Grand Rapids: Eerdmans, 2004), 3–4.

10. Based on interviews with Mark Wells in "Discipling Christian C-Level Business Executives."

12. Sherman and Hendricks, *Your Work Matters to God*, 151.

13. See Héctor García and Francesca Miralles, *Ikigai: The Japanese Secret to a Long and Happy Life* (New York: Penguin Life, 2017).

Chapter 15

1. Keller with Alsdorf, *Every Good Endeavor*, 67.

2. Matt Perman, *What's Best Next: How the Gospel Transforms the Way You Get Things Done* (Grand Rapids, MI: Zondervan, 2016), 14. See also Brandon D. Crowe, *Every Day Matters: A Biblical Approach to Productivity* (Bellingham, WA: Lexham Press, 2020).

Chapter 16

1. There are many excellent resources on this topic to draw on. For example, see R. Paul Stevens and Clive Lim, *Money Matters: Faith, Life, and Wealth* (Grand Rapids, MI: Eerdmans, 2021).

2. See Jeff Haanen, "God of the Second Shift," *Christianity Today* (September 20, 2018).

3. Theology of Work Project, *The Bible and Your Work Study Series* (Peabody, MA: Hendrickson, 2015).

4. Theology of Work Project, *Provision and Wealth*, 81.

Chapter 17

1. Dorothy Sayers, "Why Work?," *Creed or Chaos?* (San Diego: Harcourt, Brace, 1949), 56–57.

2. William Diehl, *The Monday Connection: On Being an Authentic Christian in a Weekday World* (Eugene, OR: Wipf & Stock, 2012). See also David W. Gill, *It's About Excellence: Building Ethically Healthy Organizations* (Eugene, OR: Wipf & Stock, 2011).

3. For those with a similar struggle, note that Matthew 24:39–41 makes it clear that when Jesus returns, he will expect to find believers in their place of work.

4. Theology of Work Project, "1 Corinthians and Work," *Theology of Work Bible Commentary*, 752–53.

5. Andy Crouch, "Why Ethical Work Is Not Enough," *The Praxis Journal* (September 3, 2020), https://journal.praxislabs.org/why-ethical-work-is-not -enough-1d4a42296fc5.

6. Potential books on this topic include: Lisa Sharon Harper, *The Very Good Gospel: How Everything Wrong Can Be Made Right* (New York: WaterBrook, 2016); Timothy Keller, *Generous Justice: How God's Grace Makes Us Just* (New York: Penguin Books, 2012); Jessica Nicholas, *God Loves Justice: A User-Friendly Guide to Biblical Justice and Righteousness* (Los Angeles: S&E Educational Press, 2017); and Emmanuel Katongole and Chris Rice, *Reconciling All Things: A Christian Vision for Justice, Peace and Healing* (Downers Grove, IL; IVP Books, 2008).

7. For example, there is an economic cost to racial discrimination in the workplace. See Chris Fleisher, "Putting a Price on Prejudice," *American Economic Association* (June 29, 2018); see also *Racial Justice: The Insights You Need from Harvard Business Review* (Boston: Harvard Business Review Press, 2020).

8. In *Kingdom Calling*, Amy Sherman identifies three facets of justice for vocational stewardship: rescue, equity, and restoration. Rescue involves "identifying, exposing and transforming situations where there is an abuse of power, typically perpetuated through coercion and deception." Equity "denotes fairness and impartiality. . . . It is about avoiding policies that unfairly burden the poor and weak." Regarding restoration, "The justice of God is all about restoring wholeness in relationships—with God and with other human beings" (29–32).

9. Tom Nelson outlines policies for business leaders to consider in *Work Matters*, 137.

10. Scott Rae and Kenman Wong, *Business for the Common Good* (Downers Grove, IL: IVP Academic, 2011), 187–88.

11. Theology of Work Project, *Ethics at Work*, The Bible and Your Work Study Series (Peabody, MA: Hendrickson, 2016), 76–77.

12. Theology of Work Project, *Truth and Deception*, The Bible and Your Work Study Series (Hendrickson, 2016), 59.

13. Keller with Alsdorf, *Every Good Endeavor*, 210.

Chapter 18

1. We do not minimize the financial struggles faced by many workers. including around 7 million adults considered "working poor." "A Profile of the Working Poor, 2018," Bureau of Labor Statistics, July 2020, www.bls.gov/opub /reports/working-poor/2018/home.htm.

2. Ken Costa, *God at Work: Living Every Day with Purpose* (Nashville: Nelson, 2016), xv.

3. Sherman, *Kingdom Calling*, 54.

4. John Rinehart, *Gospel Patrons: People Whose Generosity Changed the World* (CreateSpace, 2014).

5. See Shannon Deer and Cheryl Miller, *Business Doing Good: Engaging Women and Elevating Communities* (Lanham, MD: Rowman & Littlefield, 2021).

6. M. Melendez, "5 Ways to Encourage Employees to Volunteer," January 15, 2016, www.pointsoflight.org/blog/author/mmelendez.

7. "Social entrepreneurship" means developing business applications to solve local or global problems. See https://growensemble.com/social-entrepreneurs; also see Robert A. Danielson, ed., *The Social Entrepreneur: The Business of Changing the World* (Franklin, TN: Seedbed, 2015); Grant Smith, *The Accidental Social Entrepreneur* (n.p.: KREGE, 2019); and Nina Vasan and Jennifer Przybylo, *Do Good Well: Your Guide to Leadership, Action, and Social Innovation* (San Francisco, CA: Wiley, 2013).

8. See examples in Andrew MacLeod, "Why Go it Alone in Community Development?," *Harvard Business Review*, June 13, 2012, https://hbr.org/2012/06/why-go-it-alone-in-community-d.

Chapter 19

1. Compiled from excerpted interviews with Mark in "Discipling Christian C-Level Business Executives."

2. "Bill Hull and Brandon Cook, "Transformation: Discipleship Practices for Everyday Life," October 14, 2019, www.navigators.org/transformation-discipleship-practices-for-everyday-life/.

3. Nelson, *Work Matters*, 112–13.

4. See Chris Evans, *Fruit at Work: Mixing Christian Virtues with Business* (Wake Forest, NC: Lanphier Press, 2012).

5. One great resource is Denise Daniels and Shannon Vandewarker, *Working in the Presence of God: Spiritual Practices for Everyday Work* (Peabody, MA: Hendrickson, 2019).

6. A few sample devotional resources include: Theology of Work (www.theologyofwork.org/devotions), Faith at Work (www.faithatwork.ca/devotionals), and The Word before Work (https://jordanraynor.com/twbw).

7. See "Uncovering the Blessing of Fixed-Hour Prayer," http://worship.calvin.edu/resources/resource-library/uncovering-the-blessing-of-fixed-hour-prayer.

8. Brother Lawrence modeled this discipline in his devotional, *Practicing the Presence of God*: "We can do little things for God; I turn the cake that is frying on the pan for love of him, and that done . . . I prostrate myself in worship before him, who has given me grace to work; afterwards I rise happier than a king. It is enough for me to pick up but a straw from the ground for the love of God." Hendrickson Christian Classics (Peabody, MA: Hendrickson, 2004).

9. Source unknown. For the full text of this prayer and other workday prayers see https://prayerist.com/prayer/workday.html.

Chapter 20

1. An excellent resource for exploring the purpose of the Sabbath and how to apply it is *Rest and Work* in The Bible and Your Work Study Series by the Theology of Work Project (Peabody, MA: Hendrickson, 2016).

2. See D. A. Carson, "Are Christians Required to Tithe?," *Christianity Today* (November 15, 1999).

3. "What Is a Tithe?," April 17, 2019, www.christianity.com/wiki/christian-life/what-is-a-tithe-meaning-and-importance-of-tithing-in-the-bible.html.

4. "God's Law Calls People of Means to Provide Economic Opportunities for the Poor (Ruth 2:17–23)," *Theology of Work Bible Commentary* (Peabody, MA: Hendrickson, 2016), 232–33.

5. Andy Crouch, *Playing God: Redeeming the Gift of Power* (Downers Grove, IL: InterVarsity Press, 2013), 247.

6. Crouch, *Playing God*, 248–49.

7. The "cliff effect" occurs when low-wage workers can't afford a pay raise because they would lose public benefits, such as housing subsidies, that cancel out the gains. For more on the "benefits cliff" and how employers can help, see www.benefitscliff.com.

8. See Erica Campbell, "Gleaning While She Waits," *IPHC* (May 31, 2018), https://iphc.org/discipleship/2018/05/31/gleaning-while-she-waits/.

9. Crouch, *Playing God*, 248.

10. Sherman, *Kingdom Calling*, 20. See also the practical resources from www.vocationalstewardship.org and the handout "Vocational Stewardship," http://denverinstitute.org/wp-content/uploads/2017/09/Vocation-4-Vocational-Stewardship.pdf.

11. Adapted from the list in Sherman, *Kingdom Calling*, 120–26.

12. Sherman, *Kingdom Calling*, 125.

Chapter 21

1. Randy Alcorn coined the term "Christoplatonism" to describe "the unbiblical belief that the spirit realm is good and the material world is bad." For more details on the history and rebuttal to Christoplatonism, see *Heaven* (Carol Stream, IL: Tyndale, 2004).

2. Keller with Alsdorf, *Every Good Endeavor*, 181.

3. For example, the 1987 book, *Your Work Matters to God*, reported a survey finding that 90 percent of Christian respondents had never heard a sermon relating business principles to their work life. In a 2018 Barna study, over half (53 percent) of working church attenders agreed strongly that "their churches help them understand how to live out their faith in the workplace." See "Christians at Work, Part 3: The Church's Role," Barna Research Release, October 2, 2018. See also Lifeway Research, "More Pastors Preaching about Faith and Work" (November 5, 2015), www.lifewayresearch.com.

4. Sherman and Hendricks, *Your Work Matters to God*, 46.

5. Alcorn, *Heaven*, 52.

6. James Roseman, "Toward a Theology of Work & Business: Reflections on Christianity, Calling & Commerce," Dallas Baptist University Symposium (October 3, 2003).

7. Helen Howarth Lemmel, "Turn Your Eyes upon Jesus" (1922).

8. Darrell Cosden, *The Heavenly Good of Earthly Work* (Peabody, MA: Hendrickson, 2006), 23.

9. David Miller, *God at Work: The History and Promise of the Faith at Work Movement* (New York: Oxford University Press, 2006), 9–10. If you are a church leader looking for ways to close the Sunday–Monday gap, see the resources from Made to Flourish (www.madetoflourish.org). See also the books written for churches in Appendix C.

10. David Jensen, *Responsive Labor: A Theology of Work* (Louisville, KY: Westminster John Knox, 2006), 2.

11. Keller with Alsdorf, *Every Good Endeavor*, 131.

12. Barry Rowan, quoted in Rae and Wong, *Business for the Common Good*, 94.

13. Keller with Alsdorf, *Every Good Endeavor*, 135.

14. Cheryl Stone, excerpt from an essay written for Kingdom Purpose Workshop (2021).

Chapter 22

1. Witherington, *Work*, 67.

2. A key resource is the *Theology of Work Bible Commentary* (Peabody, MA: Hendrickson Publishers, 2016), www.theologyofwork.org/resources/the-theology-of-work-bible-commentary. See also, for example, R. Paul Stevens, *Work Matters: Lessons from Scripture* (Grand Rapids: Eerdmans, 2012).

3. For a list of references to work in Jesus' parables and analysis of work-related themes in his teachings, see Klaus Issler, "Exploring the Pervasive References to Work in Jesus' Parables," *Journal of the Evangelical Theological Society* 57/2 (2014): 323–39; also "Examining Jesus' Inclusion of Work Roles in His Parables," https://tifwe.org/wp-content/uploads/2014/04/Jesus-and-the-Parables-1.pdf.

Chapter 23

1. James M. Black, "When the Roll Is Called up Yonder."

2. John Eldredge, *The Journey of Desire: Searching for the Life You've Always Dreamed of* (Nashville: Nelson Books, 2000), 111.

3. Alcorn, *Heaven*, xx.

4. Tom Nelson, *Work Matters: Connecting Sunday Worship to Monday Work* (Wheaton, IL: Crossway, 2011), 72–73.

5. Note that we are *not* saying that humanity can bring about the kingdom of God by our work; only Jesus can establish the kingdom of God. Nor are we denying the reality of a final judgment, from which our good work alone can't save us; only those in the Lamb's book of life will be allowed entrance into heaven (Rev. 21:27).

6. Quoted in Sherman, *Kingdom Calling*, 104.

7. Steve Hawthorne and Graham Kendrick, *Prayer Walking: Praying on Site with Insight* (Lake Mary, FL; Charisma House, 1996).

Chapter 24

1. Theology of Work Project, "The Sabbath Year and the Year of Jubilee (Leviticus 25)," https://www.theologyofwork.org/old-testament/leviticus-and-work/the-sabbath-year-and-the-year-of-jubilee-leviticus-25.

Chapter 25

1. Keith E. Webb, *The COACH Model for Christian Leaders: Powerful Leadership Skills for Solving Problems, Reaching Goals, and Developing Others* (New York: Morgan James, 2019), 40, 53.

2. See Webb's resources on the Creative Results Management website, https://creativeresultsmanagement.com.

3. Patrick Choi, essay written for Kingdom Purpose Workshop (2019).

4. Pope, *Insourcing*, 136.

5. Online resources for equipping the person you are discipling to be a disciple maker include: discipleship.org; navigators.org; wearemakingdisciples.com; and justdiciple.com.

6. See also Chris Chancey and Katie Gibson, *Refugee Workforce: The Economic Case for Hiring the Displaced* (Amplio Recruiting, 2019).

7. Webb, *The COACH Model for Christian Leaders*, 30–31. The COACH Model® is the registered trademark of Keith E. Webb. Copyright © 2004 Keith E. Webb. Used with permission.

8. Adapted from Webb, *The COACH Model for Christian Leaders*, 17.

9. Webb, *The COACH Model for Christian Leaders*, 53.

10. A few resources for powerful questions and a coaching approach to discipleship include: Marilee Adams, *Change Your Questions, Change Your Life* (Oakland, CA: Berrett-Koehler, 2016); Richard Boyatzis, Melvin Smith, and Ellen Van Oosten, *Helping People Change: Coaching with Compassion for Lifelong Learning and Growth* (Harvard Business Review Press, 2021); Michael Bungay Stanier, *The Coaching Habit: Say Less, Ask More & Change the Way You Lead Forever* (Toronto, ON: Box of Crayons Press, 2016); Tony Stoltzfus, *Coaching Questions: A Coach's Guide to Powerful Asking Skills* (Virginia Beach, VA: Coach22 Bookstore, 2008); Will Wise and Chad Littlefield, *Ask Powerful Questions: Create Conversations That Matter* (Deerfield, IL: Round Table, 2017); Charles E. Worley, *Creating Ministry Champions: An Introduction to Developing and Coaching Leaders for Churches and Christian Organizations* (Minneapolis: NextStep Resources 2021).

11. Webb, *The COACH Model for Christian Leaders*, 32.

12. Webb, *The COACH Model for Christian Leaders*, 159.

Chapter 25

1. Lutz, "Discipling Christian C-Level Business Executives," 75.

2. Lutz, "Discipling Christian C-Level Business Executives," 77.

3. Lutz, "Discipling Christian C-Level Business Executives," 72.

4. Excerpted from a paper written for Tom's Kingdom Purpose Workshop (2019).

5. Barna Group, *Christians at Work; Examining the Intersection of Calling and Career* (2018), citing David Kinnaman, *You Lost Me: Why Young Christians Are Leaving Church . . . and Rethinking Faith* (Ada, MI: Baker Books, 2011).

6. See Matt Rusten, "Vocational Discipleship: A Universal Desire among Workers," March 1, 2019, https://greenroomblog.org/2019/03/01/vocational -discipleship-a-universal-desire-among-workers.

About the Hendrickson Publishers/ Theology of Work Line of Books

There is an unprecedented interest today in the role of Christian faith in "ordinary" work, and Christians in every field are exploring what it means to work "as to the Lord" (Col. 3:22). Pastors and church leaders, and the scholars and teachers who support them, are asking what churches can do to equip their members in the workplace. There's a need for deep thinking, fresh perspectives, practical ideas, and mutual engagement between Christian faith and work in every sphere of human endeavor.

This Hendrickson Publishers/Theology of Work line of books seeks to bring significant new resources into this conversation. It began with Hendrickson's publication of the *Theology of Work Bible Commentary* and other Bible study materials written by the TOW Project. Soon we discovered a wealth of resources by other writers with a common heart for the meaning and value of everyday work. The HP/TOW line was formed to make the best of these resources available on the national and international stage.

Works in the HP/TOW line engage the practical issues of daily work through the lens of the Bible and the other resources of the Christian faith. They are biblically grounded, but their subjects are the work, workers, and workplaces of today. They employ contemporary arts and sciences, best practices, empirical research, and wisdom gained from experience, yet always in the service of Christ's redemptive work in the world, especially the world of work.

To a greater or lesser degree, all the books in this line make use of the scholarship of the *Theology of Work Bible Commentary*. The authors, however, are not limited to the TOW Project's perspectives, and they constantly expand the scope and application of the material. Publication of a book in the HP/TOW line does not necessarily imply endorsement by the Theology of Work Project, or that the author endorses the TOW Project. It does mean we recognize the work as an important contribution to the faith-work discussion, and we find a common footing that makes us glad to walk side-by-side in the dialogue.

We are proud to present the HP/TOW line together. We hope it helps readers expand their thinking, explore ideas worthy of deeper thought, and make sense of their own work in light of the Christian faith. We are grateful to the authors and all those whose labor has brought the HP/TOW line to life.

William Messenger, Executive Editor, Theology of Work Project
Sean McDonough, Biblical Editor, Theology of Work Project
Patricia Anders, Editorial Director, Hendrickson Publishers

www.TheologyofWork.org
www.HendricksonPublishingGroup.com